Bless Me,
Father,
For I Have Sinned

Bless Me, Father, For I Have Sinned

Catholics Speak Out About Confession

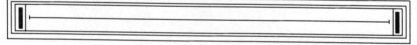

Quentin Donoghue & Linda Shapiro

Primus

DONALD I. FINE, INC.
New York

Dedicated To

*Sean, Siobhan, Gregoire, Alexandre and Katia
and
Pearl and Benjamin Geneen*

With Special Thank You To

All the people of this book for letting us into their lives, as well as Ann David, Jean Eaton, Sharon Ellis; Aaron Milrad, Deborah Wilburn and the memory of John Cushman.

Contents

Contents

Preface

Bless Me, Father, For I Have Sinned began as an ordinary search for knowledge and ended as an extraordinary personal adventure.

Linda Shapiro and I, friends and business associates, met for lunch on the last day of 1980. Linda casually remarked that she often used the day for yearly review and self-confession. The word "confession" struck a chord in me. Like so many American Catholics, I assumed I knew everything about Confession, so I began to pontificate about the Sacrament of Penance. Linda was fascinated, and started asking a lot of questions. I very quickly ran out of answers.

At a meeting the following week, the topic of Confession was coincidentally raised once again. Everyone within earshot was

9

Catholic, either practicing or lapsed, and everyone had something to say about Confession. Universal chords were struck.

Realizing then my own lack of knowledge about the subject, I went to a nearby Catholic college library in the hopes of finding an accessibly written book about Confession that would answer Linda's questions as well as my own. When I couldn't find such a book, the seeds were planted for the collaboration which resulted in this one.

Throughout our research, I developed a profound respect for my Irish ancestors who had contributed so greatly to the history of the Sacrament, as well as to Western civilization. Equally important, and somewhat surprisingly, I also developed a tremendous admiration for the Church's ability to confront its weaknesses and to adapt to the times, where before my reactions were largely of a critical nature.

For Linda, a practicing Jew, the entry into the world of Catholicism was intriguing. She had always been curious about Confession, perceiving it as both awesome and compassionate.

We extend a most sincere thank you to the people whose voices are heard in this book. Together, they tell, and are, the story of the Sacrament of Confession.

—Quentin Donoghue
Linda Shapiro
Toronto, 1984

General History

Chapter 1

The Early Years (. . . to A.D. 500)

───────────────────────────────────────

Bless me, Father, for I have sinned," are the first words spoken by
Catholic penitents as they begin their confession to a priest. The
origin of the phrase is unknown, but many believe the oral tradition
can be traced to the Irish monks of the Dark Ages.

Much of the history of the early Church, including the practice
of Confession, is muddled since accurate records were not kept, but
the story that emerges from preserved documents and other
sources is a lively one, nothing less than an adventure, an extraordinary tale replete with heroes and villains, plagues and famine, emperors and heretics. It begins in the Holy Land, travels the breadth
of Europe and eventually finds its way to the shores of North
America . . .

*   *   *

13

Bless Me, Father, For I Have Sinned

To begin at the beginning, the first confession was Adam's when he said to God in the Garden of Eden, "The woman whom Thou gavest to me to be my companion gave me of the tree, and I did eat." In the book of Genesis we're told that because of that first willful act of disobedience, man and woman were banished from Paradise, stained forever with Original Sin. Woman was branded as an occasion of sin, and both were condemned as sinners, burdened forever with the compulsion to confess.

From the dawn of time, every civilization has utilized some form of confession to placate its gods. Calamity spurred devotion. Just when an enemy appeared at the gates or a natural disaster devastated a crop, primitive man was quick to flatter his gods. By humiliating himself as a sinner, man exalted their power.

And as man evolved, so too did his confessions. The Sumerians, around 3000 B.C., were the first people to confess their sins to gods through intermediaries. A thousand years later the Babylonians turned to women, those thought to be mother goddesses who interceded on behalf of prostrate sinners, seeking mercy from their deities.

The ancient Egyptians confessed to their countless gods sins which they did not even commit. These unique negative confessions, as expressed in the Book of the Dead, contained lists of sins which were recited to enhance their afterlife: "No little child have I injured; no widow have I oppressed." Since their agriculture was in such a precarious state, it was natural for farmers to confess, "I have not turned back the water in time." The Egyptians were also the most advanced of the early civilizations in their concept of an afterlife, believing that good deeds performed on earth would be rewarded after death. Initially, only the well-born could enjoy an afterlife, but this was to be subsequently democratized. The early Egyptians exerted more effort in their attempt to attain an afterlife than any people before or after them.

In the Judaic tradition of confession, the High Priest acted as the intermediary between Jehovah and the children of Israel. Each year, on *Yom Kippur*, he sought forgiveness for the sins they had committed throughout the year. One tradition claimed *Yom Kippur*,

14

1311 B.C., was the day God gave Moses the second set of tablets containing the Ten Commandments. Moses had broken the first set in a rage when he saw his people reverting to the idolatrous ways they had known in Egypt. God had, nevertheless, given them a second set and along with it a second chance.

The Hebrew words *Yom Kippur,* when translated into English, become "Day of Atonement"; when translated into Spanish, they become *el Dia de Perdon,* the "Day of Forgiveness." The word *kippur* derives from the Babylonian, and in that language combines both meanings—atonement for sin by the penitent and forgiveness of sin by God. It was from this heritage of combined atonement and forgiveness that Christian confession would begin.

Jesus Christ, born into the world of this tradition, granted the power to forgive sins on the evening of His Resurrection when He said to His joyous Apostles, "Receive the Holy Spirit. For those whose sins you forgive, they are forgiven; for those whose sins you retain, they are retained." With these words, Jesus granted to those who would follow Him the power to forgive sins. For those stained with Original Sin, Heaven was once again attainable.

His awesome gift entailed an equally awesome responsibility. Christ bestowed the power to forgive sins, allowing His disciples and their descendants to determine the most effective way for it to be practiced. This freedom to choose how the ritual would be performed would challenge His Church throughout its history, and would stimulate Confession to evolve in unimagined ways.

The history of early Confession abounds with confusion and contradiction. There is very little written material from the period, no concrete record of how the first Christians utilized Christ's gift to forgive sins. The first followers of Christ were a messianic cult anxiously awaiting the end of the world. As they waited for Armageddon, the early Christians found themselves an outlawed sect on the run, struggling to survive wave after wave of Roman persecutions. It simply was not the climate in which to chronicle the details of their lives.

The threat of persecution would plague them for nearly three centuries. Still, this constant threat from their pagan overlords

15

actually helped the first believers, who banded together into a passionately loyal community that cared for all its members, as they were all part of the mystical body of Christ.

The new religion was severely tested in the year A.D. 67 when Peter the Apostle died. Soon after, Nero launched the first large-scale attack on Christians when he accused them of setting Rome afire. With a combination of rage and political savvy, the emperor ordered that believers of the new faith be "burned, crucified and exposed to wild beasts." That tragic year also marked the death in Jerusalem of St. Stephen, the Church's first martyr.

The small, besieged communities of converts in the first century A.D. were extremely sensitive to sin, because it jeopardized their tenuous existence. They believed, as did the Jews, that the sin of one man could infect the entire community, just as Adam had brought sin to the entire world.

Sin for the early Christians was defined as an act contrary to the Ten Commandments. As well, sin was emphasized from a communal point of view, judged as to whether it threatened the safety of the group. When sin occurred, it was crucial that it be excised as judiciously and as promptly as possible. Some scholars contend there was only one ritual within the limited liturgy of the early Church that forgave sin after Baptism. Venial sins were publicly confessed as penitents prayed together as part of the Eucharist celebration. The three mortal or grievous sins—murder, fornication and apostasy—generally prompted swift excommunication. The early Christian Church just couldn't afford any backsliders in their ranks.

The beginning of the second century marked an enormous philosophical shift for the new religion. Three and four generations of believers had now entered the faith since the time of Christ. The imminently expected Second Coming had not occurred and, reluctantly, the Church had to acknowledge the possibility of an extended wait on earth. With this they began to reassess communal discipline and the harsh dogmatism of excommunication of serious sinners. At this time as well Christians began to see themselves evolving from a group of self-acclaimed saints to a community of

16

self-accusing sinners. This shift in emphasis was gradual, but it coincided with the first use of the term "the catholic Church," the word "catholic" derived from Greek, meaning universal. As the new religion braced itself for an uncertain future, it acknowledged the sinfulness of human nature and the need for a second forgiveness after Baptism. A new rite for the confession and absolution of sin began to evolve—instead of simply excommunicating serious sinners, the Church sought a way to forgive—but not forget.

During the second century it was customary that mortal sins be publicly admitted to the bishop in the hope that the sinner could be reunited with the community. The rite more often resembled a court trial than a religious service, and once judged, the sinner was expected to perform harsh acts of public penance which could include years of prayer and fasting. Harsh as it was, it still reflected Christ's commission to His apostles to offer sinners a second chance.

There is some debate today as to what constituted mortal or serious sin for the early Church. Some theologians argue that the mortal sins of the times were those that threatened the cohesion and security of the Church—apostasy, murder and fornication. Other theologians claim those three were held in such disdain that they were beyond being classified as mortal; they were absolutely unforgivable.

This unbending dogmatism was understandable in view of the early Church's struggle for survival, even though it ran counter to Christ's example of all-encompassing mercy. Fornication, for example, was proscribed for reasons beyond illicit sex. One theory suggests that fornication was interpreted during the first two centuries as being sexual intercourse with pagan temple prostitutes. Fornication was thus an interdiction against sexual relations with the enemy, a fraternization that might tempt the sin of idolatry and weaken the security of the group. Their interpretation of fornication as adultery was crucial, too, for if a member were feuding with another member for having coveted the other's wife, it would be difficult to sustain cohesion.

Whether forgivable or unforgivable, mortal sin could only be

17

confessed once in a lifetime. A second-century book called *The Shepherd,* written by Hermas of Rome, succinctly captured the Church fathers' belief that just as there is but one Baptism, there should be but one Confession: "If anyone, after that great and holy calling of Baptism, is tempted by the devil and sins, he has but one penance. For if anyone should sin and do penance frequently, his penance will do him no good, for such a person is not likely to live." Jesus had preached that sins should be forgiven seventy times seven, but the early bishops only allowed for it once.

The first man to drastically influence the evolution of Confession was a most unlikely penitential innovator. A man of extraordinary contrasts, Callistus, a former Roman slave, embezzler, and convict, became the sixteenth pope of the Church in A.D. 217. This rogue —who would eventually be canonized a saint—accomplished the unimaginable by forgiving the unforgivable.

Details of his life are sketchy. All that is directly known of the once-bankrupt cemetery administrator was written by Hippolytus, his archenemy, who dismissed him as a profligate charlatan. When Callistus was elected pope (217–222), Hippolytus, in a monumental fury, initiated the first Church schism and became the first antipope. Ironically, Hippolytus, too, was later canonized, making it difficult to draw a clear distinction between the accuser and the accused.

Hippolytus' chief complaint against Callistus was that he "was the first who planned to make concessions to men regarding sexual pleasure." The accusation is accurate. Pope Callistus did remove fornication in all its forms from the trio of unforgivable sins and decreed absolution for repentant prostitutes and adulterers. Hippolytus snidely demanded to know where Callistus was going to hang his decree: "On the doorposts of the brothels?"

Callistus' challenge to the established doctrine of the day, however, was more likely an attempt to protect Christianity than to promote promiscuity. When he dared to enlarge the marriage law of the early Church to allow well-born ladies to marry slaves and freedmen, he was, in actuality, trying to turn the countless concubinages of the time into valid, Christian marriages.

Neither of these enemies died easily. Callistus was reputedly thrown down a well by a rampaging pagan mob; Hippolytus, in turn, was killed by the Romans and his remains were buried in a Sardinian cesspool. In an ultimate irony, years later, Hippolytus' bones were laid to rest in a Roman cemetery bearing the name of his nemesis.

Apostasy, the renunciation of the faith, was another unforgivable sin soon to be transformed as a result of the most pervasive attacks the Church had yet encountered. In 249 Emperor Decius, wanting to consolidate his empire and gain further favor with his gods, initiated the first empire-wide persecutions of Christians. Describing the Christians as poisonous, he sought nothing less than the total eradication of their faith. To root them out, Decius decreed that every inhabitant of the Roman Empire had to publicly perform an act of pagan worship, assuming that all devout Christians would refuse to do so, thereby incriminating themselves.

Over the following two brutal years, tens of thousands of terrified Christians apostatized themselves in order to survive. When the persecutions ceased on the death of Decius in 251, the Church was besieged by repentant apostates, or *lapsi*, seeking readmission into the fold. Existing doctrine, however, was adamant: apostasy was an unforgivable sin.

St. Cyprian of Carthage, sympathetic to the apostates predicament, arranged for their return to the faith through a theological back door called the martyr's privilege. During the first century there was no distinction between the terms confessor and martyr; Cyprian was now going to cleverly meld the two together again.

The men and women who had severely suffered for their faith and survived were automatically elevated to presbyter, an ecclesiastical promotion into the ranks of those who governed the Church. Cyprian believed that the Christians who survived the torture of the persecutors would be more likely to forgive the *lapsi* than their entrenched, stubborn bishops. His plan worked, and the Church survived another crisis by granting the *lapsi* a second chance and allowing apostasy to be forgiven through confession.

With two out of three unforgivable sins now acknowledged as

forgivable by the majority of bishops, the dogmatism of the early Church was weakening. Tertullian, a priest of the African Church, made one last-ditch attempt to preserve that stern tradition. He argued that perhaps God would be willing to forgive the unforgivable, but the Church should not; to do so was an incentive for licentiousness, an encouragement for sin.

Even though confession was used to reconcile the *lapsi*, it was never popular. The penances demanded by the bishops and their appointed priests were often so stringent that a penitent's life was radically altered by years of fasts, chastity, poverty and mortifications—penances frequently imposed on those guilty of mortal sin. The life of the penitent often resembled that of the monks and nuns who were voluntarily undergoing the rigors of monastic life. Because of these similarities, public penance became known as the Order of Penitents.

The sinners were universally recognizable, dressed as they were in sackcloth rags over which the bishop would sprinkle ashes. On completion of the penance, which lasted from months or years to a lifetime, the reconciliation of the penitent with the body of the Church was celebrated when the bishop laid his hands upon the prostrate sinner. While a member of the Order of Penitents, his community supported the sinner by offering prayers for his spiritual healing and providing his family with food and necessities.

A confession in the latter part of the third century might have resembled the following:

The members of the Christian congregation gathered in a room in the small home of the town baker. In the center of the white wall there hung a simple wooden cross. Everyone stared at the penitent who remained still, his head bent. Some felt no pity for the man who was about to confess, feeling that he had shamed their community, but a few sympathized, imagining themselves in a similar situation. The man they had elected to be their priest nodded. The men separated from the women, on opposite sides of the room, all falling to their knees. The priest, gazing intently at the penitent, whispered a prayer. He then gestured for the man to begin his confession.

20

In a humble voice, the sinner told how he had made a sacrifice to the false god. Describing his shame, he explained that he had committed the sin of apostasy because he feared brutality from the Romans who had threatened him because he was a Christian. The priest bowed his head. He would relate the confession to the bishop, who would then pronounce the sinner's penance. Until that time, which could be as long as a year, the sinner could not partake of the Eucharist, nor could he expect absolution until he had successfully completed his penance.

The congregation struggled to its feet, the sinner relieved. Although he knew he could never again confess in his lifetime, he gratefully realized that, until recently, his sin had been considered unforgivable, and had he not confessed he would have been doomed to an eternity in Hell.

For the weak-hearted, there was one other method by which a man could save his immortal soul. Christians who were about to be martyred were asked by other Christians to sign letters of peace, certificates which stated that those who were about to die for their faith would intercede in Heaven on behalf of designated sinners still on earth.

One cannot imagine the audacity it took to thrust a paper and quill in front of a man quaking in a dungeon as hungry lions roared nearby! The letters of peace were, nevertheless, a painless way for some to circumvent public confession for the sin of apostasy. Many bishops regarded these letters so highly that they often reconciled the repentant apostate immediately upon their presentation. Most Christians, however, avoided the tyranny of public confession and public penance, not by such luxuries as letters of peace, but by putting off their confessions until they lay on their deathbeds; some never bothered to make a confession at all. As a result of these two extremes in practicing the rite, confession was, for the most part, rarely used from the third to the sixth centuries. Although few people considered themselves saints, still fewer considered themselves mortal sinners.

As the Church moved into the fourth century, the penitential system was on the verge of breaking down. All sins were now

21

forgivable, including the previously unforgivable ones, but the people confessing were mainly those whose serious sins were publicly known.

Curiously enough, the Sacrament was next influenced by a man who never himself practiced it. In 312 the Roman Emperor Constantine claimed to have seen a cross in the sky and heard a voice, "In this sign will you conquer." He immediately attached his emblem to the monogram of Christ and granted full religious freedom to all Christians. The Church was no longer an endangered outlaw sect, and by 322 the entire Roman Empire had joined the body of the Church. As the religion took root and flourished throughout the Western world, men and women would confess their sins in a different way.

By the beginning of the fourth century Christianity boasted more than three million members who worshiped in their own specially constructed churches. The first had been erected in 232 in eastern Syria. A century later, church architecture was standardized so that the priest at the altar faced the congregation during the Mass. The building of the first churches also encouraged a stricter codification of doctrine. A hundred years after the death of Constantine, the word "sacramentum" was first used to describe rituals that bestowed the grace of God.

As the Church grew, so too did the monastic community nestled within it. The first Christian monastics were not men banded together in the pursuit of God, but were isolated hermits, avoiding temptation so that they might worship God with their entire consciousness. These silent men would soon exert enormous impact on Confession, the most vocal of the Sacraments. The earliest monastics sought God in the desert wasteland, believing that only in the arid wilderness could they most boldly confront the forces of evil and test their own spiritual strength. They became known as the desert fathers.

St. Anthony, the founder of the Christian tradition of monasticism, wanted nothing more than to live a prayerful life in seclusion. But word of his sanctity and spirituality spread to the masses, drawing hundreds of faith seekers to his side. While he never succeeded in living the life of isolated contemplation he longed for, his sterling example encouraged many thousands of men and women to seek a solitary, contemplative existence.

Anthony's message of how to regain God was as severe as it was simple. He demanded that every monk "tell his elders confidently how many steps he takes, and how many drops of water he drinks in his cell, in case he is in error about it." This scrupulous sharing of faults would eventually become an important part of the monastic discipline. St. Pachomius promoted cenobitic monasticism, communities of men banding together to share the spiritual life. St. Basil, synthesizing their doctrines and disciplines, wrote the first requirements for a monastic order. The ranks of monks and nuns were also increased by penitents whose severe penances forced them to live apart from their communities. Frequently, these members of the Order of Penitents would take the monastic vows, and monks and penitents alike would carry out their penances together, each supporting the other.

Until the fourth century monasticism was primarily an Eastern tradition. The Western Church would not feel the effects of the contemplative life and the eventual impact it would have on confession until the time of St. Jerome. Born in 331 in what is now Yugoslavia, the son of prosperous Christians, Jerome dedicated himself to the ascetic life after a dream in which he envisioned himself brutally beaten and dragged before the Lord for having read pagan literature. Jerome is revered today for having translated the Bible from Hebrew into Latin, a language he mastered to distract himself from temptation. His work became the basis for the Vulgate, the standard Latin version of the Scriptures.

Despite his own lusty nature, which proved a constant stumbling block, Jerome was eloquent in his defense of celibacy. At the age of twenty-eight he joined an ascetic community in the Syrian desert. To purge themselves of sin, these monks slept on bare ground, wore chains and spent years in prayer as they endured the rigors of the sunbaked land. Recalling his periods of mortification, Jerome wrote:

Although my constant companions were scorpions and wild beasts, time and time again, I imagined myself watching the dancing of Roman maidens as if I had been in the midst of them. Alone with the enemy, I threw myself in spirit at the feet of Jesus, watering them with my tears, and tamed my flesh by fasting whole weeks.

Jerome's contribution to Confession is circuitous. From the bitter experience of his own desert temptations, he fashioned advice for novices plagued by their own temptations and demons. He suggested that they not confront the devil alone, but instead seek the compassionate assistance of another member of their religious community. Together, they could share prayerful advice on how best to fulfill the monastic ideal. These conversations between members of religious orders eventually became a cornerstone of monastic discipline—and of the rite of Confession.

Jerome died in 420, a decade after Alaric and his Visigoths had sacked Rome and plunged Europe into the Dark Ages.

Chapter 2

The Irish Years (500–1300)

647, Connemara, Ireland

The moon was rising over the low circular walls of the monastery nestled in the hills of southwest Ireland. A young monk waited outside the beehive-shaped hut of his *anmchara*—his soul friend, his father confessor.

When it was his turn, the young monk bent, entered the rough ash door and knelt by the side of the older man. Straining to recapture the details of his temptations and weaknesses, he began to confess.

He told of how he wanted to lie longer in bed before the night vigil and how he allowed the birds' singing to distract his prayers. He whispered of his impatience with his fellow monks when they

25

worked so slowly in the fields. He nodded to emphasize the shame he felt at his pride when lauded by the abbot for his melodious voice.

His *anmchara* gave him, as his penance, the task of awakening two hours earlier than required for the night vigil, as well as additional mortifications designed to strengthen his commitment to prayer. The young monk also had to volunteer to assist his brothers in the fields. He would do all of these things until his next meeting with his *anmchara* the following week.

During the Dark Ages, it was the Irish who brought the Word of Christ to the pagan tribes of Europe. They were also the innovators who revolutionized the way in which the Sacrament of Confession was to be practiced for more than a millennium to come.

To the north, at the edge of the known world, Ireland was swathed in magic and superstition. Druids ministered the fertile land with a perverse blend of wisdom and barbarism. A Latin writer described them as a harsh race who drank the blood of their conquered and stained their faces with it. It was on the point of a sword, he recounted, that a mother offered her newly born male child its first food. Julius Caesar depicted the Druids of Gael as philosophers and theologians who believed that man's soul was immortal. Others condemned the Druids for their human sacrifices. Scholars today still dispute the meaning of their name, which varies from "one who knows" to "magician."

Ireland in the first centuries after Christ was an island steeped in fables, where sea monsters guarded the shores and giant cannibals marauded the land. Such tales evidently provided a reliable defense because the country was never conquered by Rome.

In the early years of the Church, the Irish had little firsthand experience with the new religion called Christianity except for a tale told by a wandering strong man named Conall Kearnach, who is said to have witnessed the Crucifixion of Christ. When Conall Kearnach described the event to King Conchobar years later, the pagan monarch reportedly flew into an unexplicable rage.

Pirates were indirectly responsible for Christianity finally reaching the shores of Ireland. At the beginning of the fifth century a sixteen-year-old Englishman was kidnapped by bandits and sold in Ireland as a shepherd slave. For six dismal years, he tended his flock until a voice in his dreams drove him to escape. He fled to France and joined a monastery, where his captivity kindled a passionate conversion. At the age of forty his dreams spoke to him again as he heard "the voice of the Irish" calling him back.

Thus did St. Patrick, second bishop to Ireland, arrive in 432 to an island whose barbaric inhabitants had previously resisted all attempts at conversion. Patrick's mission was shockingly successful. His feat astounded even the British bishops who had initially opposed him, claiming that his education was defective as a result of the 6 rustic years he had spent as a shepherd instead of as a scholar. But this extraordinary man of action belied his superiors' fears and worked wonders. Within 30 years the country boasted 365 churches, 365 bishops and 3,000 priests. One day in Connaught, Patrick is reputed to have baptized over 12,000 pagans, including seven kings.

Patrick's success on the island was attributable to a combination of eloquence and determination. As a missionary, he used the three-leafed shamrock to explain the Holy Trinity as having three Persons in one God. As a subverter, he unabashedly bribed for souls. Although his British superiors complained that the bishop was spending far too much money in his campaign to proselytize the island, it is known that he took nothing for himself; instead he used the money to bestow gifts on kings and to bribe lawgivers, effectively neutralizing any opposition to his message of Christianity.

Coupled with his enormous energy and missionary zeal was Patrick's political acumen. Ireland in the fifth century had no towns—following the Roman pattern—so he shrewdly imposed his French monastic tradition onto the web of clans that linked the country. By appointing the *coarbs,* or heirs apparent of the clans, as abbots of the new monasteries and later elevating these abbots to bishops, St. Patrick peacefully meshed clan with monastery, two seemingly disparate social and religious institutions.

The early Irish monasteries were nothing like the monasteries of the East. The monks lived in accessible clusters of beehive-shaped huts among the people, often assuming the cultural responsibilities of their former Druid teachers.

The common denominator that linked the Irish monasteries with their desert predecessors was discipline—the vows of poverty, chastity and obedience bound all. The other important similarity was the spiritual conversations encouraged by St. Jerome and St. Augustine, who had also cautioned that "no man can walk without a guide." These informal talks in which faults and weaknesses were shared took place as the need arose, and as they became more uplifting and effective, they became more frequent.

This soul-scouring soon created its own hierarchy of people best suited as spiritual counselors and they became known as *anmcharas,* Gaelic for soul friend. During these formative years of Confession, these meetings with *anmcharas,* both men and women, were not sacramental and offered no forgiveness or absolution, only spiritual guidance.

For five hundred years after the arrival of St. Patrick, Ireland remained solely monastic. All churches continued to be connected to the monasteries and the convents; the division into parishes or dioceses was yet to come. Because the religious communities were central to the clans, there was a neighborly familiarity between the laity and their priests, monks and nuns.

The Irish were in justifiable awe of their devoted clergy, particularly admiring their single-minded pursuit of salvation. While the Irish laity sought the same goal, they didn't necessarily want to subject themselves to the rigors of the monastic discipline. Another means of salvation, short of monasticism, was sought—and subsequently found. The regular conversations between the members of the monastery and their *anmcharas* stood out as an appealing way for the devout laymen to attain their clergy's spiritual goal. For the laity, these spiritual encounters were a pleasant way of examining their consciences, discussing their sins and guilts and receiving counsel on how to cure their faults. As the Irish Christians began to seek guidance from spiritual counselors, the history of confession had begun.

Initially, the connection between this spiritual counseling and the Roman practice of the Sacrament of Confession was vague. The two were superficially quite dissimilar. In the confession practiced by the early Roman Church, the penitent publicly confessed his mortal sins to his bishop, who prescribed a lengthy and stringent public penance. Absolution came only after the completion of the penance, and the Sacrament could only be practiced once in a lifetime. The Church remained adamant in its belief that, as there is only one Baptism, there should be only one Confession.

In contrast, the Celtic tradition was a private, frequent conversation between the *anmcharas* and the penitents. The penitents sought their counsel as often as they wished, sometimes daily. "As a floor is swept every day or oftener," went an adage of the times, "so the soul should be cleansed once or oftener every day by confession." Subtly and steadily, the role of the soul friend evolved into that of sacramental confessor. When Roman Church authorities heard that penance in Ireland was taking the form of a private, frequent sacrament, they were aghast and quickly condemned the practice, hoping the abomination would be restricted to that strange, remote island.

This new form of confession, however, was not a well-kept secret in the rest of the Christian world. In Spain, in 589, the Third Council of Toledo issued a stinging criticism of this heretical concept: "We have come to learn that in certain Spanish churches, men do penance for their sins not in accordance with canonical precedent, namely unicity, but in a most offensive manner, namely as often as they are pleased to sin, so often they demand of the presbyter to be reconciled."

As the Irish innovation, then called *reconciliation with the altar,* spread throughout the island, it became apparent that guides were needed. From monastery to monastery there was enormous disparity as harsh or lenient penances were meted out for the same offense. The need for a set of written guidelines became obvious and resulted in the tradition of the penitentials called "medicine of the souls." Soon these penitentials would have enormous impact not only in Ireland, but throughout the entire Church. The early penitentials were eclectic, highly individualized moral dictionaries written with a blend of personal judgment, Scripture, canonical law and monastic discipline. Their vast influence colored the Middle Ages, establishing the strict morality that governed most of Europe for the next five centuries.

Finnian of Clonard, the venerated teacher of the Irish saints, wrote the first of the famous Irish penitentials, which fixed penances according to the nature of the sin. Some penances were even graded according to the status of the sinner. Finnian, for example, held the clergy to account for its offenses far more strictly than those not bound by vows.

He wrote:

> If a cleric sinks so low as to have a child and kill him, the crime of fornication and murder is a grievous one. But he can be absolved by the penance and by God's mercy. He shall do penance on bread and water for three years, and be deprived of his clerical office and exiled from his country for seven years. Then the bishop or priest can decide to restore him to office.

Finnian's penitential is also remembered for its remedial penance as opposed to the vindictive penance of other writers. He sought to help the penitent heal himself, not merely atone for his sins.

The vast horde of penitential literature existing today reveals a tradition laden with as much romance as remorse. Another penitentialist wrote:

> If a cleric lusts after a virgin or any woman in his heart but does not utter his wish with his lips, if he sins thus, but once, he ought to do penance for seven days with an allowance of bread and water. But if he continually lusts and is unable to indulge his desire, since the woman does not want him or since he is ashamed to speak, still he has committed adultery in his heart. It is the same sin though it be in his head and not in his body. Yet penance is the same. Let him do penance for forty days with bread and water.

Other penitential prose offered a social tapestry of the period:

> The blood of a bishop, a superior prince or a scribe, which is poured out upon the ground, if the wound requires a dressing, such men judge, let he who shed the blood be crucified or pay the value of seven female slaves.

The penance for one unsavory sin stipulated:

> He who gives to anyone a liquor in which a mouse or a weasel is found dead shall do penance with three special fasts.

Many of the penitentials reveal their author's eccentric imagination or, perhaps, his concern for hygiene:

> He who eats the skin of his own body, that is a scab, or the vermin which are called lice, or his own excreta, with the imposition of hands of his bishop, shall do penance for an entire year on bread and water.

The period seethed with superstition, and the penitentials often reflected fear of the diabolical:

> Hast thou done what some women do at the instigation of the devil? When any child has died without Baptism, they take the corpse of the little one and place it in some secret place and transfix its little body with a stake, saying that if they did not do so, the little child would arise and would injure many. If so, do penance for two years on the appointed day.

The majority of the penitentials, however, dealt with everyday matters in just, sympathetic ways. If someone assaulted or broke the arm of a farmer, the guilty person was obliged to tend the farmer's fields and reap his harvest.

Most of the relatively short penances involved fasting on bread and water and the recitation of the hundred and fifty psalms. By the twelfth century the vast number of illiterates caused the Church to devise a substitute for the reading of the psalms. Specified numbers of *Pater Nosters* and *Ave Marias* were said in their place, later becoming known as the poor person's Psalter, or the rosary.

Finnian was but the first of many penitentialists. St. Columban, who also wrote his own inspired list of sins and corresponding penances, is best remembered as the towering missionary who epitomized the Irish zeal of bringing the Word of Christ to the pagans. His conversions were legion, spurred by his gift of a more gentle vision of the Sacrament of Confession.

A monastic at Bangor in Northern Ireland, Columban was strongly attracted to the tradition of *anmcharas,* and one of his own early soul friends was a woman. Another conviction to which he held fast was the notion of "white" martyrdom, which proclaimed that if a person could not shed his own blood for Christ, then he could, at least, give up what he held most dear. For Columban, that meant leaving Ireland. At the age of forty, imitating Christ in the number of His disciples, Columban arrived in France with twelve monks, many of whom were to join their leader in the ranks of sainthood.

His arrival on the continent was propitious; Europe was festering with countless gods who were perceived as anything but merciful deities. Columban, offering the ferocious warrior tribes the gift of mercy and the Celtic form of private, frequent Confession, was rewarded with waves of conversions exceeding even Patrick's success.

The breakdown of civil authority in the Dark Ages also contributed to the speed with which Columban's penitential was accepted throughout Europe. Because the Church frequently had to administer law as well as faith, punish crime as well as sin, the penitentials became the law books of that desperate era.

Columban's impact, along with that of all the Irish missionaries, is incalculable. This aggressive, argumentative man founded more than sixty monasteries, each becoming both centers of religious faith and the vaults which preserved knowledge of Western civilization.

The irresistible spread of the Irish form of frequent, private Confession throughout the Dark Ages coincided with the decline of its Roman counterpart. By about 600 public penance was almost nonexistent. Irish penance, however, flourished, the lure being the frequency of forgiveness, and the counseling and compassion with which it was administered.

Although sinners could now confess more frequently, penances for mortal sins were as harsh as ever. According to some penitentialists, the public penance for willful murder was twenty-seven years of prayers and fasting. Lifelong penance was imposed on those guilty of apostasy, as well as on monks and consecrated virgins who were unfaithful to their vows of chastity. Other penitentialists dictated that adultery and sodomy netted fifteen years of penance, while grave robbery was worth ten.

Soon a way to avoid these arduous penances was developed. Called the system of commutation, it allowed for the softening of the penance in return for a donation to a church so that masses could be said for the penitent.

However innocently devised, the system of commutation led to some extraordinary abuses. In the French town of Souest there was a priest who invented a foolproof spiritual swindle. During Lent, husbands and wives were expected to abstain from sexual intercourse. If a penitent confessed he had strayed, the pastor would demand a donation for masses to be said for him in lieu of severe penance. Conversely, if another penitent stated he had observed the custom of Lenten abstinence, the corrupt clergyman accused him of the sin of birth control and demanded a similar sum for penitential masses. Other commutational abuses included hiring someone else to perform the penance, usually a monk who turned over the fee to his monastery. In tenth-century England one prosperous sinner fulfilled his penance of a seven-year fast by hiring an army which completed it for him in three days.

Still, confessors were faced with the demanding responsibility of meting out suitable penances. To fully understand the sin, it was necessary for the priest to understand the circumstances which influenced it. So began the practice of priest probing penitent, seeking to uncover the nature of the sin, as well as the number of times it was committed. This exercise, often fraught with great anxiety for the penitent, was considered obligatory to the rite of Confession in the Middle Ages. The severe penances imposed as a result of this probing resulted in many people often avoiding Confession until the end of their lives.

The deathbed confessions of the Mediterranean region ironically resembled the Celtic confessions of northern Europe. Deathbed confessions were performed privately and did not involve rigorous public penance, since the penitent usually died soon after receiving the rite. Because death was imminent, absolution was given immediately after Confession. This reversal in the established order in the practice of the Sacrament was to drastically change the rite in subsequent years. But not everyone was willing to take a chance on a deathbed confession. Those in grave sin who feared losing the race to the priest at their moment of death still subjected themselves to severe public penances by joining the Order of Penitents.

Witches abounded in the superstition-ridden Dark Ages. Confession of sorcery received a full twenty years of public penance, and each day of those two decades was strictly regulated. The repentent witch or wizard spent the first four years of the penance as a "weeper," forced to stand outside the church during services. He further signaled his guilt by wearing sackcloth and ashes, the still traditional uniform of penitents.

The next five years were spent as a "hearer." The self-acclaimed sorcerer was allowed back into the church, but was relegated to the rear and allowed to stay for only certain initial portions of the Mass. It was a period in which the penitent was tantalized by being close to the source of grace and forgiveness, but not close enough to benefit from its spiritual warmth.

For the following seven years, the sinner became a "prostrator" or "kneeler." He was allowed to attend the entire Mass, but was segregated from the rest of the congregation, both by virtue of the place he was to occupy and the position he was ordered to adopt.

The former witch, by this time almost accepted back into the community, was then allowed to attend Mass with the rest of the congregation—but for the final four years could not receive Holy Communion. Such stringency was reserved only for extraordinary mortal sins. Despite the millions of words written in the penitentials, mortal sin was still considered to be murder, apostasy and fornication, or variations on those acts.

Full forgiveness and the completion of the penance by the witch, the murderer or the apostate did not mean the books were closed —there was never an end. Even after reconciliation with the Church, the penitent was expected to spend a lifetime in wariness of relapse. Often one was prohibited for life from carrying arms, engaging in commerce or having marital relations. The mortal sinner might as well join a monastery—and many did.

Throughout the eighth and early ninth centuries, the Irish form of Confession gradually became accepted within the entire Church. The Sacrament was to be received, at the initiation of the sinner, as often as he required. The Church itself encouraged the faithful to confess twice annually, at Lent and Advent. Because the new form was private, the Church fathers now had to confront the challenge of absolute privacy. With a decree in 874 which stated that priests were in no way to betray the confidences of penitents, the Seal of Confession which continues to this day was added to the growing tradition of the Sacrament.

Another key shift occurred which would affect the way Catholics practiced the Sacrament for centuries to come. During this period many confessors began to regularly grant absolution before the completion of the penance. This innovation, begun as a natural part of deathbed confessions, was now slowly becoming the new thrust of the Sacrament's evolution. Obtaining absolution was, for the first time, taking precedence over the completion of penance.

In the eleventh century this reversal of the once-rigid confessional order raised several theological issues. For instance, what if the penitent who had received absolution died with only half his penance completed? Would he, having been absolved, go to Heaven with only half his debt paid to God? Did the grievous sinner who repented on his deathbed ascend to Heaven just as quickly as the lifelong saint? The Catholic theologians of the time neatly answered these perplexing questions which dogged eleventh-century sinners and church fathers. Purgatory was not a new solution, but it offered a viable explanation to this theological dilemma.

The Church defined Purgatory as:

> the state, place or condition in the next world where the souls of those who die in the state of grace, but not yet free from all imperfection, make expiation for unforgiven venial sin and for the temporal punishment due to venial and mortal sins that have already been forgiven. By so doing, they are purified before they enter Heaven.

Initially Purgatory was not an overly threatening place—cleansing, en route to Heaven, was stressed over punishment. All too soon, however, the place of purging was transformed into a place of terrible pain. Purgatory came to resemble the fires of Hell with the only relief being the limited amount of time spent there.

The notion of time continued to taunt the theologians of the Middle Ages as they endlessly debated how long a sinner must spend in the expiation of sins. Before the revival of Purgatory, theologians were limited by the lifespan of the sinner in deciding the length of time and manner in which sins should be repented for and purged. Now, they had eternity to play with.

The Second Council of Lyons, in 1274, resolved the matter by officially establishing the existence of Purgatory:

> If those who are truly repentant die in charity before they have done sufficient penance for their sins of omission and commission, their souls are cleansed in purgatorial or cleansing punishment.

Because the pain and punishment one could expect in Purgatory was almost as terrifying as Hell, sinners of the time quickly looked for a means of avoiding it.

The solution was found again in the teachings of the early Christians. St. Paul described the Church as a form of the body of Christ. Tertullian in the third century argued, "The body cannot rejoice over the misery of one of its members; rather the whole body suffer and work together for a cure." Hugh of Saint-Cher in the thirteenth century spoke of a "treasury of merits" and the concept of vicarious satisfaction. St. Thomas Aquinas later defined the "treasury of merits" as the accumulation of satisfaction derived from the suffering of Christ, who had never sinned, and the charity of the saints, who had endured an abundance of suffering.

This merit, contended Aquinas, could be shared by other members of the Church to help them attain the ultimate goal of Heaven. A portion of this treasury was called an "indulgence," derived according to some sources as "forgiveness." The Church would administer the sharing of this merit, donating quantities of it to certain repentant sinners to enable them to spend less time suffering the punishment of Purgatory.

Neither the size of the treasury of merits nor the time to be spent in Purgatory, nor the number of saints who contributed these merits, were dogmatically counted. Saints originally were only those men and women who had been martyred for their faith. In the Middle Ages their ranks were swelled by the canonization of famous ascetics because of their good example.

Securing an indulgence soon became a welcome alternative to penance and punishment in Purgatory. To all Christians who fought in the First Crusade against the forces of Islam in 1095, Pope Urban II offered a plenary indulgence, the remission of all penance to be served in Purgatory, which meant an immediate ascension into Heaven upon death. "Whosoever out of pure devotion and not for the sake of gaining honor or money shall go to Jerusalem to liberate the Church of God, may count that journey in lieu of all penance." A partial indulgence remitted part of the punishment.

Soon the Church began to sell indulgences, their sale believed to be for a good cause. Most of the initial monies generated by the sales contributed to the construction of Europe's great cathedrals, and subsidized some of the period's greatest works of art.

As with the earlier practice of commutation of penances, the potential for abuse was realized early as people began to purchase more indulgences than they could ever use. In the twelfth century Peter Abelard condemned indulgence sales, claiming they fostered

37

greed in the bishops and laziness in the penitents. A century later Hugh of Saint-Cher argued indulgences were not alternatives to penance.

The sale of indulgences soon joined Confession in the contest for people's souls. While the Sacrament provided forgiveness and absolution, the treasury of merits provided a quick and painless way to expiate sin—and avoid penance and Purgatory.

Despite the popularity of indulgences in the thirteenth century, the Irish form of the Sacrament officially became the norm for most dedicated believers. Frequent, secret Confession to a priest, with absolution preceding penance, was accepted by the entire Roman Church. The Fourth Lateran Council in 1215 formalized the Sacrament, making it mandatory that every Christian confess his mortal sins at least once a year in order to receive Easter Communion. Up to this time, the initiative to confess was left entirely up to the penitent. The age at which confession could be made was also modified. The Council stated:

> Let everyone of the faithful of both sexes, after he has reached the age of discretion (fourteen), devotedly confess in private all his mortal sins at least once a year to his priest in order to take the Pascal (Easter) Communion.

It appeared that, as widely accepted as the Sacrament was, confession had finally obtained a stability that would carry it forward over the centuries unchanged and unchallenged. This, however, was not to be the case.

Chapter 3

The Plague Years . . . 1300–1600

1347, The Chapel of St. Gregorio, Messina, Italy

"Holy Mary, Mother of God, born without sin . . ." The young fisherman reverently enunciated each word. He was going to be married in two weeks. The fat, white-haired priest to whom he was confessing hardly moved from his chair; his stole was draped over the penitent's shoulders.

"I approach my marriage bed blemished, Father," the young man whispered.

"Your contrition can purify you anew if you are truly contrite. How did you sin?" The voice of the priest was low and monotonous.

The young man glanced about the tiny chapel as if to ensure the total privacy of his confidences. *"First, with a widow . . ."*

"Did you lie with her often?"

"Yes, Father, but no longer, not since I was betrothed to Carla."

"Was there anyone else with whom you endangered your immortal soul?"

The young man nodded, but the priest had his eyes closed.

"Yes Father, there were others."

"With whom?" the priest asked, his voice reflecting the indifference of a weary teacher.

"With the women of the sailors."

The priest nodded, taking a long time to consider this admission.

"Have you ceased this abomination?"

"Yes, I have, Father . . ."

The two of them paused, both remembering.

"For your penance, Benito, I want you to recite a rosary every day for a year, taking time to consider the perfect chastity of the Blessed Virgin."

The Church in the Middle Ages was corpulent. Confession had evolved into a scourging sacrament—the lack of compassion with which it was practiced reflected the general malaise of the Church. The most terrible natural calamity in the history of Western civilization was about to occur, and the way Catholics would confess their sins to a priest was about to be drastically changed.

On an October day in 1347 twelve galleys bearing spices and silks from the East entered the harbor of Messina on the island of Sicily.

The Plague Years. . .1300–1600

When the first of the boats scraped against the quays, the condition of the sailors was recognized with horror. Most of them were gaunt, gave off a terrible odor and many had egg-sized black swellings on their necks and under their arms. They pleaded for help in vain. The people of Messina had heard rumors about "a fierce pestilence coming out of the East, caused by a corrupting cloud that would rain snakes and scorpions, leeches and lizards . . . Syria was a carpet of corpses and India was depopulated."

The Black Death, the bubonic plague, had arrived in Europe. There is no way to exaggerate this natural holocaust. "The buboes or boils were sometimes described as knods, kernals, biles, blaines, blisters, pimples or wheals," Boccaccio wrote. "In men and women alike, it first betrayed itself by the emergence of certain tumors in the groin or armpit, some of which grew as large as an apple, others as an egg. All the matter which exuded from their bodies let off an unbearable stench, so foetid as to be overpowering."

Medicine in the fourteenth century was more superstition than science, lending nothing in the way of an explanation, much less a cure for this horrendous disease. Some said it was caused by the movement of the stars. Others raged against the perfidy of the Jews and brutally extracted false confessions from them, persecuting them for their so-called guilt. The Church blamed God's rage at his sinning people for the plague and the people countered by pointing to the Church's corruption as the cause of God's fury.

The list of accusations against the hierarchy was as long as it was accurate—immorality, rivalry, pluralism, absenteeism, nepotism and avarice all characterized the Church in the Middle Ages. So greedy had the Church become that there were counters in the Vatican where one could buy a bishop's seat or a cardinal's hat. It was not necessary for a prelate to live in or even occasionally visit his bishopric to collect taxes from it. Some relatives of popes hoarded as many as five dioceses, using the proceeds of the churches to line their own pockets.

The full force of the Black Death subsided by 1350, after having killed one third of the population of Europe. The grim survivors became bitter realists. Many recalled neighbors who had refused them food, and brigands who had ransacked their homes. They glorified the priests who had stayed among them, hearing confessions and giving last rites to multitudes of the stricken who were about to be buried in mass graves. Clerics who had fled their parishes for safer havens were reviled by survivors of the Black Death. As the stunned populace looked back, many held to the maxim, "The best of the clergy died, and the worst survived."

As the Black Death ended the Church was radically changed, forced as it was to fill its ranks with second-rate replacements. Rough, uneducated men with no other vocation than poverty were ordained to fill the parishes. Most of the men who sought the solace of the Holy Orders could neither read nor write. Moral laxity, which before had mainly been the province of the privileged, spread throughout the Church from pope to priest. Another adage of the day among Catholic believers was "If you want to go to Hell, become a priest."

The Sacrament of Confession must be numbered among the principal casualties of the Black Death. The Fourth Lateran Council in 1215 had encouraged the frequent practice of the Sacrament when it declared it a ritual to be received annually by those in grievous sin. Now Confession was once again becoming a sacrament to be avoided. The survivors of the plague were less concerned about the mystical concepts of Heaven and Hell than they were about surviving, and Confession was regarded as a deterrent to the few pleasures they felt they had earned by simply staying alive.

Confession in the Middle Ages continued to become more and more inquisitional as priests probed deeper and deeper to discover the source of sin in order to better confront and defeat it. This led to inevitable abuses, as celibate men listened to the details of sexual sins committed by their penitents. One of the formulas used by confessors to extract information about sexual sins went as follows: "Friend, do you remember when you were young, about ten or twelve, if your rod or virile member ever stood erect? Friend, wasn't that thing indecent? What did you do, therefore, that it wouldn't stand erect?"

Still, there were attempts to limit the extent to which a priest could question a penitent on sexual matters. In *Memoriale Presbiterorum* confessors were warned about questioning sailors too closely about their sins. "You must be very cautious in inquiring because you should know that the pen can scarcely suffice to write the sins in which they are involved for such is their wickedness that it exceeds that of all other men." At the other extreme, priests were taught not to probe too deeply into sexual areas with less experienced men lest they teach them things they didn't know in the first place.

Despite the tales of wildly licentious behavior of the times—Rome boasted more than 10,000 prostitutes—the Church's attitude toward sex in the Middle Ages was determinedly conservative. Sexual organs were called *turpia,* shameful things. Pleasure from sex, even in the marriage bed, was something to be avoided and could be judged a mortal sin. According to the confessional guides of the period, a man could be deemed guilty of adultery with his own wife if the act he performed with her was such that he would have performed it even if she were not his wife. Such sexual ethics of the period originated with celibate monks who praised virginity over marriage, and who taught that procreation, not pleasure, was the purpose of the marriage bed. This exaltation of reproduction so influenced the theologians of the day that it became the barometer in judging all sexual sins. According to this moral code incest and rape, which could result in a pregnancy, were lesser sins than masturbation or homosexuality, in which the seed was spilled.

The all-pervasive dominion of the Church at this period is difficult to imagine today. The pope and his bishops were able to dictate the policies of kings as well as the sex lives of parishioners. The Church reasoned that it had to be a temporal power in order to be a better spiritual one. Innocent III (1198–1216), the 177th pope, who presided over the Fourth Lateran Council, also presided over the pinnacle of Church power. During his reign, it was said that Europe could not be conceived without a pope. The continent came as close to a total theocracy as it ever would, as the Church feuded with emperors, pitting Church against nation, king against pope.

43

Calls for reform were cautiously whispered, but they had not yet found full voice. The first of the dissenters to speak up on behalf of those disgruntled with Church policy was the Englishman John Wycliffe, born in 1329. A survivor of the Black Death, he sought to lessen the Church's involvement with temporal matters, and spoke out against the exportation of British wealth at papal whim. A master of Balliol College, Oxford, and the translator of Jerome's Vulgate Bible into English, he wrote in his *English Works*, "Privy confession made to priests is not needed but brought in late by the Fiend." On New Year's Eve 1384 he died of a stroke before the Church could directly refute his heresies against it.

A second voice was soon heard coming from the Bohemian priest John Hus, born in 1369. Hus had been directly influenced by Wycliffe, whose teachings were carried to Bohemia by the scholars who accompanied King Richard II's queen, Anne of Bohemia. He had been a respected reformer in Prague, but when he started quoting Wycliffe he touched a painful nerve in Rome. In 1412 he sharply criticized the arrival in Prague of a papal agent who was sent to raise money for the Church by selling indulgences; Hus was promptly excommunicated. The stubborn reformer was then guaranteed safe passage to the Council of Constance, where he continued to defend his beliefs. When Hus refused to recant, he was burned at the stake. The torch was then turned on the long dead Wycliffe, whose remains were exhumed from his grave in Lutterworth, England, set afire and thrown into a river. Hus's incendiary execution stifled dissent for the next century, but the seeds of reform had been sown.

The fifteenth century was a fertile period during which many stimulating ideas and innovations took root. Feudalism declined in favor of mercantilism; Columbus and Da Gama discovered new worlds, and after them, sailors in great ships, guided by new compasses, charts and astrolabes dominated the seas.

It was an era of extremes, harboring both the Inquisition and the rise of rationalism. The 100 Years War ended in 1453, and prosperity spread almost as quickly as the Black Death a century before. The Italian Renaissance flowered, enlivening the arts with classical inspiration. The wealthy took their many pleasures, dressed as gaudily as birds, and Dante described Hell with foreboding genius.

The most important event of the era was Johann Gutenberg's invention of the printing press in 1454. Suddenly, accessible knowledge fueled inquiry, and universities flourished in most of the great cities. Literacy filtered down to an expanding middle class enabling people to read their own bibles, and priests were once again reading confessional guides. One such guide, *Manipilus Curatorum*, went through ninety editions in Madrid, London and Paris and was still selling well a hundred years later.

The impact of the new literacy was felt in the Church as the printing press made information more readily available to all. Court scandals were tittered over in cafes, and Church gossip was whispered simultaneously in Rome, Prague and Lisbon. Corruption within the higher reaches of the clergy was not a new phenomenon, but now reports of such corruption were available to commoners, to the men and women who had been taught to revere their priests and accept their word as divine doctrine. Two popular topics of discussion in mid-fifteenth-century Europe were, most likely, which papal bastards were elevated to the Curia and which new indulgences were the current rage.

The promise of indulgences had helped recruit armies of Crusaders in the eleventh and twelfth centuries and helped finance cathedrals in the thirteenth and fourteenth. Now those promises degenerated into a most venal corruption. One example of sixteenth-century indulgence huckstering was the "confessional letter." A direct descendant of the letters of peace following the Decian persecutions, confessional letters enabled purchasers to insure themselves against punishment in Purgatory for any sinful acts they might commit.

Another clerical abuse of the time resembled a spiritual gift certificate, in which a blank space was provided for filling in the name of the person to whom it was made out, living or dead. If the certificate were purchased for someone who had already died, he or she was entitled to instant absolution from all sins and all punishment. Armed with these plenary dispensations, many men and women rarely bothered to make confessions, believing that at the time of death they would be guaranteed an immediate ascension into Heaven.

Although it had long subsided, the Black Death continued to haunt the era. An outbreak occurred in 1500 and was particularly virulent in the German town of Eiselben, where it struck the two elder sons of Hans Luder. Whereupon Luder's youngest son announced he wanted to become a priest, but the father argued that "a celibate begging friar would be no son of mine." After the death of his first son, however, Luder relented and permitted his youngest son to join a monastery, if only because it was far from the infected region. Thus was Martin Luther allowed to become a Black Friar of the Augustinian Hermits. His choice of vocation would later change the world, and the Sacrament of Confession along with it.

Indulgences continued to be a popular substitute for Confession. Pope after pope encouraged their sale, providing a steady source of income for Rome. But the campaign for the sale of indulgences would seem tame until the time when Albert of Hohenzollern, an ambitious twenty-one-year-old who was not even an ordained priest, decided he wanted to become an archbishop. In the bargaining sessions for the purchase of three bishoprics, both Albert and the Church displayed a wry sense of spiritual values. The Pope's agent asked 12,000 ducats for the sees, an appropriate figure reminding one of the twelve Apostles. Albert's representatives countered with a bid of 7,000, recalling the seven deadly sins. A compromise was achieved at 10,000 ducats, in memory of the Ten Commandments.

All in all, Albert's lofty ecclesiastical ambitions cost him 34,000 ducats, a sum he hoped to recover by selling indulgences and sharing the profits with Rome. To ensure brisk sales, Albert hired Johannes Tetzel, prior of a Dominican monastery. "Drop a few coins in the box and you can rescue the souls of your friends or relatives from the flames of Purgatory," was Tetzel's glib promise. In 1516 Tetzel's indulgence-selling campaign arrived near the university town of Wittenburg where the scrupulous young novice Martin Luther had become an even more scrupulous friar.

Luther, not in tune with the spiritual fashions of the times, preferred confession as a means of attaining salvation rather than the questionable route of indulgences; he was reputed to confess for six hours at a stretch, driving his spiritual directors to distraction. It so happened that Tetzel was selling his indulgences one day at the same time Luther was scolding a group of students for their sinful ways. The students bantered that they didn't have to worry about sin staining their souls; salvation, they claimed, was guaranteed—they had just purchased some of Tetzel's indulgences.

Luther responded by channeling his anger into a finely wrought criticism called *95 Theses*, which he nailed to the door of the castle church at Wittenburg on the eve of All Saints' Day, October 31, 1517. Arguing that the sale of indulgences demeaned the already weakened Sacrament of Penance, he wrote that contrition should be the cornerstone of a good confession, not the evasion of punishment.

To everyone's surprise, including his own, Luther's *95 Theses* sold an amazing 4,000 copies in three weeks—with his indictment he had unwittingly captured the anger and disillusionment festering within Germany.

The Church's initial reaction to the attack was calm, reasoning that the young cleric was simply overexcited, given as he was to becoming overwrought. The Church fathers hoped to contain the incident while the friar's ardor cooled down and he could be set back on the road to ecclesiastical correctness. Luther, however, was not about to be cooled. The following year he published *Resolutions Concerning the Virtue of Indulgences,* in which he amplified the points made in *95 Theses.* To ensure that no one could accuse him of heresy, he dedicated the tract to Pope Leo X.

The patience of the Church began to wear thin as Luther became more radical and threatening every day. At the Leipzig Debate in 1519 the Church expected that the rebellious friar would exonerate himself and the whole matter would be dropped. Instead, Luther all but ensured his excommunication by arguing that "in the Sacrament of Penance, sins were forgiven solely because of God's presence, not because of repentance." On May 8, 1521, the Edict of

Worms accused him of heresy, heir to the blasphemies espoused by Wycliffe and Hus. It was a heritage he would be proud to bear.

The public by now was clamoring to hear everything Luther had to say. He described Rome as "a city of buying, selling, changing, exchanging, tippling, lying, deceiving, robbing, stealing, boasting, whoring, knaving." He pungently described his nagging effect on that city: "If I break wind in Wittenburg, they hear it in Rome."

As Luther's words raged throughout Holland, Denmark, Sweden and Switzerland, a more lasting effect was realized as the Protestant Reformation was born.

Even in Martin Luther's death, on January 23, 1546, there was controversy. One doctor reported he died of apoplexy. A second opinion argued that that was impossible since apoplexy was believed to be the result of divine wrath and Luther was holy. A compromise was speedily reached, and the official cause of death was listed as a heart attack. His departure from earth was also subject to dispute—some swore that devils hauled him away in clouds of sulphur and brimstone while others claimed to have witnessed his ascent to Heaven in a fiery chariot of the Lord.

Regardless, his death had enormous impact on the Church— riddled with dissent and weakened by revolt. Word was rushed to a small Tyrolean town where bishops and cardinals were meeting in council to rid the Church of Luther's abominations.

The site of the council had been chosen with Machiavellian care: Trent, in northern Italy, was a charming little city situated at the opening of the lowest pass in the Alps. Emperor Charles V had wanted the conclave be held on German soil to avoid papal domination, but the Pope insisted on Italy—and he won.

The Council of Trent, begun in 1545, a quarter of a century after Luther first planted the seeds of the Reformation, took eighteen years to complete. The Council was to be a momentous achievement for Roman Catholicism, for here the "modern Church" was born, resulting in decisions that would guide the Church as well as Confession for over four hundred years. The Council defined the sanctity and the discipline of the sacraments forevermore and forbade, in no uncertain terms, the sale of indulgences. It was at this

time that the tenth-century oral tradition in granting absolution—
"I absolve you in the name of the Father, the Son and the Holy
Spirit"—was codified. The Council reestablished that Confession
prior to receiving communion was mandatory only for those who
had committed mortal sin. At Trent, a marked emphasis on the
legalistic nature of the Sacrament emerged and, with it, absolution
came to resemble an act in which the priest, seeing himself as judge,
passed a sentence on the guilty penitent.

On November 25, 1551, at the fourteenth session, the Council
declared that the Sacrament of Penance was never again to be
questioned by anyone, in any way. The language was defensively
adamant:

> If anyone denieth either that Sacramental Confession was
> instituted or is necessary to salvation of divine right; or
> saith that the manner of confession secretly to a priest
> alone, which the Church hath ever observed from the
> beginning and doth observe, is alien from the institution
> and command of Christ and is a human invention let him
> be anathema.

For Confession, the case was closed.

Ironically, this most auspicious Council began rather inauspi-
ciously. Of the 700 bishops eligible to attend, only thirty-one arrived for the opening ceremonies. The majority of those that did
come held the interests of their own monarchs in greater esteem
than the interests of the Pope. They squabbled and bickered, and
on one occasion even resorted to beard-pulling. Yet Pope Paul III
(1534–1549), who pronounced that American Indians had souls,
had his way at almost every turn. The European rulers were aghast
at the power they lost in that little Tyrolean town. Spain's King
Philip II, in the lisp that, according to legend, has influenced Castil-
lian pronunciation ever since, complained that his "bishops had
gone to the Council as bishops and returned as parish priests."

Throughout its eighteen-year duration, Trent was in constant
turmoil as a result of infighting and political maneuvering. When
Emperor Charles V overtly attempted to influence the Council,

Paul III took advantage of another outbreak of the plague and hastily shifted the assembly to Bologna. Many bishops, allies of the monarchs, claimed the epidemic as a mere papal rumor and demanded to see medical certificates. In the following years, the Council withered away in Bologna, and when Paul III died, it was suspended.

Trent was reconvened in 1560 by Pope Pius IV (1559–1565), a man who had fathered three illegitimate children in his youth, but who was later genuinely committed to girding the Church against further encroachments from Protestant heresies. His ascendancy to the Throne of St. Peter was greeted with rejoicing by his relatives. Twenty-eight cousins and in-laws arrived in Rome, all clamoring for appointments. All were refused.

One nephew, however, who had made no petition, was chosen to serve. His name was Charles Borromeo, a twenty-two-year-old who had received his doctorate in canon law from Padua University. Pius IV appointed his young relative as head of the *consulta*, effectively making him Secretary of State. Known as the "cardinal nephew," he soon became the Pope's "right eye."

Despite the nepotism in the appointment, Borromeo proved a spectacularly wise choice. At Trent he represented his uncle's views and assembled groups of bishops to ensure that their final decisions coincided with those of papal policies. In effect, this young unordained cardinal became the driving force of the Council, the whip of reform.

Borromeo, excited by the attitude of retrenchment at Trent, was anxious to inaugurate the new disciplines. In 1565, 2 years after the termination of the Council, he begged his uncle to give him the Archbishopric of Milan. A sprawling domain of more than 1,000 parishes, stretching over vast regions of northern Italy and into Switzerland, it was infamous for its corruption.

For all its need of reform, Milan could never have anticipated the holy whirlwind about to engulf it. At 27 years of age, newly ordained, with no diocesan experience, Borromeo entered Milan, the first archbishop to actually reside there after almost a century. Borromeo quickly established himself as a stern but respected prelate as well as an innovative reformer. His zeal, coupled with his inventiveness, would change the way Catholics confess their sins for the next 400 years.

Legend recounts that Borromeo's birth was accompanied by celestial light. When he was born a bright illumination reportedly filled the room, heralding his sanctity. He began to fulfill this glowing prediction at an early age by building tiny altars and insisting on taking the sacred tonsure at the age of seven.

Like Luther, Borromeo was a man of contrasts. Although well noted as a preacher, he stuttered. Born to a Medici mother and a family of enormous wealth, he spent his adult life fasting and inflicting bodily mortifications. Elevated to power through the nepotism of his uncle, he scrupulously appointed his own aides on merit alone. He seemed to have little joy in life beyond the spiritual; under his cardinal's robes, he wore rags. He rarely laughed, hardly slept. Although not blessed with a major intellect, he succeeded through a combination of ardor and blind ambition to become a saint.

Nowhere was Borromeo's passionate determination to succeed better seen than in his attitude toward the plague which struck Milan, yet again, in 1576. The idea of running from the Black Death never occurred to him; he confronted it head-on. To combat the pestilence, he brought the people to the streets, and God to the people, despite strong medical arguments suggesting avoidance of large crowds. He erected altars throughout the city, and ordered Mass to be celebrated daily. Priests were to walk the streets carrying chairs so that they could hear the confessions of the afflicted while seated outside their windows.

Borromeo, the relentless reformer, insisted that his priests confess once a week, cut off their beards and cease carrying firearms. Parties, along with all other forms of gatherings except for religious reasons, were banned, and the only music permitted was that of the church organ. While many welcomed his vigorous reforms, others wished him dead. On two occasions, would-be assassins, members of religious orders he was attempting to reform, tried to kill him. Their failure only added to his saintly legend.

Bless Me, Father, For I Have Sinned

The ascetic cardinal vigilantly defended his sanctity, ever on guard against the temptation of women, whom he regarded as occasions of sin. As an additional guard against them he erected a giant curtain in the center of his cathedral so that women would not distract men during religious services. Pleased with this innovation, he made it a permanent fixture by building a wooden screen along the length of the nave.

According to history, Borromeo once spotted an immodestly dressed woman and furiously lashed out at her: "Miserable creature, you give no heed to your salvation." When the woman was found dead in her bed the following day, the faithful spoke in awe of his special powers.

Like so many of the Church fathers before him, Borromeo worried about the dangers of hearing women's confessions. He believed there was great moral jeopardy, both for the priest and the penitent, when a woman whispered the details of her intimate life into the ear of her confessor in a secluded part of the church.

Penitential and confessional guides had repeatedly contained prohibitions regarding the place for hearing the confessions of women. There were specific warnings never to be in a "hidden place with a female." Two hundred years before, the Church had commanded that women's confessions be heard "extra velum," meaning that a veil to safeguard decorum was to be placed between the female and the priest.

Borromeo, the astute inventor, had previously devised a box, a *capsa incertorum,* which was placed at the door of all churches to enable thieves to make secret reparations. He now addressed his innovative skills to the centuries-old problem of women's confessions. By combining the wooden screens of his cathedrals with the boxes for reparations, he solved the riddle of keeping Confession both private and public, and finally succeeded in protecting the decorum of the Sacrament.

Borromeo fashioned an ingenious chamber, constructed entirely of walnut, elaborately ornamented with a trelliswork door, closed on three sides, covered on top, but entirely open in front, curtained, divided by two walls, each with small grilled windows. In the year 1576 Charles Borromeo created the confessional.

Borromeo died on November 3, 1584. Twenty-six years later his lifelong ambition was achieved and he was canonized.

As the fifteenth century came to a close, so, too, did the controversy and rebellion to which the Sacrament had been subjected. The Council of Trent had decreed the Sacrament inviolate; the injunction set forth appeared secure. The evolution of its practice had been completed . . . at least for the time being.

Chapter 4

The American Years (1850–1962)

Not until the nineteenth and twentieth centuries would dramatic change once again affect the Sacrament of Confession, innovations brought about once again by the Irish—only this time on American shores. Unlike their contribution centuries before, the changes to come were not spurred by scholarship or spirituality, but by a natural tragedy that none could foresee—or avert.

Ireland in the 1840s was a disaster waiting to happen. Hindsight captures the early warning symptoms easily, but no one at the time could foretell the calamity about to strike.

The country's dependence on agriculture was both its bane and its boon. Ireland's lack of mineral resources had slowed its industrial start. Local industry could not compete with British manufacturers, further exaggerating the economy's dependence on the land. Landlords led gentrified lives far beyond their means, exhausting the capital that more sensibly should have been invested to encourage more efficient use of their farms.

The primary product of Ireland's small farms was the potato, an ideal food, wonderfully nutritious, but one with a major drawback —unlike grain, the potato could not be stored and preserved for future needs. The Irish poor, who composed the bulk of the population, were dangerously dependent on the potato.

The first hint of the looming catastrophe occurred 3,000 miles away. Potato blight struck the eastern seaboard of the United States and Canada in 1842, and a year later, it ravaged the crop in England.

Two thirds of Ireland's eight million people depended on the potato for their livelihood, and for many it was their sole sustenance. In 1845 the potato blight struck the island. With a killing instinct as brutal as the Black Death, the entire potato crop was spoiled, devastating the nation. Nature's fury, however, did not rest that year—the winter was one of the harshest ever. Typhus, dysentery and scurvy soon attacked the weakened populace. The proportions of the blight echo like Armageddon arithmetic. One million Irishmen died.

As hordes of survivors fled the countryside for the cities, the pestilence in the already crowded slums spread even further. Thousands rushed to the coasts, where they waded into the water to devour seaweed which soured their stomachs. The sea, however, offered a different kind of lifesaving solution . . .

Over the next six years two million people left Ireland, the majority of them emigrating to the United States. Many by far found that the thirty-five-day Atlantic crossing was as arduous as the life they had left behind. The vessels which carried the broken survivors of the famine for fares as little as ten dollars became known as "coffin ships"; at least one in nine of its weakened passengers died. One of those who survived the journey was John Rock, a man whose future grandson was to change the world.

The Irish in the mid-nineteenth century were not alone in fleeing Europe for the haven of America. Eighteen forty-eight was a year of revolt. Within months, most of continental Europe was shaken by a series of uprisings. In Italy, Germany, France and Austria, rulers were overthrown, forcing hundreds of thousands of political exiles to seek safety in the new democracy.

When the "potato famine" Irish arrived in America they discovered that their countrymen who had preceded them had already established a foothold in the Church; by 1830, four of every ten bishops were Irish-born or native-born Americans of Irish descent. Soon, the bulk of the clergy would come from these new immigrants.

Many of these Irish considered themselves American as soon as they set foot on U.S. soil. Since they already spoke the language, they soon dominated the police, the firefighters and the priests of this new land. They fashioned the Church in their own image, which was resolutely Catholic after years of English Protestant domination of Ireland. The Irish Church, from its monastic beginnings, had always been tightly organized, and this cohesiveness was brought to the American Church as well. For many of the new Irish immigrants the Sacrament of Confession was a source of compassion, a welcome haven for those men and women harshly uprooted from their native land and confronted with a startling new culture. In the confessional, they could find a little bit of Ireland.

Contrary to myth, the Irish were not welcomed into "the American Dream" with open arms, although anti-Catholicism in the United States did not begin with the arrival of the famine Irish. A New York law drafted in 1700 had decreed that any ordained priest who practiced Catholic rites would be deemed and accounted an incendiary and disturber of the public peace and safety and was to be banished from the colony. Seventy-six years later the plight of Catholics had not noticeably improved. Of the fifty-six men who signed the Declaration of Independence, only one was a Catholic. The Penal Laws, universal in the thirteen colonies, were based on the assumption that Catholicism was a political conspiracy. Only four of the original states—Pennsylvania, Delaware, Virginia and Maryland—granted Catholics equality with other Christians.

Religious resentment simmered during the early years of the

Republic, flaring occasionally into violence. In 1834 a mob raided a Boston convent on the premise of rescuing an unwilling novice. A decade later, in Philadelphia, bigots raged when a bishop sought to exempt Catholic children from reading the Protestant Bible at school. In the ensuing riot, churches, convents and rectories were set afire and thirteen people were killed.

Anti-Catholicism was blind and irrational, although it had originally sprung from seeds of distrust. The early English settlers were wary of their original competitors for the continent, the Catholic French and Spanish. This natural wariness continued to grow, especially by 1850 when Roman Catholicism had become the country's largest religious denomination.

Thrust into this emotional climate of suspicion, the Irish who came seeking security were confronted instead with hostility and humiliation. Eager to work for a pittance beyond the normal twelve-hour day, they met signs that warned, "No Irish Need Apply." Their willingness to toil for meager wages in America's fledgling industries endeared them to no one but unscrupulous employers.

In 1852 Pope Pius IX (1846–1878) donated a block of stone for the Washington Monument. An anti-Catholic mob later hurled it into the Potomac River. That same year, the First Plenary Council of Baltimore was held and Catholics were urged to build their own schools. These councils were to shape the entire American Church for more than five decades. Bishops from every diocese in the United States, adhering to the norms laid down by the Council of Trent, set the tone for almost all aspects of Catholic life in the United States. From 1829 until 1894 seven provincial and three plenary councils were held in Baltimore, which was called the "Yankee" Rome of the times.

The decision of 1852 to create a separate educational system was the first official Church reaction to bigotry, and to the secularization of schools, started by Horace Mann in 1840. If American society was going to be hostile to the Church, then the Church would protect its own. As they began building their schools, the first bricks of fortress Catholicism in America were being laid. It was this educational entrenchment, spurred by prejudice, that would, over the next hundred years, influence how North Americans would confess their sins to their priests.

As the North and the South edged closer to war, Abraham Lincoln was quoted on the issue of anti-Catholicism: "When the Know Nothings get control, it will read 'All men are created equal except Negroes, foreigners and Catholics.' When it comes to this," Lincoln warned, "I shall prefer emigrating to some country where they make no pretense of loving liberty—to Russia, for instance."

Father Charles Chiniquy, a Canadian born in 1809 and ordained a priest in 1833, was the most notorious anti-Catholic activist of the nineteenth century. He was responsible for misquoting the President and forging the following foreboding words in Lincoln's name to further incite other Americans against Catholics: "I see a very dark cloud on our horizon, and that dark cloud is coming from Rome. It is filled with tears of blood."

The excommunicated Chiniquy is more famous for a scurrilous bit of literature called *The Priest, the Woman and the Confessional,* published in 1880. It was a stunning example of how words can be used as weapons. Chiniquy wrote:

Why is it that the Irish Roman Catholic people are so irreparably degraded and clothed in rags? Why is it that people, whom God has endowed with so many noble qualities, seem to be so deprived of intelligence and self-respect that they glory in their own shame? The principal cause is the enslaving of the Irish woman, by means of the confessional. Everyone knows that the spiritual slavery and degradation of the Irish woman has no bounds. After she has been enslaved and degraded, she, in turn, has enslaved and degraded her husband and her sons. Ireland will be an object of pity; she will be poor, miserable, riotous, bloodthirsty, degraded, so long as she rejects Christ, to be ruled by father confessor, planted in every parish by the Pope.

Bless Me, Father, For I Have Sinned

One of the most infamous examples of anti-Catholic tracts was "The Awful Disclosures of Maria Monk," a fabricated account of a captive in a Montreal convent, replete with lurid depictions of the infanticide of nuns' children. The author and reputed victim of these outrages was a female, who was later arrested as a pickpocket in a brothel and died in jail. These lurid "disclosures" were to resurface many times throughout the nineteenth and twentieth centuries.

A Who's Who of Anti-Catholicism would be a thick book. From Ulysses S. Grant to telegraph inventor Samuel Morse to writer Mark Twain—who offered another example of venomous anti-Catholicism in his *Letters from the Earth*—the insidious prejudice was a nineteenth-century success story as it flourished and grew stronger. Slogans such as "rebellion, Catholicism and whiskey" and "rum, Romanism and rebellion" helped achieve the bigot's goal, the gradual separation of the Church from mainstream American life.

Fortress Catholicism started raising the drawbridge most doggedly in 1884 at the Third Plenary Council of Baltimore. The language of the bishops was strong and the instruction was clear: "Parents *must* send their children to parochial schools unless the bishop should judge the reason for sending them elsewhere to be sufficient." A note of urgency was evident as well: "No parish is complete until it has adequate schools to satisfy the needs of its children." That same year James Cardinal Gibbons prepared the *Baltimore Catechism,* the basic text for religious education which would be used for more than a century.

The decision to require a Catholic education for every Catholic child proved to be a watershed for both the American Catholic Church and the way the Sacrament of Penance was to be practiced. The energies and resources of all Catholics were greatly taxed as parochial schools were built—the Church was becoming a temporal as well as a spiritual power in America. More importantly, however, this insular Catholic education would eventually result in the creation of a child-rooted mentality that American Catholic men and women would bring to their priests in the confessional—a lack of understanding that would plague the Sacrament as adults continued to confess as children, seeking approval from their confessors as father figures. It was here that confession became passive and reward/punishment oriented, instead of a dynamic encounter inviting love and growth.

As Gary Wills perceptively wrote in *Bare Ruined Choirs: Doubt, Prophecy and Radical Religion:*

> That one decision entailed many things. It meant a poor body of immigrants would have to make great sacrifices to build their own schools. It meant nuns would have to be recruited and trained in large numbers to staff the schools. It meant that these nuns would have at least as much formative influence on Catholics as priests did. . . . It meant that nuns would not be contemplatives in America, nor merely the teachers of young ladies from the upper class, but teachers of all Catholics, young and old, girl and boy. It meant Catholicism would be in large part child-centered, its piety a feminine sort.

And so began the American Catholic experience of shared knowledge and shared ignorance.

While the defensive Church continued to cloister itself, an ally to American Catholicism was elected to the throne of St. Peter in 1903 on the seventh ballot—with a crucial assist from Cardinal Gibbons of Baltimore. Guiseppi Sarto's elevation as Pius X was a relatively quiet one, because the new pontiff posted notices at his coronation forbidding the faithful in St. Peter's to applaud him.

This humble son of a postman, however, was soon to make enough noise on his own as he dug in his heels and confronted the new century's headlong rush toward the future. He tackled modernism and, in so doing, focused unwanted secular attention on the Church, rekindling suspicion of a reactionary religion worthy only of ridicule.

Pius X (1903–1914), the first pope to be elected in the twentieth century and the first to be canonized since the sixteenth, was to have the greatest influence on the practice of the Sacrament of

Confession since St. Charles Borromeo. Coincidentally, Pius X revered the memory of the sixteenth-century Milanese innovator and dedicated an encyclical to him.

Opinion about his eleven-year pontificate is divided. Some historians scorn his intransigence in the face of modernism and his ostrichlike response to the realities of science. Others softened their appraisal, seeing him as a guardian of Catholicism in changing times who wanted scholarship stimulated from within rather than from outside the Church. Pius X was a man trained entirely in a theology that suspected science might undermine the faith of his least-educated believers. He feared modernism would challenge and irrevocably change his Church. He was to be proven right.

In his attempt to hold back the onslaught of scientific knowledge, he espoused some untenable notions, such as insisting that Moses was the author of the first five books of the Bible; he decreed that all Catholics must believe such spurious scholarship. He forbade seminarians to read secular newspapers and magazines, fearing the contagion of contemporary secular life.

Pius X's contributions to the continuing evolution of Confession are rooted in two of his encyclicals. Both dealt primarily with Communion, but both had great impact on the practice of Penance. In 1905, in *Sacra Tridentina Synodus,* he stressed, "For daily Communion the Catholic must be in a state of grace and have a right intention of receiving. The daily communicant ought to be free of deliberate venial sin and should make a fitting preparation and thanksgiving."

He was urging, in effect, that Catholics seek their sanctity through frequent reception of the Eucharist, which required equally frequent confession even for venial sins. Five years later Pius X's *Quam Singulari* decreed that children should receive their First Communion at the age of discretion, between the age of six and eight, when they could distinguish between ordinary bread and the bread of the Eucharist.

At the time, First Confession preceded First Communion as naturally as the seasons followed one another. Traditionally, children first experienced the Sacrament of Penance when they were fourteen. By cutting the age in half, Pius X reinforced the child-rooted consciousness of the Sacrament already inculcated by the American Catholic educational system. One of the Pope's arguments for lowering the average age of First Communion to seven was that "in ancient times the remaining particles of the Sacred Species were given to nursing infants."

Pius X's reign was scarred by the beginning of the war to end all wars. In the United States, Catholic soldiers as well as priests and nuns were applauded for their loyal response to the call of arms. The walls of prejudice between Catholics and Protestants finally began to erode as the two fought alongside each other in the bloody trenches of World War I.

In the spring of 1913 the ailing seventy-eight-year-old pope voiced his concern about the future to his spiritual adviser. "I am sorry for my successor. I shall not live to see it, but it is unhappily true we are on the brink of a *religio depopulata,*" a depopulated Church. In his final year he had displayed the foresight that had eluded him during most of his clerical career. Pius X died August 20, 1914, and was canonized four decades later.

In 1928 Al Smith, the governor of New York, was nominated as the Democratic candidate for President of the United States. Curiously, this political event would in its time provide the catalyst for more change in the circuitous history of the Sacrament. Smith, a Catholic, was the wrong man at the wrong place at the wrong time; a poorly educated machine politician, his view of American society, as well as the rest of the world, was limited by his Catholic upbringing and his Irish heritage.

Herbert Hoover, the Republican candidate, soundly defeated him. The campaign, however, was marred by a new, virulent outbreak of anti-Catholicism stunning the Church which, by this time, had isolated itself from mainstream American society. The Ku Klux Klan, which had regrouped in 1915, rode into the fray like a demented cavalry, rallying the discontented to their cause. The white-sheeted hooligans mailed millions of postcards trumpeting their alarm. "Smith's success means the President on his knees in the White House, kissing the hand of a Roman cardinal and a confessional in the White House." The Ku Klux Klan also spread the fear that Washington, D.C., would be renamed Piusville or St. Patricksburg, while New York was destined to become New Rome.

Although the outlandish charges were broadcast by a discredited group of bigots, they nevertheless planted sufficient seeds of doubt to be unconsciously absorbed by the electorate.

The effectiveness of the smear campaign was impossible to gauge. While Smith clearly was beaten by a better politician, it will never be known if he was beaten fairly. Nevertheless, after the election, the Catholics of the thirties were disillusioned and retreated further into the safety of their Church-provided fortress. Ostracized by Protestants, Catholics created for themselves a society as complete as that of mainstream America—there were Catholic Boy Scouts and book clubs, bowling teams and fraternities, golf and tennis clubs, orphanages, hospitals, newspapers and magazines. Their most celebrated organization was the Knights of Columbus, so named to honor the Italian explorer who brought Catholicism to the New World. It was possible for urban Catholics to exist entirely in a Catholic cocoon, living, working and socializing only with other Catholics. There was absolutely no need to expose themselves to secular temptations.

The national Catholic football team was Notre Dame. The favorite movie stars of Catholic audiences were those who adhered to the dictates of the Legion of Decency or who played the movie image of Irishmen—such as Bing Crosby, Pat O'Brien and Barry Fitzgerald. In the maelstrom of the Depression, the American Catholic Church provided such pervasive spiritual and social shelter that it lent some truth to the accusations of a Romanist conspiracy a half century before. American Catholicism had truly become a society apart.

In their educational ghetto, Catholic children learned about Confession in ways that encouraged the grocery-list recitation of sins and perpetuated fear of the Sacrament. An excerpt from a 1935 high school history textbook, *The Story of the Church* by Rev. B. N. Forner, demonstrates why so many North American Catholics, young and old, had so little understanding and appreciation of the Sacrament:

> St. Theresa once beheld a vision of a vast multitude of souls of every age and condition falling to Hell as thickly as flakes of snow falling in a winter's storm. Horrified and shaken by the vision, the Saint exclaimed, "Oh, my God, wherefore dost Thou permit all these souls to be lost?" And a voice answered her, "They are lost because of confessions badly made."

The teaching of Confession was often illustrated with cartoons. One popular example showed Johnny going into the confessional with four big, black, mortal sins that looked like pies. Johnny, having concealed one of the four mortal sins, came out of Confession with five mortal sins: the three he confessed, the fourth he concealed and the fifth one of sacrilege, now added to the others because he told a lie.

The issue of sin and how it was confessed was black and white with no gray areas between, but this childlike innocence and complacency about morality was to be ruptured by World War II. Once again, Catholics rallied to the flag with the same fervent patriotism that brought other American religious groups into the ranks.

World War II and its aftermath would change the world indelibly, and with it, the Church. The horrors of the Holocaust challenged every faith even more than did the Black Death. Innocence was difficult to sustain after Hitler, Hiroshima and Stalin. Science and technology ushered in modernism, fulfilling the prediction of Pius X.

During the war the Church was in as great a state of upheaval as the rest of the world as many Catholics became disillusioned and experienced a crisis of faith.

In the confessional Catholics began speaking of their faith and their God in ways they never had before, as evidenced by what could be considered a typical confession of the period:

Bless Me, Father, For I Have Sinned

1943, Metuchen, New Jersey

"Bless me Father, for I . . . oh, Father, what does it matter? Nothing does anymore. Not you. Not me. Not Him!" The slim, attractive woman in her early forties allowed her forehead to fall against the grille separating her from the priest in the confessional. She tried to muffle her sobs.

"Whoa! I'm here to listen. I'm here to help, but I can't do it alone. You have to start. God knows I wish I could look into your soul, but I can't."

"What's the use, Father? All the prayers, all the novenas, the Masses, and for nothing!"

"Nothing? My daughter, I don't even know the meaning of the word. What's for nothing? What doesn't matter? Would you prefer to start again? It might be easier."

"Why? He can't hear, or won't. He's not listening because He's not here."

"You're wrong. No matter what, He's here, always here. Always with you . . ."

"With me? You must be kidding. He isn't with me. He isn't with you. He isn't with anybody. Don't you understand, Father, He isn't here. He's supposed to be, but He isn't. He left us . . ."

"That's not . . . please start again. Start the way you should."

"Why should I? He won't listen. Oh, all right. Bless me, Father, for I have sinned, it's been eleven days since my last confession, the Saturday before last. Two days before a letter from Don arrived. Eight days after, I got the telegram."

"I understand. They regret to inform you."

"Where was God, Father? He was supposed to take care of Don. He was nineteen, my only son, two months past his birthday. God agreed to take care of him."

The American Years (1850–1962)

"God doesn't agree to things like that. You know better. We can't presuppose to understand the Divine Will. There's a greater plan. Your son, God willing, is already with . . ."

"I don't care. I don't care at all. My son is dead on some beach I can't even pronounce, and you tell me about a plan. You still don't understand. Listen, Father, I'll say it just once. I am here to confess that I have lost my faith. No, that's not right; I didn't lose it, I gave it away. I don't want it. I confess that I no longer believe in God. I don't want to believe in a God who would take my son away. I'd rather God was dead than my son. I want him back. And I hate God. Oh, Father, I hate Him so much!"

"You don't. You don't know what you're saying. He loves you, and you must love Him. There's a higher reason. He lost His only son too. Please, I do understand. Will you come to the rectory when I'm finished? Please . . ."

Despite the disillusionment of many of its faithful, the postwar American Church did try to maintain the facade of business as usual. Postwar prosperity enabled many Catholics to escape their urban ghettos and settle in surburbia. New dioceses followed them, but their influence was not as pervasive as before. The new suburbanites began to mix according to social status rather than by religious affiliation. The Catholic school-building programs, however, continued apace. By 1950 the system contained more than five million students in parochial and high schools and several hundred thousand in almost three hundred Catholic colleges and universities.

Sacramental observance remained high and Catholics gave every impression that most were abiding by the Church rules. Sexuality was still held on the tightest of reins as Confession kept passion on a short lead. Dr. Alfred Kinsey counted sins American Catholics could never imagine, and divorces were still relatively rare. The most revealing statistic of the period's fervency was that some half of all American Catholics confessed their sins to a priest at least once a month.

Bless Me, Father, For I Have Sinned

What was confessed on the Saturday afternoons of the fifties reflected the legalism and the childhood-rooted mentality that continued to affect how the Sacrament was practiced. Men and women confessed, for example, that they missed Mass, ate meat on Friday, read books on the Index of Forbidden Books, went to movies banned by the Legion of Decency, received Holy Communion after they had accidentally swallowed some water when they brushed their teeth, took part in Protestant religious services or were disrespectful to their parents. Then and now, the mortal sin was, on the whole, rarely committed.

From inside the Church, at the beginning of the fifties, the impression given was that everything was just fine, and the Church fathers could point to the numbers in their ranks as evidence—there were over 60,000 priests, 25,000 seminarians and 140,000 religious. From outside, however, the first cracks were beginning to appear in the fortress walls.

The fifties were by and large a colorless decade for the Church. Ten years of national self-delusion in which people attempted to convince themselves that they had not been thoroughly changed by the experience of global war. While many educated Catholic Americans debated new doubts in the upper reaches of their colleges, most were still not ready to voice their spiritual concerns aloud.

Nuns were becoming better and better educated, but it was a well-kept secret. The only time anyone read about the good sisters was when a kindly pastor would take them out to an amusement park where they would be photographed eating ice-cream cones. Certainly, ticking was heard, but few thought to look for a time bomb.

The call for a Catholic education for every Catholic child as dictated at the Third Plenary Council of Baltimore in 1894 was never completely fulfilled. The Church came fairly close, however, as the system expanded and schools were built to accommodate the postwar baby boom. In teaching Catholic doctrine, schools created for its students a special language as identifiable as Latin or French, spoken more fluently by kids in the fifties than in any other period.

The American Years (1850–1962)

Certain phrases were badges of faith which branded one a Catholic as boldly as scapulars or St. Christopher medals. No one else on the block bandied such phrases as "the power of the Holy Spirit," "having scruples," "Epiphany," "special dispensations," "the Beatific Vision," "imperfect contrition," "rash judgment" or "occasions of sin." Words like "transsubstantiation" and "infallibility" tripped off the tongue, although the degree of comprehension for these young Catholics was debatable.

Confession, too, had its own subvocabulary within the Catholic school language as children learned to confess their sins in the most painless manner possible. Phrases were thrown like verbal spitballs that, it was hoped, might glide past the priest at bat before he could connect with the actual sin. "Impure thoughts" made boys "touch themselves in an impure manner" and boys and girls "looked at each other with bad intentions," but all were "heartily sorry for having offended God."

Within the Church, there was talk of change, but it was only talk. The recognition of the need for change would have been an admission of Catholicism's imperfections in all things, both temporal and spiritual. The Church's vulnerability first became apparent as concepts such as clerical celibacy and social responsibility were no longer restricted to discussion in the elitist reaches of colleges and seminaries. The legalism of Confession was questioned and a New Theology emerged as God, man, sin and the afterlife were all being reexamined by clergy and laymen alike. Clerical obedience to the bishops began to waver as theologians led the way to the ramparts. Clues to the imminent revolution abounded, but the Church in the fifties paid little attention to its impatient critics.

In 1953 Pope Pius XII (1939–1958) proclaimed Angelo Roncalli —a man who would provide the next catalyst for change in Confession—a cardinal. The World War I medical orderly and chaplain had risen steadily within the Church's diplomatic corps, having served with quiet distinction in Bulgaria, Turkey and Greece. Since 1944 he had tiptoed brilliantly through the minefields of postwar France as the Papal Nuncio. His elevation to Cardinal of Venice at the age of seventy-two was to quietly cap a fruitful career. After the death of Pius XII in 1958, the roly-poly prelate was elected by the Sacred College of Cardinals as Bishop of Rome, Pontiff of the Roman Catholic Church, the least expected candidate in modern times, a *papa de passaggio,* an interim pope. His election on the twelfth ballot was a compromise within the Curia, a respite while the cardinals sought a better man to lead them cautiously into the future. Roncalli chose the name of John XXIII (1958–1963).

Roncalli's rise to the papacy appears in retrospect to have been a case of the right man in the right place or more specifically, *from* the right place. Born November 25, 1881, in Sotto Il Monte, Bergamo, in the Po Valley, one of thirteen children, this farmer's son got a boost up the ladder of Church politics by virtue of his birthplace. Had he been born in some other part of Italy, it's questionable whether he would have eventually become Pope. As a nineteen-year-old seminarian at the Vatican, Roncalli was invited to attend the consecration of the Bishop of Bergamo. The bishop was so taken by the young priest that he asked him to be his secretary. Later, when the bishop died, young Roncalli wrote a glowing obituary which he sent to the prelate's patron, Pope Benedict XV (1914–1922). Impressed by the work, the Pope appointed the untested priest as director of the Italian organization of foreign missions. Roncalli's rise within the Church had begun.

Less than a year after his elevation, Pope John XXIII made known his decision to call an ecumenical council, an auspicious assembly of the College of Bishops under the aegis of the Pope. Given his age, the determined John XXIII wasted no time. He first mentioned his plan on June 29, 1959, in his encyclical *Ad Petri Cathedram.* The next day, the Pope chaired the preparatory commission charged with planning the Council. On Christmas Day, 1961, John XXIII signed the bill *Humanae Santis,* which formally announced the inauguration of the Council the following year.

The idea of staging the Council was not universally cheered. The conservative Curia adamantly opposed it and tried various delaying tactics, hoping the *papa di passaggio* would pass on. They argued that the time was not yet right to stage such an event. The rest of the Church didn't know how to react, but felt, as with previous

70

popes, that whatever he did was all right with them. The interim pope was received more as a kindly grandfather than as a theological activist. His elevation had charmed the masses, endearing him to the world, and an instant myth was created extolling his plebian virtues, his homely habits and his gargantuan appetites—while minimizing his shrewd intellect. He resembled a pilgrim peasant, and that image suited the cardinals of Rome.

His external benevolence, however, masked a cunning intelligence honed in diplomacy. His ample girth hid his hunger for reform and, in seeking to set the wheels of change in motion, his age became his greatest defense. John XXIII simply had nothing to lose. Driven by a desire to bring the Church into the twentieth century, his *aggiornamento,* his spirit of renewal and reawakening, was a philosophy whose time had come. He brought to the council the gifts that had accelerated his own rise in the Church's hierarchy —the diplomat's acceptance of reality and ability to compromise. In his pursuit of renewal, he cajoled rather than demanded. Describing the council, he declared with characteristic optimism, "We are not here on earth to guard a museum, but to cultivate a garden." The Second Vatican Council began on October 11, 1962, attended by 2,540 bishops.

The Church entered the sixties on a wave of ambition, ready to accommodate the future. As with the rest of the nation, it would end the decade weakened, compromised and confused. Confession was to be equally shaken.

Chapter 5

The Anxious Years (1962 to the Present)

A Church in Alexandria, Virginia

On a rainy April evening during Holy Week in 1984, some 1,200 people—from babes in arms to the elderly in wheelchairs, from teenagers in blue jeans to executives in three-piece suits—attended General Absolution services.

The suburban church, built in 1976, was overflowing with people, many of whom remained standing throughout the entire one-and-a-half-hour service. Above the altar was a large figure of the Risen Christ, arms outstretched and welcoming. On the rustic brick wall was a large mural with the words, "Come Be Renewed." The sanctuary was semicircular in design, with no railing separating the priest from his congregation.

Bless Me, Father, For I Have Sinned

The service, entirely in English, began with a bearded young man playing "Come Back to Me" from Hosea on the guitar. The congregation began to sing.

The priest welcomed everyone and explained that the Sacrament of Reconciliation was a celebration, like the Sacraments of Baptism and Marriage. A young woman read from the book of Isaiah. A visiting priest delivered a homily from the Gospel of St. John. The parish priest then explained that everyone sins and everyone needs forgiveness. Jesus heals, nourishes, offers compassion and renewal. The Sacrament of Reconciliation acknowledges sinfulness, but does not dwell on it. Reconciliation calls on people to set aside bitterness and suspicion; the Sacrament encourages trust, love of life and community.

During the examination of conscience that followed, a silent, reflective moment, the priest told the congregation to examine not only their personal sins but also their social sins. Throughout the world, institutions, governments, even the Church have been sinful. He reminded them that every night people go to bed hungry . . . everyone is part of the system that oppresses the poor. It is important to ask the Holy Spirit to open people's minds and hearts so they can recognize the call to work to change the system and to bring love and peace into the world. The congregation rose for the Rite of Reconciliation.

The priest raised his hands above the congregation and granted absolution with the words, ". . . and I absolve you from your sins in the name of the Father, and of the Son and of the Holy Spirit." The young man who played the guitar began once again. People turned to their neighbors, smiling, shaking hands and wishing them peace and love.

The priest concluded this newest practice of Confession by inviting everyone to share in refreshments in the lounge downstairs. While joining his parishioners for fellowship, the exuberant priest recalled that in 1977, at the parish's first General Absolution services, only two hundred and fifty people attended.

More changes have occurred in the Church and in Confession during the past twenty years than had occurred in a millennium.

The Anxious Years (1962 to the Present)

The spirit of the sixties began in the ashes of World War II when its survivors proved Malthus right and began to reproduce with awesome fertility. Western civilization reasserted itself after the gruesome Holocaust by celebrating the survival of the species. The offspring of this reassertion of life were the most precious of children—they were better fed, better educated, more loved and granted more freedom than any generation before.

The generation that reached maturity in the sixties was very different from that of the fifties: to the horror of most parents who had survived the last world war and toed the line, they questioned, they challenged, they rebelled, they indulged. Iconoclastic by instinct, they declared God dead. Permissive by nature, they became moral anarchists attacking venerated values. It was in this stormy climate that John XXIII began the Second Vatican Council.

On October 11, 1962, tens of thousands of well-wishers from around the world crowded into torch-lit St. Peter's Square to cheer the opening ceremonies of the Second Vatican Council that would take three years to complete. The beloved Pope had planned to enter the basilica on foot, the last in a procession of more than 2,500 Church fathers, to underscore his role as pilgrim. His entourage, whom he called his "crown of thorns," persuaded him to opt for pomp so that he could be seen by more people. He conceded and was regally carried into the throng on his canopied sedan chair. This was one of the first arguments lost by the popular pontiff at this decisive moment in Church history. It was not to be the last.

The Council was the most momentous gathering in the annals of Roman Catholicism, as bishops were joined by hundreds of non-Catholic theologians. The Council sought to achieve three goals: to reawaken the faith of its people, to encourage Christian unity and to promote world peace. None of these was to be fully realized.

The public has persistently misinterpreted the extraordinary reign of John XXIII. He is revered for his attempt to revitalize the Church, to open the windows and let in the air of the twentieth century. But some theologians continue to take exception to that assessment: while venerating the man, they criticize his ignorance of the New Theology that had been exciting debate for a decade

75

before he became pope. He is further cited for his refusal to listen to the distinct mutterings of discontent coming from all five continents. His critics claim he knew nothing of the doctrinal revolution being plotted in northern European and North American colleges and universities.

In retrospect, his failures with the Council were, in part, predicted by the nature of his career. In a Church that thrived on the discipline of a benevolent dictator, John XXIII introduced the concept of leadership by example and persuasion. As a lifelong diplomat, he sought to lead by compromise rather than by command. History indicates that this tack did not work.

The Pope's unbridled optimism was reflected in the eclectic agenda he set forth for the Council. Subjects that would be discussed over the three years of study and debate included ecumenism, non-Christian religions, religious freedom, religious orders, the laity, Christian education, media and communications, bishops, peace, underdeveloped countries and space exploration.

John XXIII died of cancer on June 3, 1963, nine months after he had inaugurated the Council. He was succeeded by the Cardinal of Milan, Giovanni Montini, whose last act on leaving his diocese was to establish the Academy of St. Charles Borromeo for the purpose of studying the life of this confessional innovator.

Pope Paul VI (1963–1978) could not have been a more different man than his predecessor. If John XXIII erred by overzealously confronting the challenges facing the Church, Paul VI was mistaken in believing they might simply cancel one another out. His shepherding of the Council's final years created a rare point of agreement between bishops and theologians. Conservatives, moderates and progressives concurred that the vacillations of this intellectually gifted man prevented the possibility of a determined consensus. He sought to make everyone happy, and ended up pleasing no one.

Many of the Council's reforms were put into effect almost instantly after it concluded on December 8, 1965. The most visible change occurred during the course of Vatican II when the Council decreed in 1963 that a nation's predominant tongue would be the language of the Mass instead of Latin. For many, this decision, which was not discussed with the laity, symbolized the loss of sacredness, the demise of mystery; for others, however, it was a sign of new individual freedom.

The Sacrament of Penance was hardly mentioned at Vatican II. The only official statement issued by the Church was vague: "The rite and formulas for the Sacrament of Penance are to be revised so that they give more luminous expression to both the nature and effect of the Sacrament." The phrase "luminous expression" left a lot of room for divergent interpretation.

As the Council ended, the sixties were in full flower. Aptly, the new permissive society found an ally in a newly permissive Catholicism. The pampered post-World War II baby-boom children disdained orthodoxy and were prepared to challenge the edicts of the Catholic Church that their parents and grandparents before them had complacently accepted. The Church, surprisingly, responded in kind, allowing open doctrinal debate for the first time in its history. Now, heroes were made of men who edged closest to heresy.

Chaos for the sake of chaos seemed to be the order of the day as the nation's youth turned to drugs and sexual permissiveness as expressions of freedom. An American President, the first Catholic ever to hold that office, was assassinated. The United States entered the conflict in Vietnam officially and thunderously, and Martin Luther King, Jr.'s dream of civil rights for all Americans was briefly shared. Timothy Leary glorified an hallucinogenic reality while Masters and Johnson debunked sexual myths. All of these seemingly disjointed events challenged the meaning of sin and communal responsibility for Catholicism and secular society, and influenced the way the Church would eventually interpret the phrase "luminous expression."

One man rose above the chaos of the mid-sixties and in doing so became a target for the Church. John Rock, grandson of a survivor of the Irish famine, was a respected physician and scientist who sought a cure for infertility. A victim of a formidable irony, Rock discovered not how to increase population, but how to decrease it.

Bless Me, Father, For I Have Sinned

This devout Catholic doctor invented the Pill, the oral contraceptive that offered the freedom of choice to all womankind. For this remarkable achievement he was chastised and condemned by his newly uncertain Church. Others within the Church, however, supported him, inciting a battle over birth control that still rages.

Uncertainty was the mood of the times. John Lennon boasted that the Beatles were more popular than Jesus Christ, and while some Christians were shocked, few were able to refute his claim. The decade's continuing uncertainty was epitomized by Bob Dylan's "Blowin' in the Wind," and Catholicism asked how many saints a Church had to have after dropping so many favorites from the calendar.

Catholics were further confused when it became permissible to eat meat on Fridays and cremate their dead. They also began to wonder what had happened to such services as Holy Hours, Novenas, Forty Hour Devotions and the rite of Benediction. By 1965, the sixth anniversary of the introduction of the Pill, six million American women were using it. In Catholic terms twenty-one percent of all women under forty-five were, in effect, sinning every day.

The laity's bewilderment mirrored the clergy's as the number of seminarians plummeted by 30 percent between 1962 and 1974. During roughly the same period, more than 8,000 priests renounced their vocations, 30 times more than in any other period before the Second Vatican Council. Ironically, those convents, monasteries and seminaries that slackened their standards least experienced the fewest resignations. Other faiths reportedly suffered a similar decline during the same period.

The Church was a lame duck during the last part of the decade as it studied the best ways to implement the decisions of the Second Vatican Council. Some experimentation was already under way, and many of the liturgical innovations proposed went far beyond those suggested by the Council. Some U.S. Catholic colleges offered a new way of practicing Confession on a trial basis, which did not use the confessional or private confession of sins to a priest.

For the evolution of Confession, the most important event of the decade was a totally unexpected one. It would overshadow even the

78

The Anxious Years (1962 to the Present)

Council in its shattering impact on how and what men and women would confess in years to come. On July 29, 1968, Pope Paul VI promulgated his long-awaited encyclical on birth control. Rumors were rife that the encyclical might approve artificial contraception in some form as so many of the conciliar debates had been in favor of a form of birth control. *Humanae Vitae,* however, stunned the world by stating the opposite. The Church would brook no argument: "Each and every marriage act must remain open to the transmission of life." Prior to Vatican II's spirit of permissible dissent, such an unpopular decree would have been met with discreet, intramural grumbles. Now it was met with open revolt which was nothing less than challenge to papal authority.

On the same day that *Humanae Vitae* was promulgated, an American priest, Father Charles Curran, confronted papal teaching and declared that he and many like him begged to disagree. Curran, thirty-four, a professor of moral theology at Catholic University of America in Washington, D.C., read a prepared statement to the press at the capital's Mayflower Hotel. His public statement, signed by eighty-six theologians, read, in part:

> It is common teaching in the Church that Catholics may dissent from authoritative, noninfallible teaching of the Magisterium when sufficient reasons for doing so exist. . . . Therefore, as Roman Catholic theologians conscious of our duty and limitations, we conclude that spouses may responsibly decide according to their conscience that artificial contraception in some circumstances is permissible and indeed necessary to preserve and foster the values and sacredness of marriage.

Curran was no newcomer to controversy. The year before he had been fired by Catholic University reputedly for his liberal views on birth control. He fought the ouster, and the faculty overwhelmingly supported him, voting 400 to 18 not to hold classes until he was reinstated. The boycott shuttered the school for three days before the administration capitulated and announced they would not only rehire the young theologian, but would promote him as well. In

79

1972 Curran was the first recipient of the John Courtney Murray Award for distinguished achievement in theology.

The importance of the new theological rebellion to the history of Confession is based on the postconciliar realization that most Catholics do not, on the whole, commit grievous mortal sin. Some theologians argued that it was not necessarily a mortal sin to masturbate, nor was it a mortal sin to engage in a loving sexual relationship before marriage or to practice birth control. Curran was later to write that mortal sin was not a reality in most people's lives and suggested that a new understanding of venial sin was needed.

The American Catholic Church has known no year quite like 1967. In those turbulent twelve months one unheralded event would do more to open the gates of the fortress than the sensationalism of sexual permissiveness. On July 23 twenty-six Catholic educators signed a manifesto that became known as the "Land O'Lakes Document," which pledged that the ten universities they represented would seek to improve academic freedom by cutting themselves adrift from direct Church authority. This trend toward secularization, following the pattern set by the once-Protestant Ivy League, marked a further breakdown in communication between the Church establishment and its intellectual elite.

At the 1968 Miss America Pageant in Atlantic City, some women burned their bras in the most publicized display of female anger at the failure of feminism to be taken seriously. It caused many within the Church to review their own record on women and Catholicism.

Vatican II officially committed the Church to supporting women's rights when it upheld women's "equity with men before the law and in fact . . . to choose a husband, to embrace a state of life or to acquire an education or cultural benefits equal to those recognized by men." Despite this pronouncement, the Church's attitude toward women had hardly changed since Borromeo devised the confessional to prevent women from being occasions of sin for their confessors. No women were allowed to participate in Vatican II, and when the Council wanted to hear British economist Barbara Ward's views, her paper was read to the bishops by a man.

The Anxious Years (1962 to the Present)

1968 was also the year that marked Catholicism's acceptance into mainstream America. Anti-Catholicism, a two-century-old scourge, was finally laid to rest when two Catholics of Irish descent, Eugene McCarthy and Robert Kennedy, battled for the Democratic Party presidential nomination with barely a mention of their faith.

The Church entered the seventies as a house divided. Cautious bishops were confronted by impatient theologians who looked back at the Council with divergent views. Conservatives said too much had been allowed while the progressives claimed too little had been permitted, and hardly anyone bothered to listen to the moderates. The laity lamented that the public brawling troubled their faith, which in the relatively recent past had been tranquil, reassuring and rock-firm. Not knowing what to expect next, many recalled the past with nostalgia, longing for the days when a saint was a saint and a sin was a sin.

In 1974, nine long years after the closing of the Council, the New Rite of Reconciliation was made public. It was the same year, coincidentally, that President Gerald Ford granted a pardon to an unrepentant Richard Nixon. For almost a decade the Church had engaged in exhaustive research into its history, liturgy and doctrine in an attempt to give "luminous expression" to the Sacrament.

In "The Sacrament of Penance," published that year by the authority of Pope Paul VI, it was written that the faithful

> . . . obtain from the mercy of God pardon for their sins against Him; at the same time, they are reconciled with the Church which they wounded by their sins and which works for their conversion by charity, example and prayer. . . . Men frequently join together to commit injustice. It is thus only fitting that they should help each other in doing penance. Those who are freed from sin by the grace of Christ may work with all men of goodwill for justice and peace in the world.

The official name change from Penance to Reconciliation was clearly made to stress the new interpretation of both sin and forgiveness within the rite. Reconciliation suggests sin be viewed more

81

in terms of a multiple relationship with God, fellowman and the world, where Confession stresses sin as an act solely against the law of God. Reconciliation, the Church now stated, expressed Christ's forgiving love, while Confession had emphasized punishment. Reconciliation, an active word, was to be an embrace between priest and penitent. As in the time of Christ, the ancient tradition of atonement and pardon were reunited. Sins are those acts which harm the community, as well as the relationship with God. For the Church, the challenge of the New Rite lay in taking the most private of the sacraments and making it a joyous communal celebration.

In 1975 the New Rite was instituted by the Canadian conference of Catholic Bishops for use in churches throughout the country. On the first Sunday of Lent, 1976, the New Rite became mandatory in every parish in the United States. Reconciliation was trumpeted with uncharacteristic fanfare in the American Church as a remedy for the steady decline in the number of Catholics receiving the Sacrament. The laity was, for the most part oversold on the idea, which was delivered to them with the thunder of the Ten Commandments. It was a build-up guaranteed to disappoint.

The New Rite involves no sacramental change, as it adheres steadfastly to the strictures of Trent. The change is merely external, as form was reshaped rather than essence. There is still examination of conscience, confession, penance, amendment and absolution, and only an ordained priest can administer the Sacrament. The controversy regarding the New Rite centers on the changes in the language and the performance of the Sacrament. More traditional Catholics were offended by the evangelical tone of the New Rite's vocabulary, claiming that it smacked of Protestantism.

The New Rite of Reconciliation can now be practiced in three ways. The first way, private Confession, is still available, but there is a choice of location between the traditional confessional and the new reconciliation room. The latter resembles a simple office setting, with a desk and chairs, where the priest and the penitent can face one another. For those who desire anonymity, the penitent can kneel in front of a small screen that suggests the grilled separation of the confessional.

The Anxious Years (1962 to the Present)

The Rite, which may also contain pertinent scripture readings, need no longer begin with the penitent's traditional "Bless me, Father, for I have sinned." The confessor, in the spirit of Reconciliation, can now take the initiative in greeting the penitent. On completion of the Sacrament, there is a laying on of hands with prayer, reminiscent of Confession in the early Church.

The second form involves several penitents who gather with a priest to celebrate the Sacrament both communally and privately. Penitents participate together by making the Sign of the Cross, bowing their heads, reading from the Scriptures and singing hymns. Each person then confesses privately in a confessional or a reconciliation room.

The third way, called General Confession and General Absolution, involves a larger group that comes together, recites communal prayers and expresses communal sorrow for its sins. Participants sing hymns and have a quiet moment for examination of conscience. There is no individual confession. At the completion of the service, the priest raises his hands above the congregation and grants general absolution to all who have sincerely taken part in the ceremony.

It is this third form of confession and absolution that is the thorn. By Vatican decree, it is only to be used under emergency circumstances. This could occur, for example, during such popular penitential seasons as Christmas and Holy Week. The decree further stipulates that those who are in a state of mortal sin must seek private Confession as soon as possible following General Absolution. This last reminder is to ensure that General Absolution does not replace private Confession in the minds and hearts of Catholics.

Today some pastors throughout the United States and Canada practice General Absolution by stretching the interpretation of what constitutes an emergency. They ensure a disproportion between priests and penitents by widely publicizing their General Absolution services. One American bishop took the "emergency" loophole and enlarged it beyond any conservative expectations. On December 5, 1976, Bishop Carrol Dozier, 65, of Memphis, Tennessee, officiated at a General Absolution service in conjunction with the celebration of Mass for 11,500 Catholics in the Memphis Coliseum.

Three months before the event, Bishop Dozier ordered an extensive education program to acquaint the members of his diocese with the meaning and purpose of the ceremony. One of his goals was to reach the thousands of lapsed Catholics who had turned away from the Church during the past two decades. His pastoral commitment was reminiscent of St. Cyprian's attempt to bring back the *lapsi* after the Decian persecutions of the third century.

Dozier's experiment prompted an explosion of criticism from many in the hierarchy who charged that he had taken a far too liberal interpretation of the New Rite. Hounded by many of his fellow churchmen, the Bishop justified his experiment by reporting a rise in both private confessions and marriages following the well-publicized, well-orchestrated confessional service. Dozier had also used the media effectively to get his message across, a lesson that was largely ignored by many of his peers and the Church hierarchy. The Church, unfortunately, tended to oversell the New Rite to practicing Catholics, making little effort to reach the lapsed Catholics who might benefit from it the most. Unlike Dozier, who even appeared on the NBC "Today" show to discuss the New Rite, the Church rarely made use of secular media.

In addition to the fury over General Absolution, sexuality and early first confessions became further sources of controversy in the late seventies. In 1977 a book entitled *Human Sexuality* was published which carried on the rebellion started by Charles Curran almost a decade before. Commissioned by the Catholic Theological Society of America, the book further delineated the American Catholic theologians' objections to Paul VI's *Humanae Vitae*, directly confronting many fundamental issues of Vatican teaching on morals and sexuality, issues that were never resolved to the satisfaction of many within the Church, clergy and lay persons alike. On birth control, the writers and their consultants, including Curran, wrote, "The question of artificial contraception has not yet found a definite resolution in the Church. Therefore, the use of contraception can be a morally sound decision." On nonmarital sex,

84

they argued, "Premarital intercourse may be justified if it represents a loving relationship and some measure of mutual commitment before sexual involvement." They also helped put to rest an era of teenage guilt when they stated, "Masturbation is not objectively and seriously wrong." While *Human Sexuality* clearly was not intended, nor perceived, as a license for promiscuity, it was received as a widely respected reaction to generally accepted social and moral attitudes.

The Vatican was not amused. Thousands of confessors throughout North America, however, agreed with the arguments put forth and began to counsel their penitents along those liberal lines. Still, there were many other priests who did not agree, and the result was continued confusion in the confessional.

Just before his death, Pope Paul VI found himself isolated again on the emotionally charged issue of First Confessions. In an address to bishops in New York in 1978, the Pontiff exhorted, "First Confessions should precede First Communion. The norms of the Apostolic See ought not to be emptied of their meaning by contrary practice."

Despite the Pope's stand, the contrary practice of First Confession following First Communion had been growing in popularity. Since Vatican II, concerned clergy had urged a reevaluation of Pius X's decision to lower the age of First Communion, thereby lowering the age of First Confession. Experienced confessors had long been troubled by having to introduce such a complex concept as sin to a child of seven. They sought to reverse the sacramental order by allowing First Confession to come two or three years after First Communion, when a child would be better prepared to understand the meaning of sin.

Today, in many dioceses across North America, bishops are ignoring the late Pontiff's directive and are allowing their pastors to delay First Confession until the age of nine or ten. Parents are generally enthusiastic about the reversal.

When Karol Cardinal Wojtyla became Pope John Paul II on October 22, 1978, he immediately attempted to infuse the Church with a new discipline. Speaking out for a more restrained spiritual evolution, both for the Church and for Confession, he sternly cautioned that, "General Absolution is not to be used as a normal pastoral option, or as a means of confronting any difficult pastoral situation. It is permitted only for the extraordinary situations of grave necessity." In 1979, during a visit to Ireland, the Pope rejoiced in hearing that all Catholics in the country had been asked to go to Confession as part of the spiritual preparation for his visit. "You could not have given me a greater joy or a greater gift," the Pontiff stated, making clear his position on how the Sacrament should be practiced. Two years later he asked the special confessors of Rome's four basilicas to dedicate themselves to the administration of the Sacrament. "Keep in mind that the teaching of the Council of Trent on the necessity of integral confession of mortal sins is still in force and will be in force forever in the Church." Whereas the New Theology appears to be rooted in the here and now, the Vatican speaks of a theology rooted in the forevermore, as well.

In 1983 John Paul II made an indirect reference to Trent when he reminded the faithful that indulgences, which had prompted that Council in the first place, were still available and very much part of Church tradition. All Catholics who confessed their sins, received Holy Communion and took part in a papal audience during the Holy Year would receive a plenary indulgence. Media coverage on the announcement explained that plenary indulgences "relieved the penance for sins already confessed." Four centuries later, the notion of being excused from time spent in Purgatory is still alive and well.

If, 400 years ago, the Church was almost torn apart by the abuses surrounding the sale of indulgences, today another confessional tempest is brewing—in some parishes in the United States and Canada, nuns are hearing confessions. Many do so defiantly as one of the first steps toward the ordination of women, while others hear confessions as a way of offering spiritual counseling.

Exemplifying the cyclical nature of the history of the Sacrament, these liberal sisters hear confessions very much as the Irish *anmcharas* did some 1,400 years ago. They are not necessarily usurping

86

The Anxious Years (1962 to the Present)

the sacramental role of the priest, but are serving as spiritual guides for penitents who include lay people, priests and sisters. To complete the Sacrament, these latter-day *anmcharas* encourage their penitents to attend General Absolution services so they can then receive absolution.

The eighties have not lessened the anxiety of the Church in the way the Sacrament is administered. One Catholic commentator has described the decade so far as "the dark night of the Church's soul." For many, there is no indication of a dawn. In 1983 the sixth Synod of Bishops, comprised of 212 prelates from around the world and presided over by the Pope, was devoted solely to discussion of Reconciliation. The Synod disappointed most observers by taking no firm stand on the practice of the Sacrament, leaving unresolved the issues that continue to simmer as in some parishes the Rite of Reconciliation is practiced, in others nuns hear confessions and still others continue to practice the Sacrament as sanctioned by the Pope.

As the Church moves hesitantly toward the twenty-first century, the controversy about the future of Confession remains. Some mourn the Sacrament, saying it was mortally wounded by the upheavals of Vatican II. Others are more optimistic, predicting a continued evolution toward, as yet, unimagined practices. As in decades past, time will tell.

Oral History

The recent history of Confession is brought to life through the words of penitents and their confessors. Men and women of all ages reveal their feelings and thoughts about the Sacrament, which examine its past, present and future.

In interviews with 281 Catholics, lapsed and practicing, telling anecdotes and confessional experiences were related. Many were so enthusiastic about sharing their memories that they suggested the names of family and friends to add to the lore. To protect their privacy, we have changed the names, cities and professions of all the men and women interviewed. The names of priests interviewed have been changed as well, allowing them to speak with complete candor.

Chapter 6

Penitents on Confession

Confession is an explosive topic, producing as it does a wide range of feelings, from rage to gratitude. Here penitents recall their memories of the confessional, beginning with their First Confession and wending through childhood. Some pause at adolescence to struggle with the maze of impure thoughts and impure actions characteristic of sins confessed in these youthful years. Others remember their adult sins, guilts and confessions.

Elaine, a fifty-five-year-old Boston lawyer, is passionate in describing her feelings about the Sacrament of Confession:

Confession is a spiritual cleansing, a way to start again, a way to wipe the slate clean. I love going to Confession, telling the priest my sins, having him forgive me and the euphoria that follows. When I go to Confession and the priest wants to know something, I'll tell him everything. When I was in school, I remember memorizing a quote from St. Isidore. It was about how confession heals and gives us hope and mercy. I believe every word of that.

Arthur, however, a sixty-eight-year-old retired Toronto publishing executive, is furious at the mere mention of the word.

Confession is one of the most crippling facets of the Church. It perpetuates neurotic patterns. It encourages people to hang on to their guilt and never feel good about themselves. It's a thief of human integrity and dignity. It makes people constantly respond as children, never allowing them to grow up. Being in that box, you never escape. You live, like on a paycheck, from week to week, from confession to confession. There are so many worthwhile things in life, but confession just overshadows them all.

While some have overwhelmingly positive feelings about the Sacrament, others condemn it. But the great majority of Catholics interviewed fall somewhere in between.

Wiping the Slate Clean

The men and women who speak out in the following pages are all practicing Catholics. They go to church regularly, confess at least once a year and are pleased with the sense of peace the Sacrament brings to their lives.

Adrienna is a fifty-seven-year-old seamstress from Washington, D.C., who arrived in America after World War II, orphaned and gravely ill. Through all the horrors that she and her family experienced, they never lost their faith in God or in the Sacrament.

Confession is quite moving, earth-shattering when you really understand what is going on. You are talking to

God Himself, and being forgiven! The more seriously you take it, the more joyous the experience. If you have faith and believe, there are so many benefits. Whenever I'm in the confessional, I know that my parents and my three brothers and two sisters who are in Heaven are hearing me too.

When Sister Margaret, a fifty-four-year-old Chicago professor, took her vows, she compared her General Confession to a second Baptism.

I entered the convent when I was thirty, after working for the government for nine years. When I was a working girl, I would go to Confession regularly, once a month. When I entered the novitiate, the main thing I remember was the confession I made before First Vows. Everybody made a General Confession of their whole life. I remember that confession specifically because it was a whole new beginning. Everything in the past was gone. I had a special feeling, as though I were a newborn babe. The whole slate was wiped clean, and this was a brand-new, fresh springtime of my life.

Howard, a forty-five-year-old native of Boston, is a mathematics teacher. During his five years in a monastery, his confidence in the Sacrament was cemented.

I believe the Sacrament is a magical instrument, a mysterious instrument. One of its main virtues is absolution, which is as important to me as the counseling aspect. Fortunately, in the monastery, I got both. But I always believed that absolution was the most important aspect of it. Any psychological massaging along the way was a bonus.

Lawrence, a forty-four-year-old Los Angeles actor, returned to Confession three years ago, when his marriage ended in a painful divorce.

93

Learning to forgive is an important part of life, necessary for feeling good about yourself as well as getting along with your spouse, family and colleagues. If it weren't for going to Confession on a regular basis, I doubt if I could have sustained the relationships that I treasure so much now. If I had been going to Confession all along, I think I might have been able to save my marriage.

For William, a sixty-five-year-old retired military man from New York, discipline is the thing that keeps him connected to the Sacrament.

I was in the Air Force for thirty-one years and in the academic world as well. There's something to be said about discipline in this life. Something to be said for an injection of fear that keeps people going. I'm not talking about terror, but staying enough on the edge to keep you moving. Confession gives you that little rush, that bit of fear that keeps you on your toes. It makes you go back, time and time again, never knowing if you got it right, but always striving to do so.

Peter is a forty-five-year-old New York physician, a first-generation American, who had to battle with his father to maintain his bond with the Church.

My father was born in Italy, graduated from Harvard and spent his whole life getting assimilated. He was very critical of the Church and insisted that I go to a public high school. What kept my faith, even today, was that sense of the majesty of the Church, a refuge, a source of identity where I mattered. Despite all the horror stories, the Church for me was always a womb of experience. Confession conveyed a sense of love, sometimes a neurotic love, but for me it meant I'm worth something; I have value. It nurtured my self-esteem.

Judith is a fifty-six-year-old Toronto housewife who left the Church for a brief time after the death of her husband. When she returned, it was with more gusto than ever. A compassionate confessor was instrumental in rekindling her faith.

I believe in God and I believe in the Trinity and I believe in Confession and that's it. I've given my soul and my life over to Him, and all He asks from my life is that I visit Him once a week in Church and that I go to Confession. Big deal, when you consider all the things I ask from Him every day. Confession's not a heavy trip. I'm not fightin' it, but I guess some people do. That's the way I've been all my life. You want to be a practicing Catholic, you gotta go to Confession. Certain things go with the territory. I've been a practicing Catholic all my life, and I have no regrets.

Clifford, a twenty-eight-year-old newspaper reporter from the Midwest, sums up the Sacrament in wire-service staccato:

You know why we need Confession? How many times did Jesus drop the cross? He stumbled umpteen times before he got there. We're gonna stumble umpteen times too. That's why we need Confession.

Russ, a twenty-six-year-old Phoenix, Arizona, department store clerk who spent much of his youth in reform schools, explains how going to Confession gave him a second chance:

Confession has the power to reform criminals, if you let it into your life. I never believed it could be possible. I always thought it was just a lot of churchy crap. I used to think that you could be a hit man for the Mafia, go to Confession and that was it—you'll go to Heaven. Doesn't work that way. You've got to be truly sorry for having committed the crime and really reform, promise yourself and the priest and God that you'll never do it again. The second time that I wound up inside, I began to see a priest every week. I was up for five years, so we had a lot of time to talk. I started to develop a real conscience, began to think real deep about all the things I did and didn't do. I've never been in trouble again.

Ralph, a fifty-five-year-old composer living in Los Angeles, considers his music to be yet another form of confession.

> I'm convinced that a great poet or composer is really somebody who confesses when he creates. Because he confesses, he touches someone. Confession doesn't always have to be in verbal language. I think confession even goes into the arts, and that in many ways the artistic expression is basically nothing but a confession of the very deepest kind.

Father Ellis, a thirty-nine-year-old Chicago parish priest, describes the merciful Sacrament:

> More and more people are becoming aware that if they have sinned against God and are truly sorry for it, when they turn back to God, they are back in God's graces. It's only when they go to Confession that they make it official through the Sacrament of Reconciliation. They never break away from God. He loves us regardless of what we've done. To tell you the truth, it took me a long time to learn that, and it is still something I have to keep relearning. I have to look upon God as a loving father who rarely turns His back on His child. And if I can believe that God is forgiving me, then why can't I forgive myself?

Sister Ruth, a forty-six-year-old Washington, D.C., professor of theology, introduces the Sacrament to her adult education classes by capturing its two extremes. She acknowledges the childhood-rooted consciousness that many Catholics bring to Confession, but contends that through education and effort, one can learn to truly appreciate the Sacrament.

> The Sacrament of Penance is really a small drama. There's a lot that can be said about entering into this box, the total darkness, hearing a voice coming from the other side of the wall—it is a primordial experience. For many people,

96

it heightens their sense of guilt and their sense of fear before the Absolute and Almighty God. It is generally agreed that Confession that way brought a lot of pain to a whole lot of people. But it wasn't all pain. Many people received consolation and support from it. Looking back, we're talking about a lot of shared ignorance and shared knowledge in terms of our basic life experiences. We were part of the same system.

The Smells and the Bells

You know why people come to Church? It's for the show business. It's for the smells and the bells. As for me, I love seeing my name in lights on the confessional.

—Father Callighan, thirty-five, New York parish priest

For many North American Catholics, the confessional has a life all its own. In the following pages people recall their memories of that frightening and mysterious, yet still alluring box.

Vanessa, a fifty-four-year-old housewife from Washington, D.C., remembers with fondness the familiar trappings of the confessional.

There was the grate, and straining to see the priest and wondering if he was concentrating on you. Before your turn there was always the mumbling going on on the other side. Once in awhile a muffled word would come through and you couldn't help but listen, but you tried to block it out at the same time. I remember the nervous waiting in line, the smells of the church, the incense and the acrid scent of burning candles. There was a kind of romantic half light in the confessional so that you could always kind of see inside . . . kneeling, head bent, always fearing that someone was going to open the door on you.

Frank, a sixty-seven-year-old retired bus driver from Boston, recalls that while waiting in the confessional for his turn with the priest, he always put his hands over his ears and hummed so that he wouldn't hear what the person on the other side was saying.

> Part of me always wanted to listen, but the other part of me believed that God would kill me if I did. And then the screen would open, swissssh, like the sound of a jet engine. It scared me when I was a kid. I'd get out as many sins as I could as fast as I could, and then the screen would swissssh again, like it was saying "good-bye for now."

Kenneth, a fifty-seven-year-old Vancouver journalist, based his entire evaluation of the priest's performance in the confessional on the way he smelled.

> I particularly remember this young priest who always smelled nice and spicy. It's a sorry commentary on religion that after-shave lotions were part of the liturgy.

Lorraine, a forty-three-year-old secretary from San Diego, remembers the confessional as a place of security.

> It was like cuddling in a dark closet with Daddy or someone you could trust who was going to say, "Your sins are forgiven, and all is well." It was a nice, safe place for me. It still has a mysterious ingredient to it, something bizarre which, even after these years, still excites me.

Many people recall the confessional in theatrical terms, equating confessing to "going on stage." Denise, a thirty-nine-year-old actress from Toronto, claims the reason there are a lot of Catholics in the theater is because of those formative years spent in Church.

> All those flowing things, the pageantry, that Latin droning, the drama of the confessional . . . it stays with you forever.

Carlos, a forty-five-year-old artist, born in Barcelona and now living in New York, would agree with Denise. He attributes his inspiration to his confessions.

Confession was all theater. It taught me to make use of my imagination. When I would tell my sins to the priest, I would always live them in my mind. For the sins I didn't tell, I would go home and draw them. I once remember stealing some money from my mother's purse, and I could never confess it to the priest because he knew my mother and I didn't trust him that he wouldn't tell her. I drew a picture of me, the money, my mother and her purse, and then I tore it up into a hundred little pieces and threw it away. It felt almost like I made a confession. I wish I could remember all the drawings I used to make in place of confession. It would make an interesting retrospective of my life.

For Wayne, an inventive forty-one-year-old magazine writer from New York, images of the confessional have stayed with him through the years.

Sometimes the image of the confessional flashes in my head when I have to lean down and put my mouth next to the subway token booth opening because the mike doesn't work. Speaking into it I've always felt there was a similarity there.

For Melissa, a thirty-year-old Atlanta dental assistant, the confessional evoked high romance.

Even today, I still have a crush on Father Walsh after fifteen years. I loved being in the confessional with him. It was so dark, and with his deep voice he seemed so sexy. When I was a teenager that box had to be the sexiest place on earth.

Not all recollections were as dramatic or passionate. Some remembered the priest as seeming like "a wall, something inpenetrable, something to get past." Others compared the confessional to "an obstacle course." The darkness made them so anxious they could barely speak. Many sputtered their words and whispered hoarsely.

Jack, forty-one, a Chicago realtor, recalls the terror he felt in the confessional:

> I felt exposed, like I was in a shooting gallery, and I remember thinking the priest was going to shoot me. Either he or God was going to riddle me right there and then for my sins. Didn't matter. I still got these shivers of fear and I could barely get my voice loud enough to say a word.

First Confession

As a result of Pius X's 1910 encyclical, *Quam Singulari,* North American boys and girls have been making their First Confessions at the average age of seven. Fearful or confident, ignorant or knowledgeable, they received their preparation for the Sacrament from the nuns, with a few words from the priest. En masse, they were trundled off to Borromeo's confessional, waiting in line for their first encounter with a confessor. Some recall the day fondly, referring to it as their first rite of passage into adulthood. Others recall it with terror, while many couldn't recall their First Confession at all.

For Larry, a fifty-four-year-old New York lawyer, just being inside the box created such lingering fear that he describes his first time in it as if it were his last, and it was:

> My First Confession scared the hell out of me. I'm not exaggerating. I'd been prepared by the nuns, knew what I had to say and do, but once I set foot into that box I thought I was going to die, literally die. I couldn't move, couldn't kneel, nothing! When the priest slid open the grille I started to scream. My mother rescued me and took me home immediately. I was hysterical for the rest of the day and into the night. For over a month I needed something to make me sleep, which is really something for a six-year-old. Five months later I made my First Confession

in Father Whelman's office, kneeling by his desk. From then on, I only confessed directly to a priest.

Fortunately, not all First Confessions left such an indelible mark. Sister Agnes, a thirty-four-year-old Vancouver social worker, recounts that she could hardly wait for her auspicious day to arrive, whether she was ready or not:

> I was five in the first grade and when they started preparing for First Communion and First Confession, I wasn't at the age of reason. But I sat in on all the classes and I was determined that I was going to go to Confession too. When the priest came to give the final examination to determine if you could make your First Confession, the teacher said that some of us had to pretend that we were going to Confession. When she asked who wanted to go first, well, I was all get-up-and-get-'em, and threw up my hand. The teacher said, "Father, I think this child is a little too young to make her First Confession," and I said, "No, I'm not. I know what I'm going to do."
>
> "All right, then what's the first thing you're going to do?" Well, I'd already examined my conscience, so I went in, knelt down and he made me believe he opened the screen. I said, "Bless me, Father, for I have sinned, this is my First Confession. I murdered three people, I committed adultery four times, I stole ten times." He said, "What did you steal?" I said, "I stole a car." The priest turned to the sister and said, "She's ready!"

Several people described their First Communion along with their First Confession. Renata, a fifty-seven-year-old real-estate broker from Baltimore recalls:

> The most exciting Sacrament was Communion because you got something in your mouth. Confession was sort of low-key compared to all the arrangements for first Holy Communion, like getting the white dress, the veil, the rosary beads—we got a lot of things—the little purse,

101

a prayer book, a holy card and crosses. I remember that all the boys got their suits rented and had to return them, but the girls got to keep their dresses. Confession wasn't as exciting because we didn't get dressed up. It was a regular school day, and we just stood in line in the church.

Siobhan, a forty-seven-year-old housewife from Miami whose family is devout Irish, remembers:

First Confession and First Communion were really big deals in my house. I was made to feel very special by the nuns, the priests and, of course, my family. It was probably the high point in my six-year-old life. All my older cousins, nine of them, came to my house and quizzed me on the catechism. My mother and father were so proud when I answered everything perfectly. And then there was my dumb cousin Richard who always made fun of me and never got anything right . . .

Some men and women recalled that it was important that they please their families as well as their priests. Leonard, a forty-five-year-old teacher from Detroit, recalls:

I really made my parents proud on that day, and I even got a free candle. My parents told me that Confession was the most important thing about being a Catholic and that if I confessed my sins, I'd go to Heaven. I believed everything they told me, at least I did then.

For Sandra, a thirty-two-year-old public relations consultant from Toronto, her brother's approval was as important to her as the priest's.

I remember making my First Confession, which I did very nicely. Well, when I came home afterwards, my seventeen-year-old brother insisted that I get down on my knees at the corner of the bed. He made me repeat all the sins I told the priest. He said only then would I truly be forgiven. I believed him for years.

Although most people were unable to remember their First Confession, some had instant replay.

Jill, forty-six, divorced, is a prominent Boston lawyer.

I knew it was a sin to hate my sister. The nuns talked about childish hate that emanates from fighting over a doll or a dress. I'm talking about the kind of hate that made me want to kill her.

Laura was born when I was seven. Up until that time, there was just my mother, my father and me, and I liked it that way! Looking back, I could have been better prepared for her arrival—no one talked to me about what it meant to have a sister or prepared me for the changes in the family. All I knew was that my mother was getting fatter and fatter, then she suddenly left home for what seemed an interminably long time.

Then my mother came back to the house with this "thing." My rage became even greater when I saw my mother breast feeding it. I wanted to jump on my mother and rip my sister away and throw her against the wall. Later that day, when my sister was in her crib, I spilled ice-cold Kool-Aid all over her and she got pneumonia. I remember praying to God that she wouldn't recover. I tried to break her medicine bottle, but I couldn't reach the shelf even when I stood on a chair.

It was around this time that I had to make my First Confession. The nuns prepared us very thoroughly, but I never took it seriously because I never committed any sins except for wanting to kill my sister. And because I hadn't succeeded in killing her—yet—I never felt I had committed a sin.

When I was in the confessional, the priest asked me if I had anything to say about my family. I told him everyone was fine, that I loved my mommy and daddy and that my sister was going to die. He expressed his sorrow and wanted to know the cause of her affliction. "Me," I told him, because I was going to kill her the very first chance I got. I clearly remember that he was about to chuckle but stopped himself midway when he realized that I was serious. He asked me again to tell him about my sister. I described her size, the color of her eyes, her hair, her smell when she needed a diaper change and that she just didn't belong in our house and was going to die very soon. By this time, the priest realized that he wasn't hearing one of those "I stole three cookies" confessions. He left his side of the confessional and came into mine and immediately took me to one of the nuns who was waiting at the back of the church.

For the next three months, once a week, I met with the priest, and we'd talk about what it meant to be a good sister and a good Catholic girl, as well as the meaning of sin. He kept trying to convince me that even thinking about murdering my sister was a sin. He never did convince me. But I never did kill my sister, either.

All the First Confessions described so far were heard at the average age of seven. The following two women made their First Confessions at fourteen when they converted to Catholicism.

Alissa, a twenty-three-year-old Atlanta hairdresser, converted because her stepfather was Catholic and she wanted to please him.

When you convert at my age, you've got a lot to confess because you've been a heathen for such a long time. The confessional was so dark and it had a churchy smell, not at all like incense. The priest had terrible bad breath. Even though it wasn't pleasant, I overlooked it because I was a convert and believed everything came from God. I remember being very nervous, and scared. When I was through, the penance I got seemed lenient, like nothing.

Penitents on Confession

I thought I'd been really bad, and all I got was three Hail Marys.

Anne, a forty-five-year-old nurse from Los Angeles, converted to Catholicism because she yearned for a sense of spiritual belonging. Her parents, Protestants by birth, were atheists and offered no resistance to her decision. Still, there was a sense of being let down in her first confessional experience.

When I knelt down in the confessional box I was really nervous, thinking that the priest was taking my message right to God and I had to get it right. The first thing I did was to say, "hi!" which was just about the worst thing to do. There was dead silence. Usually when I tell someone about something I've done I expect them to understand, show some reaction. It was like talking to a wall. I remember saying, "Bless me Father, for I have sinned . . ." and then I told him about hitting my brother three times, stealing ten dollars from my mother, and I knelt there for fifteen minutes with everything pouring out of me, and he kept asking me how many times I did everything. I told him everything, thinking that otherwise God was going to punish me. I was expecting something really fantastic to happen—bright lights, or God talking directly to me, but it was nothing at all, nothing.

When asked to describe his First Confession, Kevin, a thirty-two-year-old Edmonton dentist, said he couldn't remember it, but offered his sister's confession instead.

I must have blocked mine out, but I can tell you about my younger sister. She never had any trouble with her First Confession, but as soon as it was over, she started to cry uncontrollably. I couldn't understand why. I thought she should be happy. When I asked her what was wrong, she said she didn't know what she was going to tell Father O'Neill for her second confession.

Adolescent Confession

The men and women in this section had no trouble recalling the confessional tales of their youth. Many spoke at great length; a few even telephoned after the interview with a story they'd forgotten.

For all of them, growing up Catholic in America meant living with the folklore of the confessional. Confession seemed a source of solace for some and frustration for many as they developed their own working vocabularies for making their confessions, eager to find a priest who couldn't "read between the lines."

In the confessional, pubescent boys would lower their voices to avoid recognition by the priest who undoubtedly knew their parents. Kids, full of guilt or mischief, would always be on the lookout for a priest who didn't speak English or who, better yet, was deaf. Everybody lived in fear of that phantom bus that drove up and down the streets knocking down Catholic kids who made good confessions, mercifully sending them on to Heaven. And everybody was always talking about sin. Was it a mortal, a venial, a sin of omission, an occasion of sin . . . ?

For most of Mark's adolescence, sin was not a topic for scintillating conversation; it was his dreaded daily reality. The shy, thirty-seven-year-old accountant from the Midwest tells his story:

> At one stage in my life, I thought I committed a sin too horrible to confess. There was a kid who lived across the street from me, and we were always fighting. As soon as we had a fight, the whole street would divide right down the middle. Some people would be on John's side and some would be on mine. There was this other kid, Joey, who was a year younger than me, and in the middle of this fight, he hauls off and hits my little brother, just because he was my brother and this Joey was on John's side. I was on the porch and I saw this. I took off after him, and I grabbed him from behind and threw him down. He hit his head on the side of the curb, and then there was this big hullabaloo when his dad wanted to take him to the hospital.

106

Penitents on Confession

Two months later, we heard that Joey was sick, a month later that Joey was dying and then he died. It was the day after Joey's funeral, and John came up to me and said, "He died of a lump on the side of his head and you killed him when you threw him down on the curb." At nine years old, I was a murderer. I couldn't face his parents because he was an only child and I'd killed him. I certainly couldn't tell a priest in Confession that I murdered this kid. So for about four years, from nine to thirteen, I went through a real depression. I finally confessed it to a priest at a retreat. I felt comfortable going to him because he was from Detroit. I figured murder wouldn't seem so bad to him.

The week after my confession, I overheard my mother talking to a friend and I learned that Joey died of a brain tumor and that I had nothing to do with it at all. Confessing to that priest was probably the most important thing I ever did during my entire adolescence.

Frank, forty-eight, a high school teacher from Brooklyn, left the Church thirty years ago, but there was one confession that has had special meaning for him:

I've always been fond of Confession because of one I made when I was nine. There was a legless black man who used to push himself along on a red wagon. He didn't beg, but he had a metal cup tied around his neck. He came to our neighborhood once a month, always on Saturdays. I felt a tremendous sympathy for this man, and I always gave him something, a nickel maybe or a dime. I would even go home to get something for him if I didn't have any money on me.

This one Saturday I had a quarter, and I was on the way to the movies. He smiled when he saw me. I think he recognized me. I liked to think we had something of a friendship going. I was late for the movie, and I had no change. No time to go back home and borrow an advance

107

on my allowance. So I took the coward's way out and I crossed the street.

After the movie I went to Confession as I always did. I can't be sure now, but I think I realized then I had committed my first real mortal sin that day by stiffing that poor legless man who was almost my friend. I told the priest about him and he said he knew him. The priest talked about charity and selfishness. I expected that. Then he asked me what I thought my penance should be. I was floored. "How should I know," I said, but he persisted. "Put yourself in my place. What would you say to a young fellow like you?"

I remember saying, "Please, Father, I don't know," but he kept pushing. I finally thought about it. I said I would give me for my penance, or somebody like me, a full month of not going to the movies. Plus, I should save the money and give it to that man when I saw him again. The priest said, "Not bad, young man. Now do just that for your penance."

I only felt half good when I left the confessional, of course. The other half had to come when I finally completed my penance. I had to wait a month. I remember I was almost crazy waiting for him. I gave him a dollar and I smiled, he winked and I finally felt absolved.

To prove the existence of God, some Catholic kids put their Maker through some pretty rigorous tests. Allen, a forty-four-year-old physical education teacher from New York, a devout Catholic, recounts his confrontation with God and his confessor:

When I was sixteen, I made a confession that was really difficult because I was questioning my faith. I challenged God to come to me, to prove His existence to me. I guess I was afraid of ever being without Him. It was during those days when you couldn't eat meat on Fridays. I remember buying a White Castle hamburger, taking it to the church and leaning on the wall, looking up at the sky as I ate it.

I expected lightning, a sign of some kind. Nothing happened. So the next Saturday I went to Confession and told the priest what I did. He was silent for a long time. Probably strangling himself to keep from laughing at this crazy kid. He finally explained that I was guilty of the sin of presumption, and that God had more important things to do than worry about my hamburgers.

If you were lucky, some sins might be worth a buck or two. Carl, forty-five years old, a plumbing-supply salesman from Detroit, recalls an incident familiar to most Catholic boys:

As sophomores, we attended this retreat and the priest who was conducting it was fabulous. He missed his calling. He should have been a comedian. On the last day of the retreat he said, "We're all going to Confession tomorrow. You think you've got a sin we haven't heard before, well, I want to tell you . . . I've got this wad of nice, crisp twenty-dollar bills. I'll give every boy who tells me a sin I've never heard before a twenty-dollar bill. And I hope you don't have those sins, because I could be broke in an hour." At the end of the day, he said, "See, I've still got all my twenties." I thought that was the funniest thing I'd ever heard.

When Monica was fourteen she went to the priest to confess something she thought was a sin, but wasn't quite sure. The forty-nine-year-old San Francisco policewoman recalls desperately wanting the advice of her priest. With a broad smile, she tells her story:

I was fourteen and confessed to a priest that while I was dancing really close with a boy, he suddenly developed a lump in his pants. I thought there was something sinful going on there, but I wasn't sure. The priest said that the boy must have had a wallet in his pocket and that I shouldn't dance so close anymore. So much for sex education in the confessional in the fifties.

109

Bless Me, Father, For I Have Sinned

The men and women in the following pages recount the sins of their youth with absolute clarity—stealing a chocolate bar, playing basketball in a Protestant gymnasium, hating your cousin and much more were all part of the confessional tapestry.

Herbert, a thirty-nine-year-old dentist from the Bronx, confessed petty thievery.

When I was nine, I confessed I stole a Mounds bar. It wasn't a big thing. I had confessed to a little stealing before. But this time was different. The priest told me for my penance I had to return the dime to the candy store and that I had to tell the owner what I had done. It didn't hit me right away, but on the way home I realized I would have to confess to stealing again, only this time outside the confessional.

It was the worst month of my childhood. Because I couldn't bring myself to confess to the owner of the store, in my mind I wasn't forgiven by God. I couldn't receive Holy Communion, and if I died suddenly, I would go to Hell. I had nightmares about Hell, but for an entire month I couldn't bring myself to tell the candy-store owner what I'd done.

Finally, I did—it was either that or go crazy. I ran in, dropped a dime and blurted out I had grabbed a Mounds bar because I was starving. I said I was sorry and ran away. You know how everybody says they feel elated with the slate clean after Confession? I sure felt it that time as I ran away from the store. It was a pretty good penance.

For Sal, forty-six, a New York attorney, sports became a sin.

The most ridiculous penance I ever got was having to say a rosary because I played basketball in the gymnasium of a Protestant school. I was sixteen. That's thirty years ago, and I remember it like it was yesterday.

We were taught that going to a non-Catholic religious service was a threat to our faith, and therefore an occasion of sin. That teaching certainly doesn't say much about the ecumenical spirit of the times. What I'm lamenting now is how totally we accepted that kind of dogma without a single word of dissent or questioning the reasons behind it.

I can't ever remember being told that I'd lose my soul if I played basketball on a Protestant court. But somehow the mortal danger implicit in attending other religious services spilled over and I felt so guilty that I was compelled to confess. The fact that the priest gave me a rosary means that either he wasn't listening to me and gave everyone a rosary that day, or he really believed that walking on Protestant ground was as contagious as athlete's foot.

For Ralph, forty-six, an insurance salesman from Los Angeles, his cousin proved to be an occasion of sin.

If sibling rivalry is jealousy between brothers and sisters, what's hatred between cousins? In any case, from the age of six until I was sixteen, I hated one of my cousins with an all-consuming passion. Every time something bad happened to him, it was like a Christmas present for me. I hated him because he had a better family than I had. They were richer, nicer, better-looking and had more fun. He also had older brothers and that was what I envied most. Hating him had become part of my life, like having freckles.

When I was 16 I went on a retreat and one of the topics we discussed was jealousy. I had learned about jealousy before from the nuns and the priests, but it never clicked that hatred was related. I suddenly realized that I had been guilty of a serious sin for the past ten years. How do you think that hits a teenage kid, finding out he's been a mortal sinner for a decade, day in, day out? My mind started to reel . . . How many sins did constant hatred count for? If I hated him 6 times a day that meant 6 mortal sins, times 365 days in the year, times 10 years. I figured out I had

111

over 20,000 mortal sins on my soul. I had to be about the worst person alive.

Because I couldn't dare confess being such a sinner, I suddenly became sensitive to my own mortality. I crossed the street looking both ways at least fourteen times. I called my aunt to inquire about my cousin, praying that he was well, hoping he had made the football team. I even began to hope that he'd get laid before I did.

After about a week of this weird behavior, I decided to exorcise my guilt by doing something fabulous for him. I was going to buy him a suit, a real good suit, a suit good enough to get rid of 20,000 mortal sins. After I did that, I'd be able to go to Confession and tell the priest something innocent like, "I was envious of my cousin," and hope he wouldn't ask me any more questions. If that worked, I'd be off the hook with God.

I took all my savings, fifty-five dollars, and bought him a blue serge suit from Mason's. I left it in front of his doorstep, with a note that I didn't sign, the way people leave babies. When I called my aunt the next day, she said somebody must have played a joke on them and left a suit at their doorstep. Everybody thought it was probably full of bugs, so they burned it.

Nevertheless, I still felt relieved. It was the best spent fifty-five dollars of my life. Then I went to Confession and managed to slip the jealousy sin right past the priest and I was free. Guilt gone, forever.

For many teenage penitents, the amount of penance they received often became the measure of a successful social life. Sometimes, the confessional even provided a matchmaking incentive. Billy, a forty-seven-year-old Chicago writer, remembers:

We used to feel really proud if saying our confession took a long time. If a kid only got one Our Father as penance, we figured he must have been so good that he wasn't having any fun in life. We always measured the time the girls were in the confessional, too, poking each other and laughing. The girl who was a scholar, wore a dress—she'd be in there for two and a half hours. The girl who wore a black leather jacket and hung out at the roller rink Friday nights—she'd be in there for two and a half minutes.

Had to be something wrong there, we thought. The thing is, we could never really judge. The second one could have walked in there, said "I did everything" and left. When a good girl was in there forever, we'd always try to get a date with her afterwards.

Many Catholic kids considered committing certain sins a rite of passage into adulthood.

Harold, a twenty-five-year-old San Diego truck driver, confides some of his confessional growing pains:

When I was thirteen, I went through a period where I thought that I was an adult and so I should be committing adult sins. I'd go to Confession and make up big sins like it was a badge of honor. If I came out of that box and had to say a whole rosary, boy, I was laughing. But I always told my friends what I got. "Hey, I was in church an hour just getting rid of the penance."

For many kids, lying in the confessional became a finely honed craft. A few lied because they wanted to shock the priest and boast about it to their buddies on the street. Others were afraid to tell the priest the truth because they feared he might tell their parents. Still others were too embarrassed to reveal all their intimate thoughts and actions.

Adelle, a thirty-five-year-old marketing consultant from Boston, describes a priest who forced her to lie:

As a kid, I only went to Confession once or twice a year. So I would go in and say, "Bless me, Father, for I have sinned. It's been eleven months since my last confession." and I knew right away I was in big trouble. Priests don't like this, you see. So then he starts yelling at me, real loud,

so that everybody in the church can hear. Well, there was
no way I was ever going to repeat that performance again.
So the next time I went, about nine months later, I lied.
I was fourteen. I remember that age specifically. I decided
that there was no way I was getting that abuse from the
priest again for not going to Confession regularly. So I
made up something like "one week." The priest was
happy and so was I.

Lying in the confessional affected the following two women in
very different ways. One believed that God forgave her regardless
of what she said. The other believed that God had doomed her to
an eternity in Hell for her sins.

Janice, twenty-eight, a Brooklyn court stenographer, recalls with
a grin:

> I don't think you tell the whole truth in Confession. When
> we were kids, the girls and me, we'd go to the store for
> french fries and a Coke and we just had to have enough
> money. I had no idea how much money I took from my
> mother's purse, but in confession, it would always be in
> terms like "some quarters." There was always that ele-
> ment of not telling the whole truth of it, but you felt that
> God would understand anyway.

Millie, a thirty-eight-year-old security guard from Chicago,
remembers her confessional experiences with anger:

> Confession teaches you to lie, because there are some
> things you just can't bring yourself to tell the priest, the
> fear is so great. When I was about fourteen, I remember
> sitting on my bed after confession, terrified that demons
> were going to come after me. I felt so guilty because I
> went to Communion without going to Confession first.
> Then I lied to the priest afterward because I didn't tell
> him that sin. I was convinced I was going to burn in
> Hell.

The Bloom Is Gone

Many kids became cynical about Confession because of boredom, unfilled expectations, ignorance of the Sacrament, fear, peer pressure, mistrust of the priest and other reasons known only to themselves. Their confessions dissipated into disappointment, tinged with anger.

Gina, a thirty-eight-year-old artist from Toronto, laments the time when going to Confession became nothing more than a weekly routine.

> When I made my First Confession at eighteen, as a convert, I felt honored at being allowed into the confessional. The priest had such a deep voice. I told him about the things that happened in my family and how many times I did something wrong and how much I wanted to be better for him the next time. But the next Saturday when I went back, I had nothing new to say. It was a different priest and a different voice, and it didn't feel special anymore.

Bob, a fifty-six-year-old Detroit high school principal, made up his own sardonic definition of the Sacrament.

> Confession was like bringing all your luggage full of sins up to the customs man at the airport. He asks you questions about your sins and then he lets you go through after paying something for the luxury items you bought while you were abroad. I was a teenager, and even then I didn't take it seriously.

Part of the reason for incipient confessional cynicism can be traced to the indifferent attitude of some priests. Diane, a twenty-four-year-old doctoral student from Boston, explains:

> The priest always said the same things over and over. If I'd taped myself on my parents' tape recorder and handed my confession to him, it would have been just as good. I

never got any wisdom or direction, not even a good reprimand. The only time it seemed he was really listening was when I was telling him a juicy, sexy story. He'd say, "Give me all the details, my child. Try a little harder for God." It was almost as if I had to appeal to his own weaknesses to get his attention.

Andrea, a thirty-six-year-old Detroit sales clerk, was petulant as she recalled the priests who never really listened to her adolescent woes.

It always happened so fast—there I was saying three little prayers for something that burdened me all week, and that made me feel really low. Sometimes I think it would have been better if I'd told a real person and not a priest. Maybe I would have gotten something more out of it.

For David, a thirty-five-year-old Halifax, Nova Scotia, waiter, the age of his priest was a prime concern.

I always went to older priests. Maybe it was because the priests always said, "We are Christ on earth." And since Christ is 2,000 years old, I always wanted somebody as close to that age as I could get.

Louise became disenchanted with Confession when a priest forced her to implicate a third person. The twenty-four-year-old ballet dancer from San Francisco recalls:

The sin I felt guiltiest about was reading dirty magazines when I was in grade school. My father had a couple of those magazines and I'd sneak up to the top of the garage and look at them. When I confessed to the priest that I really enjoyed looking at those magazines, he wanted to know where I got them. It was really awful because he made me squeal on my father and I felt guilty for weeks.

Jerry, a forty-five-year-old advertising executive from Calgary, Alberta, became bored with the Sacrament out of a genuine fear of it.

You see, the Catholic Church exists on a premise of terror, and you can't be terrorized and bored at the same time. Most of my confessions were lies. The sins I was supposed to confess were so terrible that I couldn't confess them, so I made up other ones. I thought if I ever confessed the real ones, the priest would vomit blood through the grille and a plague would descend upon my head.

For some of the men and women interviewed, the cynicism bred in their teenage years has kept them away from the Sacrament for a lifetime. The following two women don't go to Confession. Even as adults, they still blame their priests. Delores, forty-five, a social worker living in a Chicago suburb, remembers:

When I was eleven, I decided that I hated Confession and would never go back again. I was a secretive person and objected to telling the priest personal things that he wouldn't help me with anyway. My mother was insane— she'd overdose on sleeping pills and I'd have to prop her up so she would vomit. I told the priest that I thought my mother was crazy, but all he wanted to hear was that I had been a naughty girl. He never gave me any advice or consolation. When my mother finally committed suicide, I never told the priest, but I held him responsible.

Angela, a twenty-three-year-old Toronto cocktail waitress, reveals a certain cynicism:

My father died suddenly of a heart attack and I was terrified that my mother was going to die too. So I went to Confession, and I told the priest I was willing to make a bargain with him. If I went to Confession every week for the rest of my life, I wanted him to promise me that my mother wouldn't die and leave me. All he said was, "God doesn't make bargains." I expected some sympathy, but he gave me nothing. So I never went back to Confession again.

Bless Me, Father, For I Have Sinned

Many teenagers became confused, blasé or angered by the way the Sacrament was administered. Some claim they never understood what a sin was and were equally confused about the purpose of confession, while others understood the meaning of sin but never felt they were sinners.

Caroline, a fifty-six-year-old Washington, D.C., public school teacher, recalls her youth:

> I never liked Confession because I could never think of anything that I did that was bad enough to tell the priest. There must have been something wrong with me. I was very obedient, a real goody-goody. Soon I began to take Confession as seriously as if my mother had told me to go to the store and pick up a dozen eggs.

Barry, a thirty-two-year-old Toronto accountant, recalls his confusion about sin and the way he solved it:

> I remember one confession; I was about nine or ten. It centered on the fact that even though in retrospect I knew I had committed a sin, at the time I thought what I was doing was right, so it wasn't a grave sin. I remember sitting in church before going into Confession and thinking to myself, "What am I doing here? Why am I going to Confession if what I did at the time was what I thought was right? It's not a grave sin." That was my first germ of rebellion against the Church and it certainly wasn't my last. My way of coping with sin and confession was to avoid both.

Chapter 7

Sin and Guilt

The Young "Scrupes"

There are two dictionary definitions for the word scrupulous. The first is "having moral integrity"; the second is "punctiliously exact." *Scrupulus,* the Latin root, means a unit of weight as well as a small sharp stone that the more scrupulous monks would place in their shoes as a penance to cause mental and physical discomfort. Scrupulous penitents have not only caused great discomfort to themselves but also to their confessors, as they have punctiliously and repeatedly weighed their sins.

Some priests call them "scrupes," those obsessive penitents—men, women and children of all ages—who attribute a scrupulous sense of sinfulness to everything.

Bless Me, Father, For I Have Sinned

Confessional folklore has always included the story of the child who forgets to tell the priest a sin and immediately runs back, saying, "Bless me, Father, for I have sinned. It's been ten minutes since my last confession."

This story, although full of charming naïveté, unfortunately contains the seeds of a neurosis capable of stunting a child's emotional development into mature, responsible adulthood. Overscrupulous penitents are, for the most part, the result of religious instruction begun at an early age that overemphasizes sin, guilt, feelings of unworthiness and fear of the afterlife.

The following people echo the words of many others as they recall the religious training that encouraged scrupulosity.

Robert, forty-five, a computer analyst from Boston:

> We were weaned on the milk-bottle theory of sin and confession. There were these three milk bottles and they represented your soul. You would get one pure-white milk bottle, which is what your soul looked like after Confession and after Baptism. One pure-black milk bottle is what your soul looked like after committing a mortal sin. And one speckled milk bottle was what your soul looked like after committing venial sins. Naturally, we always asked if you could make a speckled milk bottle into a black milk bottle by committing a lot of venial sins. And if so, what would happen to the other two bottles?

Mark, forty-five, a Toronto film producer:

> I took Confession very seriously as a teenager. I would never just casually arrive in church on Saturday afternoon like some kids did. I'd be up most of the night before writing down the number of times I did it, the date and how sorry I felt. I'd give myself an "A" for very, very sorry, a "C" for so-so sorry and a "B" for somewhere in between. I'd take the paper with me and review it carefully before going in. I would also write down what I wanted to accomplish from my encounter with the priest. After the

confession, I would take my piece of paper out and check off all the sins, just to make sure I didn't forget any. I'd do this every week, sometimes two or three times a week, if I thought I was a really bad sinner that week.

Joyce is a fifty-five-year-old Brooklyn housewife who has not been to Confession in twenty-five years. She speaks with rage when describing the nuns, the giants of her childhood, who first instructed her in the Sacrament:

The nuns used to drum the notion of guilt into us pretty early. I remember a nun who used to encourage us to write in the margins so that we didn't waste paper. When I went to Confession, I always told the priest about the paper I wasted because I thought if I didn't, I'd end up burning in Hell. There was another nun who said that every time we committed a sin, we added another lash to the back of Christ. How would you like to deal with that at the age of seven? God knows I tried to be as sinless as possible but I didn't always succeed. And I felt extremely guilty about every sin I *did* commit, no matter how minor . . .

Angela, a forty-six-year-old Italian-American divorcee, lives in New York with her four children. She vividly recalls one particular sin and confession from her youth:

When I was sixteen I received Communion while I had a sin on my soul that I hadn't asked forgiveness for in my last confession. The nuns taught us that our mouths would explode if we ever did that. For months, I had visions that I would be instantly set on fire.

Meredith, who left the Church in the early 1960s, returns nostalgically for midnight Mass every Christmas. The forty-year-old Washington, D.C., librarian recalls her battle to sustain her self-esteem:

We were taught two conflicting ideas that I could never come to terms with as a kid. One was that I was a child of

121

God, created in His image and loved. The other was that I was born into the world with sin, and the only way I could be admitted into Heaven was for God to send His son to die a horrible death because of our sins. I was torn between feeling I was good, created in God's image, but at the same time someone awful because by nature I'm also a sinner.

I felt this same swinging back and forth about myself as a person. One minute I could believe in God and everything would be fine but if for an instant I fell from grace I was a sinner and therefore a terrible person. It was difficult for me to ever really feel good about myself. I believe the Church created this monster by telling us, "You're a sinner and we're going to give you a way to get rid of all that. You have to go to Confession and you have to do penance." But it was never that simple. It was something you had to live through over and over again.

Many men and women described their pattern of sin, guilt, confession, elation and sin as if they were on a Sisyphean treadmill. José, a forty-six-year-old elevator mechanic from Buffalo, New York, speaks out in despair:

When I was a teenager I remember thinking that after Confession I was all right for another week or so, maybe another day. I was taught that if I died and I had just been to Confession, then I'd go to Heaven. But if I died five days after I'd gone to Confession, then I'd go to Hell. I mean, in those five days, I must have committed a sin somewhere along the way, like saying "shit." By the fourth or fifth day I'd be terrified because I was on God's blacklist again. I could never get off that treadmill.

Maria, a forty-seven-year-old secretary in a New York advertising agency, echoes José's anxiety:

I could never keep track of all my sins and that was why going to Confession was so traumatic for me. When I was

Sin and Guilt

six years old, I can remember starting each day thinking, "Today I'm going to get it right" and before I knew it, on the way to school, I'd already have removed my mittens and scarf and thrown away my lunch. Then I'd realize I blew it again and had two more sins to confess. I always figured in eleven times for yelling at my mother and eight for everything else. Eight seemed like a nice round number. I eventually just gave up because I saw myself as an incurable sinner.

While some of the young "scrupes" compulsively confessed their sins every day, others were so consumed with guilt that they couldn't bring themselves to the Sacrament. Victoria, a thirty-five-year-old liquor store manager in Vero Beach, Florida, confides:

There were lots of times I felt so guilty that I couldn't go to Confession because I was so terrified to tell the priest what I'd done. At seventeen, I still hadn't menstruated or developed breasts and I was getting curious. I remember exploring myself, touching my breasts to make sure they were real. My friends had all been menstruating and wearing bras by the time they were twelve.

Then I felt terribly guilty for touching my body. I knew it was wrong, but I didn't know how to tell the priest, who was a man. I never had a close relationship with him. And the nuns used to skip over anything that had to do with marriage or sex. Well, the guilt about touching myself kept coming back, and I just couldn't go to Confession.

Finally I got up the nerve to tell the priest about it. I was really surprised that I wasn't immediately consumed by flames. But he was very complacent. At seventeen, I think my age surprised him more than my sins.

The way the priest reacts toward the young "scrupes" can have a marked long-term effect on their self-esteem. For many, a priest

123

who was harsh and reinforced their guilts and fears did the greatest damage. The compassionate priests, sensitive to their tender feelings, proved to be the catalyst for a healthy examination of conscience and positive attitude toward the Sacrament.

Laura, a thirty-two-year-old Los Angeles film editor, is a devout Catholic. She describes a confession at the age of eleven with a priest whom she credits with saving her faith.

My problem was that I was never sure that I'd made a thorough confession. Because of the emphasis on being totally truthful, you had to examine your conscience and tell everything to the priest. Everytime I would walk out, the anxiety would return that perhaps I had not remembered all my sins. If you forgot something, it was all right as long as you mentioned it the next time around.

I would immediately begin to build up a list of forgotten things to bring up next time, then I'd forget a few more of the new ones. The anxiety over it just kept building up to a point that when I got older I became so neurotic about it that I was going to daily Confession.

I remember walking out of the confessional one day and going right back in. The priest recognized me and I said, "I've come back, Father, because when I was stepping out of the church, I was thinking that you were an idiot. So I had to come back and tell you this." And he said, "Why don't you wait until I'm finished? I want to talk to you."

This wonderful priest called the nuns at my school and told them I was supposed to stay out of religious class, that I had to see him once a month and that I was to go to Communion on a daily basis. He helped me get out of this incredible bind I'd gotten myself into. He tried to explain that the things I thought were wrong weren't that wrong and he made me realize I was being silly about certain things. He knew that I was feeling this way because of the kind of education that I'd had. He tried to explain the important things in life. He stressed that no matter what I thought I'd done, I should receive Communion every day at school. His faith in my behavior made me feel more sure of myself.

Several people recalled that the scrupulosity of their youth caused them to suffer physically as well. Martin, a divorced thirty-four-year-old Detroit boutique manager, explains how an understanding priest helped him to become more self-accepting:

> When I was ten years old I had a lot of difficulty understanding the difference between sexual sin and mortal sin. I was so terrified that it affected my appetite. I couldn't eat, and I lost so much weight that I was hospitalized for a month. I couldn't sleep either. My guilt over sexual thoughts became an obsession for me. I finally met a priest who said that everyone thinks like that, about girls being undressed.
>
> It would be difficult to estimate the full impact of those years on my adult emotional life, but I'm sure it would be considerable. None of the other priests I ever met had such a broad concept; they were all so narrow, strictly by the numbers. That priest eventually left the priesthood and married a divorced woman. Some of those with a broader concept of life couldn't live with the strict Church rules.

Angie, a twenty-seven-year-old physiotherapist from Washington, D.C., recalls a priest who corrected her for her scrupulousness:

> When I was a little girl, I always wanted to be very thorough. I went into Confession and said that I hit my sister, I punched her, I kicked her, I pulled her hair, I ripped her shirt. There was a long line—I think it was Easter—and the priest stopped me and said, "Pardon me, would you mind just saying you fought with your sister?"

. . . and the Unscrupulous!

The opposite of the "scrupe" is the "unscrupe." Often the unscrupulous kid could be a source of frustration to a well-meaning
confessor attempting to teach the meaning of sin. Bill, a fifty-six-
year-old medical-supply salesman from Albany, recalls that during
his youth he experienced none of the guilt voiced by some of the
others in these pages.

I was ten when I confessed I wanted to kill my grandmother. Not only did I plot to kill her, I prayed to God that
He should kill her. A friend of mine overheard my prayers
and said I had to confess to a priest right away. It never
occurred to me to confess because I felt no guilt over it.
But I did worry that it might be a sin. So I told the priest
that I had been thinking about helping my grandmother
die. That seemed indirect enough for me. The priest
could tell I was only a kid, so he said, "Why do you want
her to die? Is she ill?" I realized I was stuck and would
have to explain everything. "No, she has a bigger house
than we do, she smells badly, she yells at me a lot and
complains to my mother about my bad manners!" Speaking very slowly, he explained that those were not sufficient
reasons to want somebody dead. Then he caught himself
and added that there were no reasons to want somebody
dead.

Eventually, he made me tell him everything, about how
I prayed for her to die, how I read mystery stories and
went to movies that had murders in them so I could learn
how to do it. He got so exasperated he almost screamed
at me, "Killing is wrong, it's a grave sin." He probably was
thinking, "Can't you get that through your thick Irish
head?" He told me to come to the rectory after my confession and asked permission to contact my parents. They
never convinced me that I was sinning when I wanted my
grandmother to die. When she eventually died two years

later, I never felt anything one way or the other, except glad that we got the bigger house.

Impure Thoughts, Impure Actions

"Bless me, Father, for I have sinned. I have been impure in thought, word and deed. I have touched myself in an impure manner."

The number of times that those words have been spoken by Catholic kids is incalculable. "Not only was it a mortal sin to do something of a sexual nature to others or to oneself, it was a mortal sin to even contemplate doing it. St. Augustine's fifth-century definition of sin as word or desire as well as deed, in opposition to the eternal law of God, made impure thoughts a perplexing problem.

As a result, many adolescent penitents have found a variety of inventive methods for coping with or circumventing this troubling lack of separation between thought and deed. Others have been less successful and, as adults, still remember that "even after wiping the slate clean in Confession, those bad thoughts kept coming back over and over again."

Joan, a fifty-six-year-old Boston mother of five, recalls that impure thoughts and their accompanying guilt were a constant source of anxiety:

> I first felt guilty of sins of impurity in the sixth grade. I started having "impure thoughts." I didn't know they were sexual—I didn't know enough about sex for that— but I sensed they were unclean because of certain feelings they produced in my body. What a relief it was to go to Confession . . . I felt forgiven and strengthened. I was sure I'd never have those thoughts again. But they returned and, with them, the guilt. Every time I went to Confession, I had the same unclean thoughts to confess. I remember being so discouraged, so tired of trying to fight these thoughts, that I asked the priest, "When will this end?"

The priest said they would never end and I would always have to struggle against them. It was so discouraging. I remember thinking it would be impossible for me to ever be good.

For most Catholic kids, sex as a confessable sin had a natural progression beginning with the "impure thought" and blossoming into the "impure action."

Most women described their impure thoughts in terms of sexual fantasies involving such diverse males as movie stars, teachers, the boy next door and priests. Impure actions were usually controlled kissing and petting above the waist, the Checkpoint Charlie of chastity.

Two women describe their priests and impure thoughts—a common phenomenon whispered in locker rooms and in late-night phone conversations.

Shirley, fifty-two, a mother of four, in Denver:

> When I was in high school, I got a crush on a priest. I never thought of it as an impure thought, just a crush. It certainly wasn't a sin, but I went to confession every day for a week because I was so infatuated with this man. By the third day I had nothing left to confess. At the end of the week, I told him I'd been there every day because I had a crush on him. He took it very well and gave me good advice about how that sometimes happens, but it was important for me to think of other things. He was such a sweet man. I'd had crushes on other priests, too. It was an easy thing to do because there is no possibility of any entanglements. It's safe and perfectly pure.

Peggy, thirty-four, single, an advertising agency copywriter living in Niagara Falls, New York:

> The confession which I felt most guilty about had to do with sex. It was when I first discovered that the priest, under all his wonderful tunics, was wearing a pair of trousers. That's when I first remembered having some terrible

thoughts about this man who was supposed to be representing the Divine. Somehow I found the fact that he was wearing trousers very exciting.

Masturbation was a nightmarish cycle of temptation, commission, remorse and confession, over and over again. In the thirties, forties, fifties and sixties, masturbation was considered a mortal sin, sufficient to doom the culprit to an eternity in the flames of Hell, not to mention a lifetime of hairy palms and poor eyesight.

Charlie, a thirty-six-year-old Los Angeles cab driver, recalls that he marched to a different drummer, but not for long:

> I first became aware of mortal sin as I was committing it. My buddies in the street had told—and shown—me about masturbation, but I always thought of myself as a rugged individualist. I'd do it in my own good time. Just like smoking cigarettes. Everybody else started smoking at fourteen, so I waited until I was sixteen.
>
> Some of my friends started masturbating at eleven, but I waited until I was thirteen. At that time, I had little sense of a conscience. I guess it was masturbation that did it. It was just too much fun not to be a sin. I went to Confession and said, "Father, I'd like to ask you some questions about something that I'm doing, but I don't know whether or not it's a sin." "Does it involve touching yourself?" he asked. I admitted it did, and he said, "Well, you didn't know until now that it was a mortal sin, but now you know it is." From then on, I felt guilty about it, but I kept doing it—and enjoyed it even more.

Brian, a forty-five-year-old teacher from Birmingham, Alabama, explains that he graded his sexual sins:

> Every sin I committed when I was young had to do with sex. I remember having used to stall going into that confessional because I couldn't open up to the priest. He'd ask me to list my sexual sins, and the number of times I'd committed them. I began grading them "A," "B"

and "C." I felt most guilty about jerking off. Not only was it a sin, but it was embarrassing to admit doing something that stupid. It's certainly not the noblest sin one can commit. I always gave it a "C."

Donald, a forty-five-year-old lawyer from Detroit, echoes the words of many others who wanted direction and not damnation from their confessors.

When you're a kid the most guilt-ridden sins are always related to sex. Of course, there was no sex education, and the first experience was masturbation. I was terrified that I was going to go blind or grow hair on my hands. But at the same time I couldn't believe I was truly committing a sin because it seemed so natural. I didn't want forgiveness from a priest in the confessional, I wanted an explanation. When I was about sixteen, I finally confessed to a young priest at a retreat. He said that masturbation had been preached as a sin previously, but that it was now considered a personal matter and not an act against God.

This lack of agreement among priests was another source of anxiety for the young masturbator. Different priests had different interpretations, and the kids were caught in the crossfire.

Walter, a thirty-year-old Chicago shoe salesman, reminisces:

Some priests would say masturbation was natural—so long as we didn't do it too often. Others, usually the older ones, said we would burn in Hell if we masturbated. The conflict of attitude was hell itself. I'll tell you a story about a priest I'll never forget.

Father Damian was handsome, funny and very athletic. He gave the impression he could have any woman he wanted, but chose to remain faithful to the Blessed Virgin because he loved her so much.

Father Damian knew all about jerking off. He even used the words in Confession. Sometimes he called it having an affair with your five fingers. None of that "I touched my-

Sin and Guilt

self in an impure manner" stuff. He reassured us that we wouldn't suffer any physical consequences, that it was a natural act, but still forbidden by the Church. When I went to confess after that, I felt free. Of course, I went on masturbating but I no longer felt so bad about it.

Kenneth, a forty-two-year-actor from New York, learned how to exploit this disagreement among priests.

If you were smart, you found a priest who was deaf and spoke no English except the words "three Hail Marys." Then you'd charge your friends for his name and make a couple of bucks on the deal as well.

But seriously, no matter how often I confessed to a priest that I'd masturbated, it never got any easier. I'd always leave that for the last. I'd go through the usual sins of lying, swearing, not being nice to my parents and sisters, and then, at last, quick as I could, I'd squeeze it in. When I left, did I ever feel relieved! I was ten feet high— until the next time.

Some found confessing to masturbation not an embarrassing problem but a source of inspiration. Derick, a sixty-year-old New York writer, recounts his tale.

When they told me I was going to have impure thoughts, I couldn't wait. When I finally had them—and carried them out—I started to make up terrific stories. Instead of saying I masturbated at night in bed under the covers with a Klee-nex—please God, a Kleenex—I'd tell the priest that I masturbated in full view of the Sodality of the Holy Mother!

In the confessional, masturbation was the first sexual sin, but certainly not the last. From "touching yourself in an impure manner," teenagers soon moved on to "touching somebody else in an impure manner."

Enid, a fifty-year-old Atlanta dentist, explains how in Confession, as in real life, one thing led to another.

Everytime I confessed "an impure act," the priest asked "by yourself or with someone else?" I always wondered what would happen if I said with somebody else. Would I graduate to a new level of sinning? Would the penance be different? Would I finally be an adult? His question almost made me want to do something with somebody else. The priest practically egged me on to sin. He made it sound so mysterious and desirable.

Many men and women spoke of the trauma of confessing their first sexual sin. Some said they remembered the event more clearly than their wedding night. Debby, a thirty-seven-year-old mathematics instructor from Arlington, Virginia, recalls one priest's peculiar method for cooling teenage ardor.

My memory of the Sacrament (of Confession) was that the sins you were supposed to confess were entirely sexual. There were a lot of lectures about what you were and weren't supposed to do when you kissed a boy. Well, I hardly kissed boys at that age, but all that talk was certainly preparing me to. Can you imagine how much anxiety that built up in an adolescent girl? I remember a priest telling me in the confessional that when a couple was kissing, it was the girl's responsibility to make sure things didn't go too far. She should make a pact with her boyfriend. If she thought they were kissing too much or getting too aroused, she should make a Sign of the Cross on his arm. When I got out of the box, I thought to myself, this is lunacy.

The priests were there for guidance as well as penance and absolution. Brenda, a thirty-seven-year-old nurse from Glens Falls, New York, remembers seeking direction.

I asked a priest in confession how long you were allowed to kiss a boy. Without pausing for a second, he said that the way you could tell if a kiss was a grave sin or not was to time it. If you could count to five or more, it was a

mortal sin. A shorter kiss was only venial sin. It wasn't easy
to concentrate on kissing and counting at the same time.

The sin determined the nature of the confession and penance,
but frequently the knowledge that one had to confess colored the
way in which the sin was committed. Brenda continues:

> We were taught that in order to commit a mortal sin, you
> had to be in command of all your faculties. In other words,
> you had to be committing the sin by choice. My girl friends
> and I came up with a simple solution. If we were "swept
> off our feet" the sin wasn't mortal. Many of us got swept
> away every Friday and Saturday nights. Afterward, all we
> had to confess was a venial sin.

Adolescent penitents were inventive in their confessions—and
their reasoning. Rejeanne, a thirty-year-old manicurist from Santa
Fe, New Mexico, gave sin a great deal of thought.

> When I was around fourteen, I went to Confession me-
> chanically, confessing only the most minor transgressions.
> The major ones were too embarrassing. Besides, I didn't
> think the priest ought to hear about sins that had to do
> with sex, which were the only important ones. I heard that
> French kissing was a sin, but my information didn't come
> from an official church person, and I'd never read that it
> was a sin. So I decided I wouldn't worry about it. I thought
> it would be awful if a priest found out what French kissing
> was. I couldn't believe they knew what really went on.

In the Church, the end of innocence is often defined as the
beginning of sexual knowledge. Countless men and women admitted that the beginning of their premarital sexual experiences
marked the end of their confessional ones. Constance, a thirty-
seven-year-old word processor from Baltimore, poignantly describes her sexual initiation and spiritual loss.

> When I was nineteen, I stopped going to Confession. I
> had started having sexual relations, and was too embar-

rassed to discuss the intimacies with a third person, even a priest, especially a priest. Of course, I could no longer take Communion. At first I was sad, then angry. I began to look for faults in the Church. Not long after that I left it. The experience was painful, like falling out of love with someone and trying to justify the change in my feelings by the unworthiness of the other person.

These days the thing I miss most is not being able to say "Jesus, Mary, Joseph, help the afflicted" every time I see an ambulance.

Though Catholicism puts a high and non-negotiable value on virginity, many of its sons and daughters find it an unnecessary burden. The difference in opinion has driven many away from Confession and, as a result, the Church.

Michael, a forty-one-year-old computer industry journalist from New York, explains that the euphemisms of the confessional alienated him:

Why don't they ever use the real words? Groping in the dark with my girl friend's bra strap and wanting to make love with the lady at the supermarket were both reduced to impure thoughts and actions.

At around twelve, the priest started to hint that screwing around was a sin. He didn't come right out and say it because he figured no one would think of doing it at that age. He was wrong. If he had come right out and said what he meant, we might still have sinned in the eyes of the Church, but we would have grown up with a more honest approach to Confession and sex. Because he never spoke in sexual terms, I never felt I had to explain my sexual actions. Still, I knew I was supposed to. When I started having sex in my final year at college, I stopped going to Confession.

Some Catholic teenagers continued to go to Confession, but left their sexual activities at home. Some thought the priest didn't or

shouldn't know about sex. Others knew in their good Catholic
hearts that they were doing the wrong thing and feared the priest's
wrath, the penance and, perhaps, the withholding of absolution.
Some of them tell their stories.

Joanna, thirty-six, an accountant who lives in Baltimore:

> I never thought of sex as a sin so I'd never go to a priest
> and confess anything that had to do with sex. Besides, it
> was none of his business. He was supposed to be chaste,
> so what could he know about the flesh or understand
> about desire? He might have those feelings, but because
> he denied them, because he chose celibacy, I could never
> talk to a priest about sex.

Lynne, twenty-nine, a nurse from Buffalo:

> My sex life really began at eighteen when I left the Church.
> When I was actively involved in the Church and going to
> Confession every month, no guy ever found me attractive
> enough to even make a pass.
>
> I remember my first kisses and certainly never saw them
> as sinful and certainly never confessed them. Even when
> I lost my virginity, I felt no remorse. I felt great! And I
> wasn't going to spoil that feeling by telling a priest.

Jane, thirty-six, a real-estate agent in Denver:

> I never confessed my sexual sins because I never thought
> they were wrong from a religious point of view. But I
> always thought they were wrong morally because that's
> what my parents taught me. Even now, when I'm in bed
> with a man, I'm sure my father, who is in Heaven, is watch-
> ing. I really hope he's not too disappointed in me.

Patrick, twenty-nine, a high school teacher in San Diego:

> I stopped going to Confession when I started sleeping
> with my girl friend. It was a wonderful thing, and I
> couldn't believe I was doing something I had to be for-

given for. If a priest was going to give me penance and a lot of Hail Marys for doing something that was pleasurable for both of us, then confession wasn't for me.

Robert, thirty-five, an engineer and recent immigrant from Poland:

In the Roman Catholic Church, sex is permitted only between married people and only for having babies. Everything else is sin. But I wasn't married and I liked sex—to give and receive pleasure and express love and admiration. The priests insisted it was a sin, so as soon as I started to feel like a man, I stopped going to Confession.

Raymond, a forty-eight-year-old disc jockey from Cincinnati, describes an unconfessable sexual encounter:

On my eighteenth birthday, I made love in a confessional. Even now, thirty years later, I'm reluctant to take all the blame, but I still feel guilty. My girl friend Elaine suggested we do it because she was a non-Catholic and wanted me out of the fold. It was a Sunday afternoon. We'd been fooling around on her bed and then she—I'm positive she was the one—suggested that we go to the confessional. We practically ran to St. Patrick's. Never, in all my life, can I remember being so excited. It was the ultimate experience—sex, religion, sin, pleasure and rebellion rolled into one. We were in the priest's section and she sat on my lap. Afterwards, I was truly spooked—I expected lightning to hit me at any moment—but I never confessed. Would you?

Sin and Guilt

All Grown Up

It is not the criminal things which are hardest to confess, but the ridiculous and shameful.

—Jean Jacques Rousseau, *Confessions*

The Church recognizes many sins. Some are minor offenses, common to all; others are heinous. Many Catholics, rooted in the pre-Vatican II consciousness, confess even the smallest sins regularly. Others believe minor sins need not be taken to the confessional. It's all a matter of conscience—and definition.

We began by asking people to explain what sin meant to them. Some recited phrases learned long ago. "There are the seven deadly sins," began a forty-seven-year-old Chicago lawyer, "like lust, anger, and then you're got your mortals, your venials and your omissions." A thirty-six-year-old Calgary nurse explained, "A venial sin is an everyday sin, like arguing with your husband. A mortal sin is more serious, like murder, and a cardinal sin is—I don't know—a cardinal sin is absolutely the worst thing, but I forget what you have to do for that."

Some of those interviewed claimed they had never sinned. "What do I know about sin?" commented a sixty-year-old Miami newspaper vendor. "Confession is for people with big sins, not for little people like me, little people with little sins."

Eric, a fifty-six-year-old Boston physician, takes a more theological approach.

I always found the concept of being born into Original Sin inhumane because it's contrary to human dignity. My mother, who's seventy-six, is so wonderfully open. She was lying in bed and a priest dropped by to see her. He said, "You are a sinner," and she said, "What do you mean, I'm a sinner? I'm an old woman lying here in bed. I've lived my life. I've tried to be as decent to everyone as possible, and I want to die with some peace and honor. How dare you call me a sinner?" She was quiet for a

137

moment, and when she spoke again she was smiling. "My God, it would be nice to sin a little, but I can't anymore."

Sarah, a thirty-six-year-old inner-city social worker from Chicago, found herself guilty of an unexpected sin.

When I was in college, I thought I had no sins. I admired St. Thomas Aquinas and was seriously considering becoming a nun. Sexual sublimation was easy for me. I just never had the problems others did, such as masturbation and impure thoughts. As a result, I always felt superior to the men I knew who were more needy. One day I told my brother, who was a priest, that I had no sins. "There is always the sin of vanity," he answered. That devastated me, but you know—he was right.

For Harry, a sixty-six-year-old retired flight controller from Philadelphia, sin had a Catch-22.

For a Catholic, life is a struggle, an impossible struggle that never lets up. You come in sinning. Before you've done anything there's a mark against you. You fight like crazy to get rid of those marks. You finally feel good about yourself. Then they will nail you with the sin of pride.

For Mark, twenty-nine, a Trenton, New Jersey, computer programmer, sin proved to be beneficial.

I remember all that damn confessional cataloguing. You had your worst sins, your mediocre sins and the sins that weren't sins because you never committed them in the first place. Trying to keep all that shit straight was high-level organizational training. It was hell at the time, but it must have done me some good. I'm a computer programmer now. Confession trained me to think logically.

For Annabelle, forty-seven, a security guard in Charlotte, North Carolina, belief in sin—at least in her own personal sin—floundered on logic.

Sin and Guilt

I stopped believing in mortal sin in high school. I couldn't figure out what I was supposed to confess when I went to Confession. The Church said that for a sin to be mortal, it had to be desired. There had to be an affirmation of the act before it was committed. I couldn't see how any logical or reasonable person could commit a mortal sin if he thought about it. Only deranged people commit mortal sins. Things like adultery, drunkenness and gluttony are uncontrollable acts. Therefore, they're not mortal sins. But logical human beings don't commit them.

Isabel, forty-three, a Chicago housewife, defines sin according to humane and social responsibility rather than the dictates of the Church.

Is sex before you're married a sin because it's pleasurable or because you can have children and not be able to care for them properly? When I confessed to a priest that I was sleeping with my boyfriend, he told me that it was a mortal sin, but I didn't think so. The key is the Ten Commandments. If you follow them, if you try not to hurt others, you can go through life free of mortal sin.

Mitch, thirty-seven, a New Haven policeman, also sees sin in social terms.

They never taught, at least in my day, that sin was a transgression against only yourself or even the next person. The only sin was against God. You never had to worry about your fellowman. Now, looking back, it seems selfish.

For Guy, a twenty-four-year-old Worcester, Massachusetts, cab driver, sin has to do with responsibilities to society, the family and the self.

I come from a family of overachievers. My father and mother are both self-made people. Though they came over from Italy without a knowledge of English or a penny, both graduated from college. They made a lot of money.

I'm a different story. My idea of doing something is getting somebody else to do it for you. I barely scraped by in high school, never went to college. Right now, I drive a cab because I want to work when and if I feel like it. I guess you could say I'm lazy.

Last year, I had to go to Confession because a cousin of mine was getting married and I was going to be in the bridal party. There I was, sitting face-to-face with a priest in one of the new rooms they use, and the priest settles down for a long chat. I think my cousin told him about me because he knew an awful lot—at least compared to all the dummies I've run into in the Church.

I told him I had nothing to confess, so he started to ask me about my life and what I was doing with it. Finally he said I did have something to confess. Wasting my life was a sin. I answered that it was my life, and if want to live it my way, what was it to him, or for that matter, to God? I mean, I went to Confession from the time I was seven until I was seventeen, and no priest ever talked to me about sin like that before. I was expecting a lecture on impure thought and impure action. Instead, he started to make sense. He made me feel guilty about wasting my life, especially with the example my parents had set. I realized what I was doing affected other people as well as myself. He asked me to visit him every week so that we could talk about what I was doing with myself.

A month later, I enrolled in a night course in creative writing. I still backslide occasionally, but something inside me says I'm going to make it.

But if one owes things to his fellowman and himself, in the end sin always comes back to what one owes to God. Barbara, a thirty-four-year-old San Francisco housewife, learned that difficult lesson from her priest.

A few years ago, a very young priest amazed me. He looked about eighteen, the age of my baby brother.

Sin and Guilt

I was having a crisis of faith brought on by my happiness. It seems contradictory, but it wasn't. I love my husband very much. My two daughters, brothers and sisters are the most important things in my life. I had everything and was absolutely elated. Then I realized they were more important to me than God. I was committing a sin against God because I loved them so much.

I confessed this sin to the young priest. He said my confession was a good one because I had "revealed my heart." I cherished that phrase for a long time afterward. I realized that God worked in His own wonderful ways to give such understanding to one so young who could, in turn, give it to me. My confession helped me put things in perspective. God has His place in my heart and so does my family. They're not in conflict anymore.

Elaine, a single, forty-one-year-old high school teacher from Los Angeles, sinned through self-doubt.

In my heart, I always felt like a failure. If I got eighty percent on an exam, I felt guilty it wasn't ninety; if I got ninety, it should have been one hundred. When I cleaned my room, I worried about spots of dirt I might have missed. Maybe I felt so inferior because I was always comparing myself to the saints. I grew up on the nun's stories of their miraculous works and their suffering for our Lord and the Blessed Mother. By comparison, I was worthless.

My father added coals to the fire. He said if I didn't win a scholarship to college, I wasn't good enough to go. From the first day of my senior year in high school, I did nothing but study. I never went to the movies, watched television, had a date, even talked on the phone unless it was about schoolwork. I drove myself like the saints who used to pray for days on end, living on bread and water. When I got ninety-three percent on a chemistry examination, I was so furious that I decided to punish myself. I pierced my ears in the hope I'd get an infection. Then I put myself on a strict diet in imitation of the desert fathers. When I didn't finish reading certain pages by certain dates, I'd ration my food even further.

I went to Confession every week to purify myself for my final examinations and to early Mass every Sunday to pray that God would not cause me to fail because I was still a sinner.

Early one morning, around seven A.M., I fainted as I walked out of the confessional. The priest, who had known my family and me for years, said I looked gaunt and sickly and demanded to know what I was doing to myself. He probably thought I was on drugs. When I told him about my preparations, he explained that my abuse of my body was a sin. God wants us to be healthy in mind and body so that we can be better people and serve Him better. He insisted I make an appointment with another priest who did psychological counseling.

I went to see the priest that very afternoon because I was petrified of committing yet another sin. I wanted that scholarship desperately and believed that the more sins I had on my soul, the less chance I had of getting it.

I won that scholarship and another as well, but even today, twenty years after college, I'm still driven by visions of perfection I know I'll never attain. I still go to Confession every week. But thanks to that priest, I can laugh at myself just a little bit.

To Selwyn, a forty-six-year-old oil company executive from Chicago, like the adolescents in the previous chapter, sin meant sexual sin.

I can't understand why non-Catholics marry or have relationships with Catholics. Those of us who grew up in the fifties were a crazy bunch. All we thought about was sex and sin. You couldn't have one without the other. When I was twenty, I was infatuated with a non-Catholic girl. I put her on a roller coaster instead of a pedestal. I'd pursue her passionately all week until my lust began to wane on Friday, the day before Confession.

The true lunancy was that I, as well as every other Catholic girl and boy I knew, believed we'd renounced sex until marriage. Everybody talks about wild Saturday nights. Not in my life. On Saturday afternoon I confessed all my sexual sins of the week in order to receive Communion; on Saturday night I was absolutely pure. Sunday mornings were wonderful. I felt good and cleansed. Then came the week. I'd make it until perhaps Tuesday, when I'd start the whole sin-sex cycle all over again. I forgot all about staying pure until marriage.

The girl put up with this for three years. Then she ended the relationship. Can you blame her? She said good sex and Catholicism don't mix.

Many people we interviewed were unable to define sin. Some recalled the Ten Commandments. Others fell back on the rules of the Church—meatless Fridays, attendance at Mass, proscription of Protestant religious services—rather than its concepts. The clergy told another story. As might be expected, they had a clearer idea of sin. Many were articulate, even eloquent on the subject.

Father Duarte, fifty-six, speaking from his Miami parish, relates sin to the love of God:

> Those who have a burning love for God don't commit sin when temptation comes along. They cannot and will not betray the love and trust of God. They say to themselves, "He doesn't want me to commit this sin. He has said so in black and white. He has made the difference between right and wrong clear to me."
>
> If you've got God's grace, you don't commit sin. But if you don't have the grace or love of God, then maybe the fear of God will keep you from sinning.

Father Romaldo, thirty-six, recently arrived in Washington, D.C., from Milan, where he had been a parish priest for eight years. He explains the connection between sin, forgiveness and the community:

> A lot of people feel that they have to confess before each Communion. That isn't necessary. Confession is obligatory once a year, but only for mortal sins.
>
> A priest doesn't bestow forgiveness. God does that when the penitent first examines his conscience and confesses his sins to Him. The priest merely examines the penitent's sincerity and allows him to return to the Church. That is what absolution is all about.
>
> Sins disrupt the community. The priest, as the leader of the community, absolves the sinner and reunites him with the community.
>
> Baptism admits an individual to the community. A habit of sin separates him from it. That's why Confession is called a second baptism. It reconciles the penitent with the community and God.

Lingering Guilt

Confession leads to penance, penance to absolution. The slate, as we have seen, is wiped clean. But sometimes Confession doesn't work as intended. Some people, consumed by guilt, are unable to confess. Others, obsessed by it, find that peace of mind eludes them even after Confession and absolution.

Marion, a forty-six-year-old Los Angeles insurance adjuster, with four children, couldn't confess the sins which pained her the most.

> I have felt oppressive guilt throughout my entire life because of the way in which I lost, or rather stupidly threw away, my virginity. I now realize that my guilt was debilitating at the time, and it still haunts me because I felt such closeness to the Church.

Sin and Guilt

I was twenty-two years old, in my first year of a graduate program. My father was a deacon, my mother was in charge of all the church socials and everybody thought I was going to be a nun because I was such a good little Catholic girl. But I was living a double life. I used to hang out with a group of kids who drank and slept around. They had an exotic, dangerous aura that was lacking in my home. I was fascinated. I went to their parties but always stayed on the sidelines, watching, waiting until the day I'd have the nerve to participate. Then one day, just like that, I said "Enough! I'm bored with being the Good Ship Lollypop."

I don't even remember the guy's name. All I recall is that he was the first man I ever met who said he was bisexual. I was out to rebel, and sleeping with him gave me two sins for one. To tell the truth, I never believed I'd feel very guilty about it. I assumed I'd get a slight tinge, the kind I got when I told a little white lie. Then I'd go to Confession and still be Little Miss Perfect. It didn't work out that way.

When I went to my weekly Confession, I couldn't say a word to the priest about what I'd done. I remember riding home on the bus, watching everybody, thinking they were watching me, knowing what I'd done. I felt like a leper. Unclean. Contagious. How could I ever set foot inside a church again? It was then that I realized how sex, the Church and God were so closely interrelated for me. And as I relived that sexual experience over and over again, I admitted to myself how unsatisfying and self-destructive it had been.

I never confessed my loss of virginity to the priest. I gave myself my own penance. I would always remember it and always feel guilty for it. I'm married now, and have four children. I'm a respected woman in the community, but I'm still haunted by the sexual sin I committed so many years ago.

Bless Me, Father, For I Have Sinned

Eunice, a forty-eight-year-old Miami housewife, is often troubled by her lack of charity.

For me sin is related to money. I always wanted to confess that I'd spent money when I could have given it to charity. I always wondered but never asked how one could be a really good person, a holy person, and also have money to spend. How could a frivolous, uncharitable person go to Heaven? I felt guilty if I spent two hundred dollars on a dinner or a dress. I knew there were people who needed the money, but I still spent it. I wanted to talk about it, but never believed my confessor would understand. After all, hadn't he taken a vow of poverty?

The problem still bothers me. I've been going to Confession for thirty-one years and have never mentioned the sin that plagues me most.

Though Carmella, a thirty-six-year-old Boston English professor, received absolution, she has been performing her penance for the past eighteen years.

Since the age of eighteen, I've been walking around with a volcano of guilt inside me. It erupts every time I hear one of my father's favorite songs from the old country or see a man with the same walk.

The nuns, priests and, of course, my parents taught my five sisters and me that it was a sin not to honor your mother and father. But no matter what they said I never respected my father. I was convinced he'd wasted his life. He and my mother came over from Italy when they were both teenagers. He spoke English with a dreadful accent, never learned to read properly or write, never dissolved in the big American melting pot. He embarrassed me.

In those days, I went to Confession every month, but never discussed my feelings about my father with the priest. I knew in my heart that I was committing a sin, especially when I wished that my father would die or made

146

up lies about him to explain to my friends why I never invited them to my house.

My father worked in construction all his life, digging ditches, until he died from a heart attack when I was eighteen. I went to our family priest to confess that I had hated him all my life and had not given him the honor that Catholic tradition demanded. The priest told me not to be too critical of myself. He spoke of the cultural and generational gaps that often tear families apart. For my penance, he told me to give my mother, for the rest of her life, not only the honor that was due to her but also the honor that I had never given to my father. Even though I'm doing what the priest wanted me to, I don't think anything can erase the guilt and gnawing pain I feel as an adult.

Gregory, a fifty-six-year-old Baltimore magazine publisher, is still haunted by a lie that no confession can undo.

I prepared myself for that confession with a real examination of conscience. I knew what I had done, and was trying to figure out how to say it all so it was clear but didn't take forever. There were a lot of people waiting to confess. I could probably recognize their faces today, even after thirty-six years. Everything about that confession remains crystal clear.

I told the priest I hurt somebody by lying. I said I'd told my college fraternity brothers I'd gone out with a girl named Carol and she'd put out. It wasn't true. We'd necked heavily and she'd been wildly passionate, but I hadn't scored. The point was that she had a reputation, so it was expected I'd go all the way with her. Half the house was awake when I got back and wanted the details. I lied and told them what they wanted to hear.

The next day Marilyn, one of Carol's sorority sisters, said she had left school. My lies had reached her before lunch. Marilyn said the phone was ringing constantly, guys wanting to date her, guys who'd never noticed her before

147

suddenly asking for her. She left school without saying a word, without even packing.

Her mother came for her clothes the next weekend. It was as if she had died. Everyone was quiet. The girls looked at me as if they wanted to kill me.

I told the guys in the house that I had lied, but they wouldn't believe me. They didn't want to. The fifties were like that. It was so hard getting laid that nobody would let you give one back. When I called Carol and told her I was sorry, she hung up. I called again and again for weeks, but she wouldn't talk to me. Finally I wrote her a letter. I don't know if she ever read it.

Then I went to Confession. I hadn't been for almost six months, but I was desperate. I told the priest that I had never been so truly sorry for anything in my entire life. He must have believed me and thought I'd punished myself enough, because all he gave me was one Hail Mary.

Afterwards, I felt I'd gotten rid of the sin, but not the guilt. Only Carol could absolve me of that, but she never did. It's still with me.

Ross, thirty-six, a Dallas-based airline pilot, has struggled for years with the sin of abortion.

I was in the Air Force in Spain during the early seventies. Abortion was a common form of birth control there. Women didn't take the Pill. Married women with large families, especially those with small incomes, frequently resorted to abortion. It was illegal, but everybody looked the other way. Though the police had cracked down on the illegal butcher shops, many reputable gynecologists regularly performed abortions.

A few years later I was reassigned to the States. I met a young woman and almost immediately we began a terrific affair. About six months later, she got pregnant. She didn't want to get married and neither did I. We were great lovers, but neither of us could envision retiring to Florida together someday. She wasn't a Catholic. I was the Catholic, just back from a Catholic country where abortion was as common as a cold. I said there was no need to worry, she'd have an abortion.

She did, and that proved to be the end of our relationship. Neither of us could handle the guilt. She felt guilty for aborting the child she'd been carrying. I felt guilty because I was a Catholic. Why I didn't feel Catholic before the abortion I'll never know. But I couldn't afford the luxury of a conscience then. It would have to wait until the crisis had passed.

I went to the chaplain and asked him to hear my confession. I had prepared well in advance. I don't remember ever examining my conscience with such scrupulousness since I was a teenager. I described my current life—lots of women, dozens of missed Masses, little time spent with my parents—especially my father who was very proud of me. I finally admitted that I'd encouraged my girl friend to have an abortion.

The priest interrupted me. "Aren't you a little late, lad?" he asked. My only answer was that I hadn't felt guilty before. I told him what I'd seen in Spain. The enlisted men were knocking up their girl friends regularly, but few were getting married. Finally he asked me, "Why do you think you're feeling guilty now?"

I was quiet for a while. Then I said that abortion hadn't been real to me before. It had been like a dirty weekend —an easy escape without consequences. Only after the abortion did I realize I'd killed my son or daughter, I'd killed a part of me. At that moment I thought, but didn't say, that God could have given me a just punishment by telling me I had one chance for a baby in my life and had just blown it.

The chaplain sighed. He said he was going to give me

149

a special penance. He wanted me to support an orphan from South America and pay for its education. If I could afford more than one, I should take on another.

For the first time my penance wasn't a few prayers. I'm still supporting two kids. The agency sends me letters about their progress, and the kids send me their drawings and photos of themselves. I'm very attached to them, but I still feel guilty about the abortion, especially when I hear from those kids. Maybe that's what the chaplain had in mind.

Sometimes those who cannot find solace through Confession seek it in other areas. Lora, an unmarried high school teacher from New York, turned to psychiatry to heal the wounds of incest.

I believe that Catholic girls who have sex with their fathers feel more guilt than girls of other religions, even though we can go to Confession.

My parents, immigrants from a small Polish village, arrived in America after the Second World War. My father worked in a factory, my mother worked in a bakery. They never learned English or tried to assimilate. They rarely spoke to me, or to each other, except to scream about the importance of my virginity. They never had any friends and neither did I.

I was afraid to bring anybody home after school because I never knew when my father was going to fly into one of his cursing rages. So the nuns at school and the Virgin Mary became my best friends. Every night before I went to bed I would have long, wonderful conversations with the Blessed Mother promising her that I would always make her proud of me.

When I began to mature physically at thirteen, I felt as if a strange person was invading my body. The nuns warned us about awful animalistic urges, and I believed I was turning into a wild beast. I tried to explain my feelings to a priest in Confession, but he just gave me an extra Hail Mary as penance. I was lost.

One night I went into my parent's bedroom to get something and there was my father, lying on the bed, fully clothed, just staring in the dark. He did a lot of that, lying in the dark, staring, with only the light from his cigarette letting anybody know he was alive. I sat down beside him, then I lay down, close, then closer. Then it started. He never said a word, not even when it was over, except, "Don't tell your mother." I went downstairs to the kitchen where my mother was making supper.

When my father came downstairs a half hour later, he didn't say a word, but then he never said much anyway. And that's how it started. It went on for about three years, once, maybe twice a month.

As I look back now I realized I wanted someone to notice me, to talk to me. I felt flattered that my father, somebody, was paying attention to me. And it felt so warm and reassuring to have a body on top of me. I never felt any guilt. It never occurred to me that I was committing a sin because it was with my father and not one of the boys at school.

When I was seventeen, a boy asked me out on my first date. I remember feeling very strange whenever his shoulder touched mind when he bent over for popcorn. On the way home, he held my hand and tried to kiss me goodnight on the mouth. I turned away in disgust and wiped my mouth with my hand, right in front of him. When I told my father what had happened, he yelled at me for leading him on and called me a *kurwa*, prostitute in Polish. That night when I went into my father's bedroom, he turned away and ignored me. The next night, the same thing happened. I guess the sex just ended itself—or maybe my father ended it.

Around that time, the girls in my class started talking

about getting married and having babies and suddenly it struck me like a bolt of lightning. I wasn't a virgin. I had defiled the Blessed Mother and my Church. No respectable Catholic boy would ever want me. I felt so ashamed. I'd committed the gravest sin of all. Not only was I going to burn in Hell, I was unfit to live in this world.

For days I cried, vomited and ran a high fever. When the doctor came to the house to examine me, I cringed at his touch. As soon as I got better, I took my father's car and deliberately caused an accident. The woman in the other car ended up in the hospital, but I was fine. My guilt grew worse. My torment increased. I couldn't die and I couldn't live.

There was no place in the world for me. I felt the Blessed Mother looking down on me crying because I was such a sinner. I had failed her. I wanted to go to Confession to beg the priest for forgiveness, but I knew I wasn't worthy to set foot in a church. Once I got up the courage to enter the confessional when the priest wasn't there to see if the words would come out. Sitting there alone in the dark, I felt a crushing weight on my chest, cutting off my breath, cutting me off from God.

Then I started to sleep around. Since I was so filthy, I figured I couldn't sink any lower, though I tried. Married men, older men, one-night stands and some very sick scenes along the way. I swear to the Blessed Mother I never enjoyed one moment of it. I was trying to hurt myself as much as possible. Promiscuity was my penance.

Finally, I decided to see a psychiatrist, a non-Catholic because I thought I could talk to him more easily. God wouldn't be in the room with us. The doctor sat there, huddled over his notebook, like a secretary taking dictation, never looking me in the eye. Sometimes I would make up funny stories because I was afraid I was boring him. He never asked about my family or my religious background. I told him that I had had sex with my father and asked him if he thought it was important. He never answered, just kept on writing. After ten months I left, more confused than before.

The psychiatrist that I've been seeing for the past two years is Jewish and understands about God and guilt. He explained that sex is a powerful force that must be dealt with. He's trying to make me understand that what happened between my father and me wasn't my fault. As a child, I wasn't responsible and as an adult I ought not to feel guilty.

Some days when I think about what I've done with my life, I begin to hate my father with such a passion that I fantasize about killing him. Then I start to feel guilty all over again because I was taught that hating your parents is a sin.

My psychiatrist says that I have to learn to be gentle with myself and regain my dignity. I've started to go back to Church. I still can't bring myself to go to Confession or Communion, but I do sit at the back by myself in quiet conversation with the Blessed Mother, begging her forgiveness. I haven't been on a date in such a long time, but that doesn't bother me. I've promised myself and the Blessed Mother that the next man I have sex with will be my husband.

For many Catholics guilt is inescapable. As a forty-eight-year-old waitress from Tucson, Arizona, exclaimed, "Ain't nothin' like it in the whole world." Some said they were so consumed by guilt, for imagined as well as for real sins, that they feared they'd never be entirely free of it. A forty-five-year-old Buffalo housewife laments, "How can I enjoy my life when I was taught that the life of Jesus was so painful? I feel guilty whenever I think about my own pleasure."

Some men and women traced their guilt to their youth when they were encouraged to compare their actions with those of the saints. Thelma, a forty-seven-year-old secretary from Washington,

D.C., describes her struggle with the guilt instilled in her at an early age:

> For the rest of my life I'll feel guilty about almost every-
> thing. It's a result of my upbringing and parochial school
> education. As a child, my role models were the saints
> and martyrs. In school we read the calendar according to
> saint's days, studied their stories, tried to emulate their
> deeds and their holiness. Of course, it was a losing bat-
> tle. A lot of my dreams and nightmares were about the
> deaths of the martyrs. I remember waking up in the
> middle of the night, hanging off the bed. I'd dreamed
> that I was beheaded in the presence of St. Sebastian and
> other martyrs because I wasn't worthy. In my First Con-
> fession I told the priest I wasn't as perfect as Sister
> Theresa.
>
> Now that I've been through psychotherapy, I know I will
> never shed this guilt. Guilt and the need to confess it
> shaped my life. When I make decisions I base them on this
> self-knowledge. I recognize the problem, and I also recog-
> nize that I can't change. That's pretty sad—and devasta-
> ting.

Maurice, thirty-seven, the owner of a clothing store in Dallas, Texas, speaks of the origins of his sexual guilt:

> The Church made me feel abnormal, and I don't think I
> can ever forgive it for that. I never committed a mortal sin,
> but the priests kept condemning my thoughts and feel-
> ings. They convinced me I was abnormal, dirty, sick. I'm
> very bitter about that sexual angst. I've spent a lifetime
> trying to get rid of my guilt about sex. But sometimes I
> think it's hopeless. I feel so guilty.

Some Catholics, for whatever reason, manage to fight free of Church-inflicted guilt. Philip, a thirty-four-year-old criminal lawyer from Portland, Oregon, makes his own decisions about right and wrong.

Sin and Guilt

I've got a yardstick that tells me whether I'm comfortable or not. If I feel uncomfortable, I won't do something. I don't need Church law to make up my mind for me. I've got my own very well-developed conscience and sense of right and wrong. I'll give myself my own guilt on my own time in my own way.

Not everyone finds guilt debilitating. Thomas, a forty-five-year-old St. Louis high school principal, believes it has its uses.

Guilt has gotten a bad rep. There are times when we're supposed to feel guilt. If you do something wrong and your equipment is working properly, you feel guilty. You *should* feel guilty. Guilt is like a temperature; it indicates something is morally wrong with you. Guilt keeps you on your toes and tells you where you are all the time. What's wrong with that? If you sin and don't feel guilty, you're in moral trouble. If you sin and don't confess, you go to Hell.

Chapter 8

Heaven and Hell

In fidelity to the New Testament and tradition, the Church believes in the happiness of the just who will one day be with Christ. She believes that there will be eternal punishment for the sinner, who will be deprived of the sight of God, and that this punishment will have a repercussion on the whole being of the sinner.

She believes in the possibility of a purification for the elect before they see God, a purification altogether different from the punishment of the damned. This is what the Church means when speaking of Hell and Purgatory.

The preceding is an excerpt from a letter on "Certain Questions Concerning Eschatology," addressed to the bishops throughout the world by the Congregation for the Doctrine of the Faith, May 17, 1979, approved by Pope John Paul II.

For centuries fear of damnation in the next life has been a spur to good behavior in this one. Catholic children are nurtured on descriptions of Hell that would frighten the devil himself.

A nineteenth-century Roman Catholic priest, coincidentally named Father Furniss, wrote several children's books. In an attempt to frighten his young readers into goodness, he described Hell as being "one child trapped forever in a flaming oven, screaming to be let out and beating her head against the roof." A sixteen-year-old girl who preferred the park to church on Sunday is condemned to stand barefoot on a red-hot floor for eternity. A boy who drank and kept bad company is permanently immersed in a boiling kettle. The blood of a girl who attended the theater seethes in her veins while her brain audibly boils and bubbles in her head.

We asked people if their visions of Heaven, Hell, Purgatory and Limbo played a part in their daily lives and had an effect upon the quality and frequency of their confessions. Once again the answers varied widely, but in most cases age was a factor. Older people spoke thoughtfully, as if they were finally nearing the afterlife they'd been anticipating. The young were more categorical. They described Heaven and Hell in vivid terms, as if they had firsthand knowledge. Almost all of those interviewed were resigned to an extended stay in Purgatory.

For Marianna, the fifty-six-year-old manager of a Bangor, Maine, dry cleaning store, confession leads the way to salvation:

> Of course I'm going to Heaven when my time in Purgatory is up. That's why I go to Confession every month. I was taught that you can't get to Heaven if you don't confess your sins regularly. I can't prove they're wrong, so they must be right.

William, a fifty-year-old furniture salesman from Austin, Texas, recalls youthful philosophical debates regarding the afterlife.

Heaven and Hell

When we were kids, we were always debating about what was a sin and who was going to go to Heaven or to Hell. It was a difficult problem, especially for nine-year-olds. Suppose a person was a devout Catholic and always went to Church. One Sunday he missed Mass and was killed in a car accident. Did he go to Heaven or to Hell? The conclusion we came to was that if he was on his way to Confession, he would go to Heaven. We never did agree what would happen if he was on his way to a ball game.

Karen, a thirty-four-year-old Baltimore kindergarten teacher and mother of three, talked about Limbo. Like most children she had a concrete image.

I had this picture of Limbo, where babies go. They sit in rows and rows of high chairs, and angels with wings and long gowns feed them Pablum while they wait for the end of the world. Then they all go to Heaven. So what was the point of Limbo?

Irma, a fifty-year-old housewife from Phoenix, Arizona, believes in being prepared.

Hell? You want to talk about Hell? If you get hit by a bus tomorrow, in a state of disgrace because you haven't been to Confession, you go to Hell. It's just as my mother always said. Going to Confession is like wearing clean underwear because you never know when that phantom bus is going to hit.

Ronald, fifty-five, an Atlanta cab driver, understands Heaven and Hell; it's Purgatory he has trouble with.

I'm not sure what happened to Purgatory. You get the lecherous bugger who left home when he was sixteen, had a gal in every port, committed every sin you can think of, and here he is, seventy-two, and he's put into port. He's in the hospital and the chaplain says, "Now, I under-

159

stand that you were Catholic originally," and then the guy
goes through the grocery list and dies ten minutes later.
Where does he go? Beats me.

Now we've got the other guy who has been holy all his
life. He's coming down the street, and he's got a gun on
his hip for some reason. Maybe he's been out shooting
buffalo. He sees a guy beating his wife and he pulls his gun
and shoots him. In the meantime, a car hits him from
behind, and he dies. Where does he go? Beats me. That's
why I can't understand what Purgatory is.

Priscilla, a charismatic Catholic, is a thirty-six-year-old New Orleans secretary. She describes the horrors of Hell and the salvation
of Confession:

I believe in the devil and in Hell. My vision of Hell is based
on the children of Fatima. Fire is consuming the souls,
though they're not in human form. They look like animals
swimming in fire and screaming in pain. This Hell is eternal. There is no escape. That's why Confession is so important. If you confess your sins, you're saved. You don't
have to endure an eternity of agony.

For John, a thirty-two-year-old Denver dentist, the afterlife is
equally vivid but less terrible.

From the first moment I heard about Heaven and Hell,
they became the most important things in my life. I was
determined to please God and avoid evil and sin. Heaven,
Hell and Purgatory were real places for me. I began to
pray for my relatives to get out of Purgatory and into
Heaven. If they were already in Heaven, I prayed that
they'd help me. It was all vivid in my mind and crucial in
my life.

Sister Catherine, a forty-year-old teaching nun from Hartford,
Connecticut, speaks of the post-Vatican II view of Heaven and Hell:

160

Heaven and Hell

The painful thing about the Church of my childhood was the emphasis on Hell rather than Heaven. In today's Church there's less talk about Hell and God's eternal punishment and more about God's mercy and love in the here-and-now sense. All those descriptions of Hell make colorful reading, but they have a destructive effect on children. How can kids understand the Sacrament when their minds are full of such horrible images? I remember leaving many a confessional thinking, "Phew, saved from the fires of Hell this time!"

These stories were told by men and women reared in a pre-Vatican II fire-and-brimstone Catholicism that is currently in the midst of change. Future generations may have different tales to tell.

Chapter 9

Priests on Confession

The Sacrament of Confession described by the priests we interviewed appears different from that described by the penitents. Frequently, they seem to be talking about two entirely different things.

In this chapter, priests speak about Confession from their side of the screen. They describe stints in the confessional that have tested their physical endurance and penitents who have stretched their compassion to the limit. They tell of their own failings, their dismay at being placed on pedestals and their frequent loneliness. In their commitment to the Sacrament, they reveal a haunting sense of responsibility which belies the accusations of indifference.

The Other Side of the Box

"Father, I feel the need to celebrate the Sacrament of Reconciliation. I am a priest; I am having an affair with a married woman and she is carrying my child.

"This woman and I were close friends in college. In fact, looking back on it, we loved each other even then. One day, recently, I met her on the street. We decided to go for a drink for old time's sake. Her husband was out of town on business for two weeks. Her kids were at summer camp. I started going to her house for dinner every evening while her husband was away, and that's when it started. For the past four months, we've been seeing each other at least three times a week.

"Being with her is wonderful because I am discovering things I had forgotten, things that are bringing a wholeness to me. I'm lonely. I have no sense of community with the priest I'm living with. He's much older than I and very rigid. His view of ministry is different from mine. There is a lot of silence in our home, as well as some ugly fights. This woman offers me the companionship and the warmth that I crave.

"When I am in my parish, in the hospital or the schools, I feel like such a hypocrite. Everybody thinks I'm chaste and holy, but I know the dreadful truth about myself.

"Father, help me, please. It's been five months since I've attended General Absolution."

This "confession" did not take place in a confessional or a reconciliation room; it took place in 1984 in a seminary as part of the practicum course given to final-year students in preparation for their roles as confessors. Before these weekly mock confessions begin, the professor addresses the class on certain issues which might arise in the confessional. Birth control, abortion, sexual problems, family disputes, heinous crimes, business ethics, racism and world justice present concrete problems after three years of moral theology. One student is chosen as confessor, another as penitent. The class of thirty-three seminarians and their professor act as critics.

Priests on Confession

"My son, there are a lot of gray areas here. First, tell me about your relationship with this woman. What are your responsibilities toward her? What about your child that she is carrying? Have you told her honestly about your feelings?"

"Yes, Father, I have. She thinks I have too much conscience. She's contemplating an abortion."

"What you must address immediately is your problem at home. It is important that you develop a network of healthy relationships. Come and talk to me immediately. There are programs in the archdiocese for priests who are looking for the same kind of community that you are. Find a spiritual director, someone with whom you can share conversation and prayer. I feel your deep sorrow and struggle. Will you come and see me? We must discuss your feelings about leaving the priesthood and your obligations to this woman and the unborn child. Say an act of contrition. I absolve you in the name of the Father, the Son and the Holy Spirit. Go in peace."

During the two-hour critique following this mock confession, there was heated debate. Andrew, a Midwesterner in his early twenties, felt the confessor reacted fairly because the penitent showed true contrition and was in great pain. Bob, thirty-eight, a former New York accountant who was entering the priesthood as a second career, raged at the confessor for being so lenient. He would have demanded that the penitent dissuade the woman from having an abortion. Thomas, thirty-nine, a doctoral candidate from Los Angeles, argued that the root of the problem was that the penitent attended General Absolution services and did not regularly confess to a spiritual director. The penitent was obviously not paying any attention to his prayer life. Ron, twenty-three, born in Chicago, was furious that the confessor absolved the penitent. Would he have given absolution if the penitent were not a priest? Was the confessor being lenient because the man was a member of the club? Gary, forty-three, a former military officer, contended that the penitent showed lack of discipline, no responsibility to his parish and no commitment to Jesus Christ. He must stop living in a fantasy and face the harsh reality of his reprehensible actions. Perhaps he wasn't meant to be a priest in the first place. Len, twenty-four, born in Detroit, understood the gray areas and felt great sympathy for the penitent. He hoped that counseling and companionship would ease the penitent's burden and show him the way back to God.

There were as many opinions about the sin, the sinner and the penance as there were seminarians in the room. The intention of the course is to reiterate the teachings of the Church, provide guidelines and foster understanding. Still, the personal differences and the practical and spiritual problems remain. Perhaps the only act more difficult than confessing is hearing confession.

> For I have heard these fifty years
> Confession muttered at my ears
> Till every mumble of the wind
> Is like tired voices that have sinned.

For Father Mulligan, a 67-year-old priest in Duluth, Minnesota, who has served his Church in parishes throughout North America, Confession is like a comfortable old shoe that gives a new lease on life to a tired soul. He estimates he's heard about 100,000 confessions in his time.

> Sometimes I'm amazed at all the wonderful things that have happened in the confessional. People have come in disturbed, distraught, at odds with God, and through the grace of the Sacrament, they've found peace with themselves and God. At the end, they've said to me, "I'm so grateful I've had this opportunity."

For Father Spinetti, a thirty-seven-year-old parish priest in Los Angeles, Confession is *the* most important sacrament.

> I'm not a Bible-thumping person, but I think the greatest story in the Bible is about the Prodigal Son. This young guy went off and spent all his money, got drunk, lived with women, did everything in the book that was wrong. Then when his money and luck ran out he went home. You can imagine the fear and trepidation he felt, and the jealousy

of his brother who'd stayed to work on the farm. But his father greeted him with outstretched arms and with joy. Christ didn't tell this story because it was a nice anecdote. He told it because it applies to all of us. At some time in our lives, we're all going to deny everything we were taught and fall flat on our faces. But when we're ready to come home, the Father is there, His arms outstretched, ready to give us a second chance.

Father Heinrich, forty-four, a Pittsburgh journalist, is equally fervent about the Sacrament.

Whenever I hear confessions I'm humbled. There's nothing that strengthens my faith more than to hear another human being come in and sit or kneel and open his heart to me. There's a big difference between the person that comes in with a shopping list of sins and one who comes in and pours his heart out. Every time that happens, and it happens a lot, it's humbling and frightening, but spiritually strengthening. As humans, we all have the same weaknesses. These penitents are bringing out their humanity and asking for strength and forgiveness. You have to look at the life of Christ to understand sin and forgiveness. Christ forgave as a symbol of love and peace, and as confessors it is our duty to carry out the Sacrament as Christ taught us.

To Be a Good Confessor

The traditional qualities necessary to a confessor are prudence, knowledge, goodness and respect for confidentiality. Patience, a strong back, a cool temper, an ability to withstand confinement, good hearing, a tolerant olfactory sense, a short memory and a sense of humor are secondary virtues that get most priests through.

Father Stern, fifty-three, ministers to businessmen and women in the financial section of Chicago. His parishioners are worldly but their needs are spiritual.

Because we're an innercity church, we hear more confessions than in any other church in the city. We get a lot of people who want anonymity. We get shoppers, business people and conventioneers, but never any children. We advertise in the newspaper. We're like a business, open Monday to Friday, from 7:00 A.M. to 7:00 P.M. When the buzzer rings, I get up from my office and immediately hear it. I'm available all day long.

Afternoon confessions are more trying than those that take place in the morning. As the day goes on, people become more frustrated. At 8:30 A.M., it's a brand new day. "I don't like my boss, but I'll see if I can get along with him." By noon, the guy is growling at the boss. At the end of the afternoon, he's ready to punch him out. That's when he comes to Confession. Sometimes these people get a little short with me. They can bite if they think I'm not doing my job properly.

The priest may appear to be the passive member of the Confession, but for most of them the sacrament is dynamic. Many used active verbs to described the experience. "To listen, to care and to forgive. If you do all three, you can't fail," explains thirty-four-year-old Father Conrad from Flushing, New York.

As we noted at the beginning of this chapter, no amount of theological training can entirely eradicate personal differences. Ethnic and cultural background, worldly experiences, personal interpretation of Church doctrine, even the state of his health can affect the way a priest hears confessions.

Father Morris, fifty-seven, a retired army chaplain from Orlando, Florida, recounts:

If the priest sees himself as a judge, then he's going to be dogmatic and authoritarian and behave as though he's giving a sentence to a guilty person. He'll go strictly by the penitential book. A lot of priests were taught to administer the Sacrament that way. But it's more than training, and age has nothing to do with being dogmatic. I've seen it in the young and the old.

Flexibility and sensitivity to the penitent's mentality and needs are crucial qualities for a good confession. Although Father Davis, twenty-nine, has been hearing confessions for only five years in his Phoenix, Arizona, parish, he has learned that each penitent is different.

> Experience has taught me to alter the way I deal with people in the confessional. The age of the person and his marital status influence my behavior. Some still view Confession as a car wash. Come in one side, get sprayed, come out the other side squeaky clean. Others want counseling. It's very complex—and challenging.

Father Donald, a spry seventy-two-year-old priest from Cleveland, Ohio, emphasizes compassion in the confessional:

> A priest has got to look at everyone who comes into that confessional as if he were his own son or daughter.

Penitents have often criticized priests for haste in the confessional. They want time to express themselves. Father Drake, a fifty-five-year-old parish priest in Little Rock, Arkansas, tells the other side of the story:

> Sometimes it's not easy. My stomach might be upset, I might be preoccupied, the confession might not be interesting. Your mind wanders, and you've got to concentrate on what the person is saying and hear the degree of hurt and emotion that's involved. In the confessional I always try to remember my own humanity.

Hearing the Confessions of Children

Many priests don't enjoy hearing the confessions of children. Father Franklin, a forty-five-year-old Newark priest, describes what he does to make the experience more pleasurable for the kids and himself:

> In a classroom of thirty kids, I can tell you what twenty-eight of them are going to say. Some of them are uneasy,

others downright terrified. I try to make Confession a visual celebration for them. I once asked a group of physically handicapped children to write down the names of people they had hurt. They put their lists in envelopes and sealed them. Nobody knew what they'd written, except the kids and God. After reading and some songs, we lit a candle and they burned their sins. It was a moving experience for the kids, because they could see their sins being destroyed in front of their eyes. Afterward, I went up to each one and gave him individual absolution.

Father Wharton, a thirty-seven-year-old Milwaukee parish priest, echoes the words of many of his fellow clergymen when talking about the confessions of children.

I don't like hearing the confessions of children. I don't mind the kids, only the conditions under which I have to hear them. I go to the schools—no windows, no air—just lines of children. I know a priest who's so bored by the procedure that he hears their confessions face-to-face with coffee and cigarette in hand. It's the only way he can cope. The pressure to get the confessions done in a short period of time is tremendous. Many of the kids are unfamiliar with what's happening. Some of them walk in and say, "Hi, how are you? What would you like to know about me?" You have to say, "What would you like me to know about you? How are things at home? Do you always do what your mom and dad ask you to do?" You have to uncover so much for them. It takes so much time for each child, and a lot out of the priest. Sometimes it becomes automatic. When recess comes, I'm as eager for it as the kids.

Physical Discomfort

Many priests spoke of the physical discomfort of the confessional. They recall harsh northern winters, when they wore heavy coats and gloves because there was no heat. In the stifling summers, they'd be soaking with sweat. While penitents were in the confessional for minutes, the confessor sat there for hours.

When teaching at a New York seminary, Father Francis, sixty-three, advises his students:

> Go into a closet, close the door, and sit in a chair for several hours. Then you'll begin to know what it's like. The confessional is a closet. The first thing that goes is your legs. The blood doesn't flow properly. I used to tell the students you couldn't have a one-armed priest. Open the side, close, open the other side, close, and on it goes.

Father Francis goes on to describe the training he received at his seminary for hearing confessions:

> I was ordained in 1950, so I'm really a product of the thirties and forties. At the seminary we had the standard training for hearing confessions. Four years of moral theology, four years of canon law, four years of sacred scripture. There was a great deal of discipline involved. A friend of mine, a graduate of West Point, went to my seminary and said it was more severe. But it was that discipline that prepared us for hearing confessions.

Father Cousins, a former star athlete now in his mid-fifties, is a parish priest in Baltimore. In his airy office, he mimes the reaction of a claustrophobe when describing his days in the confessional.

> The human aspect is that you're not always feeling one hundred percent. You've got the flu, an upset stomach, a headache. I developed back problems and have had six bouts of surgery. That's caused me a lot of problems in the confessional because every confessional is different. Even the comfortable ones were painful to be stuck inside of for long stretches of time with an aching back. Sometimes you get a little impatient and short, and you want to bite your tongue afterward. If I realize what I've done, I always

171

apologize right there and then, before the confession is over. I'm only human.

Father Simmons, an energetic thirty-year-old Providence, Rhode Island, priest, foundered on the garlic. "People came in with terrible breath. It's hard to concentrate on the spirit when the flesh is so intrusive."

Peer Criticism, Self-Criticism

Priests resemble doctors in that both are loath to criticize their colleagues. Father Thomas, a parish priest of long experience in the Boston area, couches his criticism diplomatically:

> When I think of all those men hearing all those confessions hour after hour, week after week, year after year, I think they were heroes. One priest had a terrible nervous problem; he fidgeted constantly. Psychologically, he had some problems too, yet he could give some tremendous advice.
>
> Sometimes it didn't seem fair. You'd get an older man, close to seventy, hearing confessions for four hours at a stretch. He might have health problems. I'm not trying to make excuses for bad confessors, but some had their problems. Then again, others weren't pleasant people, and there's no excuse for that.

Although priests rarely criticize their peers, many are quick to admit to their own faults. Father Warren, thirty-eight, a university librarian in Boston, is candid about his own failures as a confessor:

> I've made mistakes in the confessional. I've felt guilty about them and confessed them. Perhaps there's a big crowd outside the confessional and you're rushing. You say to the penitent, "five Hail Marys." Then you say to yourself, "Oh my God, what have I done? She needed more time and I failed her." Sometimes your behavior reflects your own emotional state. You're exhausted.

Priests on Confession

Easter's here and you've already had six hours of confession. But still, there's that feeling of guilt. There are times when I fail totally.

Because time is such a precious commodity when hearing confessions, many priests have learned to pace themselves carefully. The amount of time allotted to each person must be well spent. As Father Waters, fifty-nine, a veteran confessor from Atlanta, explains:

> Sometimes there's a person with a major problem on one side, you finish, and you hope you've helped him. Then you open the other side, and there's an equally big one. You can go through an afternoon, with five, six or even seven major crises. That's when I use pastoral sense. I'll ask the penitent if there are many people outside the confessional. If the person answers yes, I'll suggest he come back. I'll say, "Look, I can spend a little time with you now to help you immediately or would you consider returning to see me in my office? It's just as private."

Many priests spoke of the catharsis that is part of the confessional experience. As Father Comden, a forty-five-year-old priest from Detroit recounts:

> Within an hour, perhaps four or five people will cry because of their relief and joy at having been forgiven. Confession is not an easy thing.

When the priest hears genuine contrition, but senses the person will repeat the sin, he must struggle with his own feelings of frustration. Sixty-two-year-old Father Flanaghan from Charleston, South Carolina, knows the problem well.

> When a person comes into the confessional with a true heart it can't help but touch you. People often come to the confessional in tears. "Father, I'm discouraged because I drink too much, or I have a girl friend on the side or I'm involved in the gay scene. I keep falling into the same

traps. I really want to do right and I try, but I go for a week or ten days, and then all of a sudden, I end up sitting in a bar, and it starts all over again." You can tell the penitent is in pain, but you know he'll be back in a month with the same story.

Father Elton, whose Washington, D.C., parish is rife with drugs, prostitution and crime, is a shade more optimistic.

You have only a few moments of real openness in the confessional. These moments have to be captured. People are at their most vulnerable when they're in pain. That touches me deeply. I try to spot the moments of genuine sincerity and share them. It's a beautiful thing.

The alchoholic is a perfect example. He can drink for twenty years. The whole world tells him he's got a problem, but he doesn't listen. Then he crashes and that's the moment when you can teach him. That's the moment you can turn him on or off. It's a difficult, sacred, fragile moment.

Responsibilities and Frustrations

Most priests bring a sense of responsibility to the confessional. It is the pride and the cornerstone of their profession.

The following prayer is sometimes recited by priests before they hear the confessions of the faithful. It captures the hope of excellence they yearn to bring to the practice of the Sacrament:

Give me, O Lord, the wisdom that sitteth by Thy throne, that I may be enabled to judge Thy people with justice, and Thy poor and humble ones with true judgment. Grant me so to handle the keys of the Kingdom of Heaven, that I may open it to none who ought to be shut out, nor shut out any to whom it ought to open. Let my intention be pure, my zeal sincere, my charity long-suffering and my labor fruitful. Let me be kind without laxity, severe without harshness; let me not look down upon the poor man,

174

nor flatter the rich man. Give me sweetness that I may draw sinners unto Thee; give me prudence in asking questions; give me skill in instruction. Bestow upon me, I beseech Thee, zeal in withdrawing sinners from evil courses, diligence in establishing them in goodness and earnestness in moving them to a better life: maturity in my answers, rightness in my counsels, light in obscure matters, insight in intricate cases and victory over all difficulties. Let me not be involved in useless talk, nor corrupt by shameful avowals; may I save others, without myself becoming a castaway. Amen.

"Bless me, Father, for I have sinned. It has been twenty-four hours since my last confession, and I have sinned greatly."

The confessions of the "scrupes" are distinctive, and the discomfort they cause both themselves and the priest is considerable. Some priests become angered by their destructive obsessiveness, while others, moved by compassion, want only to embrace them and lighten the burden they carry.

Father Morris, a former chaplain, knows the frustration felt by many priests confronted by an overly scrupulous penitent.

These scrupulous people truly suffer, but there isn't much we can do for them, except be firm. There are more scrupulous women than men. When you get these kinds of confessions, you've got to pay close attention. You have to be firm but gentle. It's a fine line, and frustrating. Sometimes I'll get a scrupe who will come to me once or twice, then go on to another priest.

Father John, a forty-five-year-old Seattle priest, shook his head wearily at the mention of the overscrupulous:

A scrupulous person sees sin everywhere. It's a real neurosis, and there isn't much you can do. This is the kind of confession you hear from them. "Bless me, Father, for I have sinned. It's been a week since my last confession and during that time, Father, I have sinned greatly because I

175

went to Church and didn't pay attention. My mind wandered during Mass, Father. And my husband and I had a disagreement in front of our children, and Father, I know that disagreement was an occasion of sin for my children. And worst of all, Father, I sent my son to the store for milk and on the way home, he had to pass a video store, and you know, Father, they have those obscene pictures in the window and that was an occasion of sin for my son, and I caused it!" On and on it goes.

When I try to tell her that's enough, she begins again. "I know I shouldn't worry so much about these things, Father, but I know that Jesus died for us and because of that, Father, I know I'm a sinner and sometimes I don't really believe that I'm worthy and that I'm saved."

Many priests are ambivalent about scrupulous penitents. They realize that these troubled souls have no one to blame but themselves. On one hand, the Church celebrates the devotion of saints; on the other, it complains of the susceptible who seek to imitate them.

Father Jeffrey, forty, a Mobile, Alabama, high school science teacher, echoes the despair felt by priests who realize the Church is largely responsible for the scrupulosity:

Much of our moral theology is so restricting that people sin everywhere. It's a horrible sickness of mind and a lack of faith in the mercy of God. For example, a penitent will confess that while bathing he touched himself and that's sinful. It's not sinful, it's a necessity of bathing. These scrupes come to Confession every second or third day to confess the same sin. Confession is supposed to be a blessing, a reconciliation with God, and it ends up being a curse.

Our mental wards are liberally sprinkled with Catholics who had a scrupulous approach to their sexuality—and were destroyed by it. In the past Church teachings have produced a lot of anxiety and guilt that in turn force people to go to psychiatrists.

Priests on Confession

Father Callaghan, forty-seven, a parish priest from Sacramento, California, describes the illness as "wacko piety," a sad mixture of fantasy and faith:

The sad part is that these scrupulous people are truly suffering, and the Church has contributed to creating their pain. The scrupe doesn't believe that he's loved by God. Generally, these people are articulate, intelligent and hold responsible jobs. Ninety-nine percent of their lives are in order—except this one area. Their speech is compressed, rapid-fire. The only time you can get a word in is when they stop to take a breath. Their confessions aren't sacramental in any sense, and that makes their situation all the more sad and frustrating.

Father Merovitch, forty-six, a parish priest on Long Island, New York, acknowledges the frustration felt by his fellow clergy and explains how he attempts to reeducate the scrupulous:

Their guilt becomes exaggerated, and I have to identify that for them. I get people over forty confessing in very childish ways. "I had lust, told lies, wasn't charitable, was judgmental, hurt my sister." They make formula confessions, including the number of times each act was committed. I'll ask, "What did you do to your sister?" or "What do you mean you told lies?" You have to probe. But you've also got to treat them with kid gloves. I begin to explain, "It's not your fault that an image flashed on the television screen and you felt lust. God gave us sex for building relationships, love, pleasure and the continuation of the human race." But it's an uphill battle. These people have been taught a rigid debilitating routine, and they've been encouraged by the Church to keep this routine going. They haven't read enough, and no one has explained things to them. It's as though they're coming from another culture, and it's a culture the Church has created.

177

Even the frequency with which one can or should go to Confession can become a problem. Father Merovitch continues:

> Confession and Communion are the only two Sacraments you can receive as often as you wish. I started my priesthood under Pius XII. He confessed to a French Jesuit every morning of his nineteen-year pontificate. When asked why he confessed so often, the Pope said, "I'm a glutton for God's grace."

Father Elton, a sixty-year-old New Orleans priest, relieves the dirge of complaint with a bit of humor that captures the determination of the "scrupes" to have their guilt their own way.

> My mother recalled a situation when she was in Confession. There was another woman on the other side who had a loud voice. She confessed that she had missed Mass on Sunday because she was sick. The priest, who was also talking loud, said that wasn't a sin, but the woman kept yelling back, "Yes, it is a sin." The priest shouted, "No, it's not a sin," but she continued to insist it was. On and on it went until, finally, in frustration, the priest yelled, "Lady, will you shut up and listen! It's *not* a sin." My mother peeked out of the confessional and saw the woman wandering through the church looking for another confessor.

Almost as trying as the "scrupes" are the perfunctory penitents who come to confession with a grocery list of sins that has not varied since childhood. In these confessions the counting of sins replaces a meaningful examination of conscience.

Father DeNiro, forty-four, a parish priest raised in New York, describes these automatic penitents:

> They come in and run through the ritual. It reminds me of the old automats. They put down their money and out would come absolution and penance. I used to try to talk to them, but that bothered many of them because they

were tied to that ritual they'd learned as kids. They were getting instant relief and, as a result, had never grown up.

Father Connor, a fifty-year-old priest from St. Paul, Minnesota, believes perfunctory penitents, like scrupes, have been created by the Church.

One day I was hearing a woman confess. "I got angry with my husband eight times, and with my kids four times, and that'll be all, Father," she said. She might have been at a supermarket, saying, "That'll be five slices baloney." I would have laughed, if it hadn't been so tragic. Thank goodness, that grocery listing is giving way to a more genuine examination of conscience.

Many people stayed away from Confession because they felt the priests didn't listen, and many times they were right. Priests sometimes fell asleep. The recitation of a grocery list—even a grocery list of sins—is narcotic. Once when I'd dozed off the woman knocked on the screen and asked what her penance was. I didn't know what she'd said. I'd actually fallen asleep during her confession. I quickly gave her a light penance. I knew that if there had been anything tragic or heart-wrenching she would have caught my attention, but she'd been running the litany of sins as she'd been trained to do in childhood.

In the old days, I often wished that people would break out of that mold and speak from their hearts. The sad thing was that they didn't know they could. They thought they were confessing according to the Church's teachings. Talk about lack of communication. They thought they were doing what we wanted, and we were desperate to get them to do what we thought God wanted.

But if the scrupulous and the perfunctory annoy priests, serious sinners trouble them sorely. Occasionally, priests hear the confessions of people who have battered their infants, sexually abused children or committed murder. The public can vent its rage at these

179

despicable acts, but the confessor doesn't have this luxury. He must, in the face of every contrary instinct, hold out hope for another chance and forgiveness.

Canon Law 886 directly compels a priest to forgive. It states unequivocally that if a penitent asks for forgiveness and the confessor has no reason to question his contrition, the absolution can be neither denied nor deferred. The directive is clear, but obedience to it can be difficult.

Father Lawrence, thirty-nine, a parish priest from Spokane, Washington, speaks of the dilemma:

> When a man molests a child, he breaks the law of God. The Church says a sin hurts God primarily, then flows down to other people. We, as priests, have to keep God in mind so we don't get emotionally involved. There's no place for anger in the confessional.
>
> So a desperate penitent comes in and confesses he's attacked a child or a father says he's having sexual relations with his daughter. Inside I cringe and pray to God to love and forgive the offender. I've trained myself over the years to remember that he is coming to me as a sinner who wants help. If he weren't desperate, he wouldn't be inside a confessional. It takes courage for a man to tell me he's molesting his daughter. The agony is like a third person in the confessional. The penitent cries. He stammers. His voice cracks. He can't get the words out. Finally he confesses this heinous act he's committed.
>
> Now if for one moment I agree that he did a dreadful thing, I'll destroy him. I have to work slowly. First I try to help him get his anguish under control. Then I begin to talk, not about the sin, but about stopping it. "Look, you can't continue that. You could hurt your daughter for life. It's hard to say what effect it's already had. What you've got to do right now is stop. Not tomorrow or next week, but right now." He'll ask me how and we'll get into that. That's the approach you take with someone who has com-

mitted such a sin. God's the one that is being hurt. I stay
out of it. I control myself at all times.

Father Connor looks at another aspect of the confessor's responsibility:

To tell you the truth, I have been shocked in the confessional. Maybe a better word would be scared. Sometimes
a penitent will come in in a rage, threatening terrible
revenge, even murder. I'm terrified—most confessors are
—of panicking and not handling the situation properly.

Father DeNiro speculates on the practical efficacy of the Sacrament:

Someone comes in the confessional to admit that he's
committed a heinous crime. At first, I'm taken aback. If
there's a long line waiting, I'll encourage him to come
back to talk later, and pray that he will. But always in the
back of my mind is the worry that I may never see him
again. Some priests would tell him to return to the Church
to discuss his problem as penance.

I try to find out if he's really sorry for what he's done.
I'd like to forgive him because that's what he came for. If
you want him to go and sin no more, you've got to give
him the tools and motivation. He came to me instead of
a psychologist because of the supernatural aspect of sin.
I really believe in the power and the grace of the Sacrament to change people's lives. God can forgive. If priests
are going to err in the granting of forgiveness, it will be
on the side of being lax and granting absolution. If you
don't do that, you've lost the penitent forever.

Father Jackson, fifty-seven, a diocesan accountant from San Francisco, describes his personal reactions:

In the confessional, I never judge. I'm entirely objective.
My role is to show no distaste, no personal opinion what-
soever. A priest who shows that he disapproves of homosexuality or other sexual acts is taking away the penitent's

last chance. He's not going to go to another confessor, he's going to go out and sin again. Supposing a man says, "I'm twenty years old, and I raped a woman of seventy-five." It turns my stomach. My anger is there, but I can't show it.

Many priests, recognizing their limitations when faced with serious crimes, urge penitents to seek professional counseling. Father Elton has devised guidelines:

> If a person has committed a grave crime against society, like child molesting, I strongly recommend that he give himself up to the police. I also demand, for the absolution to be valid, that he see a psychiatrist. I never just give him absolution and send him back on the streets. I put stipulations on the absolution.

Father Merovitch explains how a priest should not behave in the confessional:

> It's essential not to panic. To handle the situation properly you must remain calm and reassure the person that if he seeks peace with the Lord, as well as professional help, he can resolve his problem. There's a temptation to overreact to someone who comes into the confessional, especially if you are repulsed yourself. You've always got to remember why the person is there and what's best for him.
> At the same time, you've got to remember the teachings of Scripture and the forgiveness of the Lord. Sometimes, the Lord is more forgiving than society, like a father with his own child.

Father O'Neill, fifty, an Irish priest assigned to a St. Louis parish, speaks of the tightrope between social and spiritual responsibility which the confessor must walk:

> There is a public aspect to the Sacraments which must also be considered. What if someone we know is involved in sin comes to take the Eucharist? We must give him the benefit

of the doubt. We cannot know the mind of God, and we might do irreparable harm to the man who is seeking God even when he is in grievous sin.

We face this problem occasionally in Ireland when someone involved in political violence comes to the altar for the Eucharist. We are forbidden to publicly condemn because we cannot presume to know the state of his soul. The danger, however, lies in the other members of the congregation who are aware the man is in the I.R.A. They might assume that we, the clergy, are tacitly approving of his violent way of life because we do not censure him and allow him the Eucharist. That is not our responsibility. We can speak out against violence, but we cannot specify our accusation.

Thus, the teaching regarding violence becomes suspect. Suppose someone who is known in the I.R.A. for having killed soldiers presents himself. He may come to confess and never mention the bombs and the ambushes, the knee-cappings and killings. He may not feel he has done anything wrong. Most of them think they're waging a just war. But you can't ask him directly about it. You're supposed to have faith in his contrition. Now, people see such a man go to Confession and assume he has confessed to some violence and that he has been forgiven for it. The danger then is in linking the Church with such men.

Chapter 10

Priests Are People, Too

Confession, as the preceding interviews reveal, take a huge spiritual, emotional and physical toll on priests.

> The most responsible office of the priest of God is the hearing of confessions. Every other duty imposed upon him is child's play compared with it, because so much depends upon it, *viz*: the salvation of immortal souls.

When these words, taken from *The Confessional* by Rt. Rev. Aloysius Roeggle, published in 1882, were shown to one young priest, he shrugged and asked, "Why do you think priests drink?"

Confession, of course, is only part of the answer, but the fact remains that the image of the lonely cleric imbibing in solitary, silent pain is not without foundation. Perhaps the numbers of alcoholic priests have been exaggerated, but they do exist. Father Brennan, a youthful fifty-four-year-old New York pastor, gives one example:

> When I was first ordained, back in the fifties, and people came to confess their drinking problems, I sympathized, told them to learn to reject it and gave them a couple of Hail Marys as penance. Now I realize the inadequacy of my response.
>
> Around eight years ago I was assigned to a parish where the pastor was, to be blunt, an alcoholic. He was a kind man, a caring minister, but a classic sucker for the demon drink. The problem was that he hated to drink alone and so he used to persuade me to sit with him for hours in the evening. We'd have wine at dinner, a few brandies afterward and even a nip during the day. To tell the truth, I was beginning to enjoy it all very much.
>
> Whether it was coincidental or caused by the drinking, I became concerned about my faith. It wasn't a question of faith in God, but in my own ability to help anyone. I began to doubt whether any priests ever made any difference. To fight back, I made a determined effort to be a better priest, and one of the ways I did that was to attempt to be a better confessor. Before, I guess I was your average guy in the confessional, taking it in one ear and letting it out the other. Then, it started to stick. The pain, the anguish, the guilts started building up in my head like silt. I was getting clogged by people's unhappiness. The solution, of course, was to drink more.
>
> When my sister became ill, I had to go home to help out the family. There wasn't a drop of liquor in the house, and I thought I'd go crazy. I can still recall the shame I felt when I sent my nineteen-year-old niece out to buy me a bottle of brandy. I made excuses about having a cold, but I saw the look of pity in the girl's eyes. Thank God, I wasn't

that badly hooked. I recognized my problem and cut myself off immediately, cold turkey.

When I returned to the parish, I assumed that if I could turn away from addiction so quickly, my pastor could do the same thing. That night, I rampaged through the rectory, smashing all the booze I could find. He begged me for a drink, got down on his knees and cried like a baby. I was so blind to his real need that I never gave him a drop. I just lectured on and on, self-righteously, about my own victory.

The next day, he went into town, got drunk in a bar and made a real scene. The policeman who brought him back suggested A. A. I don't know why I never thought of that. Pride, perhaps, in thinking that only I could change him. I was so naive about the magnitude and depth of the problem. Today, when someone confesses a drinking problem, I send him to A. A. with God's blessing.

I eventually got over my own scrupulosity as a confessor and put things in better perspective. Confession is still very important to me, much more than in one ear and out the other, but I don't bring work home from the office anymore. I still feel the pain, but I can handle it now.

Priests, as the previous interview reveals, are all too human. They put on their trousers one leg at a time like everyone else. They also confess their sins like most other Catholics. Father Brennan is typical of many priests.

I go to General Absolution at Easter and Christmas, and also have private Confession. My spiritual director is my confessor. If I were downtown and felt the need, I'd just go to a church and confess. I use all three ways of Confession.

Father Winslow, thirty-five, a U.S. Army chaplain in Chicago, describes a priest's spiritual life:

Most priests have a specific confessor. Generally someone my age will choose an older man, someone he considers

strong in spiritual or common sense, whichever he's looking for. I would think the majority of priests confess at
least once a month, if not more. Some confess as often as
once a week. It's generally done on a face-to-face basis,
just by walking into the confessor's office. Sometimes it's
even more casual. Two priests might be driving to a ball
game, and one will say, "By the way, it's time I made my
peace," and the other will say, "Sure, go ahead" and right
there, sitting in the car, he'll tell him what's happening in
his life.

Confession is essential in our lives. Too often people
put us on pedestals and think we're like Christ. The reality
is we're all too human. Most of us are weak and lonely.

Father Moratti, fifty, a parish priest from Annapolis, Maryland,
speaks of the toll it exacts over the years:

Catholics idealize the priest, and I say that despite the fact
that priests work very hard for their people, particularly in
years past when they did everything including physically
building the church and school and educating two or three
generations. A lot of demands were put upon them, but
they were still put on a pedestal. I guess it adds to the
reverence of the Sacraments. But the reality is that priests
are human, and most of them have suffered great pain in
their lives.

Some of them have problems with alcoholism or other
weaknesses. Others burn out at the ages of thirty-seven or
forty because they've given so totally of themselves. We
come out of the seminary with the illusion that we've got
to save everybody. The reality is that we're just not strong
enough. Some of us break down under the strain.

A priest is simply a human being, like anyone else, an
instrument fulfilling a role that happens to be one that
follows God. Like the guy working on the street corner or
the doctor or lawyer, he has weaknesses. If you've got
40,000 priests in North America, the odds are that 20 to

30 percent are going to end up with some sort of emotional or physical problem.

I don't think a priest today is as afraid to seek professional help as he would have been twenty years ago. Then, it would have been admitting defeat. Today, it's admitting you're part of the human race.

Since the sixties, people are more compassionate toward their priests. Twenty years ago, if a priest left the Church, his flock's faith would have been shattered. Today there's more understanding.

Other priests carry their burden more lightly. Some manage to take their duties as confessor in stride. Father Kiernan, thirty-eight, of Dallas, Texas, is one of these.

I never feel burdened by confessions, but I am troubled when a close friend confides serious problems. I become emotionally involved, and it weighs heavily on me.

Father Petrie, also thirty-eight, a parish priest in Santa Fe, agrees:

People think the secrets we hear in Confession weigh heavily upon us. Not really. Minutes after the confession, I couldn't tell you what I heard. Even when I administer the Sacrament face-to-face, I can't remember the sins. That's because of the Seal of Confession and God's grace. I'm not forgiving the penitents, I'm only the instrument, so I'm able to let go of their confessions as soon as they do. Though if I ever hear of a murder or an abortion, that might stick in my mind for a while.

Father Elton makes a statement that would have smacked of heresy two generations ago:

I don't think all priests are temperamentally suited to hearing confessions. Some just aren't built for sitting in a little closet for hours and hours. Perhaps they're the nervous type. I remember a priest who always perspired. He couldn't stand confinement. It wasn't hearing confessions that bothered him, it was just sitting still for all those hours. We used to say that he had ants in his pants. He wore out a cloth by constantly rubbing it while he was sitting in the confessional.

But in the boondocks, in a one-priest parish, what choice do we have? We're terribly short of seminarians. And it's an insult to say to a priest, "You're not good at hearing confessions." He would take it as a terrible affront. After celebrating Mass, which is the priest's biggest task, hearing confessions is the priest's number two job.

To the penitent, if not to the confessor, spiritual limitations are more important than physical. A Russian Orthodox priest who had been raised as a Roman Catholic does not believe all priests are capable of becoming good confessors. He allows only the gifted ones of his own church in Lyons, France, to hear confessions.

Many priests are unfit to hear confessions. It is an art, not a science, and a difficult art at that. I knew a Russian priest who was a great confessor. He was also a drunkard. People would come to him and say, "Father Nicholas, stop drinking. I want to confess." So he'd stop drinking for a time, they'd make their confession and he'd go back to his bottle. He was a wonderful confessor because he was able to bring people to say what was in their hearts. This is a rare gift. He was able to bring the truth out. Few men can do this.

Though the fact that not all priests make good confessors is more widely accepted today, it is not exactly news in the Church. In the eighteenth century St. Alphonsus wrote:

If all confessors would fulfill the obligations of their office, the whole world would be sanctified. Bad confessors are the ruin of the world.

Chapter 11

Penance from Heaven

The Church possesses both water and tears: the water of Baptism, the tears of penance.

—St. Ambrose, fourth century

One of the most consistently criticized aspects of Confession is the penance meted out by confessors. Penitents regularly condemn the predictable number of prayers uttered in automatic fashion by seemingly indifferent priests. "That'll be three Our Fathers and three Hail Marys," regardless of the sin or the pain involved. Many penitents long for more relevance—to the times as well as the sin —in their penance.

Father Benetto, a thirty-two-year-old parish priest from New

York, is concerned, however, with the spiritual power rather than the social relevance of penance.

When the concept of Confession was translated into practice, it became mathematical or mechanical. We numbered the sins and the species and worked out an equation. That was the mentality of the age, the Dark Ages. All the Sacraments took on this mathematical aspect. Unfortunately, most people I see in Confession have retained this mentality. They were taught that way as children. And the Church is perpetuating the problem because the teachers of today's children were trained in yesterday's modes of thought. So were the parents. How long before the mentality changes? I ask myself that question all the time.

We must strive to get away from this mechanical interpretation of Confession. Many people feel once they've committed a sin they can go in, get absolution and bang, it's gone. It's like taking a pill to be relieved of a headache.

The aim of Confession is to enable you to take charge of your life and your responsibilities. After Confession you should feel more anxious rather than less because now you're responsible for taming your evil inclinations. The more you suffer from that tension, the more anxiety you have, the more in touch you are with yourself. Today, Confession is perceived as relief, but it shouldn't be that way.

The ultimate goal is to change your behavior and you can't do that without pain. This is why people resist the true Confession. It's too painful.

If you go into that box with a sincere heart, you are going to have to confront your true nature. And the priest will have to make you suffer if you want to be free. Confession is the pain and suffering of changing your behavior and your evil inclinations.

The idea of praying every day as penance is really an

exercise in discipline to make sure that through prayer you are getting in touch with yourself and are growing. The purpose of prayer makes sense. Three Hail Marys doesn't.

Father Merovitch believes the Church has changed, and penance with it.

What would the priest give as penance today to a serious sinner, an adulterer for example? Today the penance would be negligible. Penance is practically gone. Today's priest must judge the penitent's motives. Has he confessed because he's afraid of going to Hell if he gets hit by a car? Or does he understand that he has committed a sin against the community? If he doesn't understand the true sin, then he's likely so thick-headed that he hasn't got any spiritual pain either. He's only worried about being hit by that car and the fear of going to Hell.

The kind of penance that a priest gives is often determined by the times in which he was ordained. Father Carlson, sixty-two, a parish priest in Cleveland, is decidedly prayer-oriented.

Priests trained in the thirties and forties—my years of training—tend to give the same type of penances, not because we're static, but because we've learned that some of the more sophisticated penances don't work. Some people can't handle penances like helping someone who is physically handicapped. They get embarrassed by it and complain that they don't "feel right" doing it. They'll come back, feeling distraught, and say they couldn't do their penance. So I'll commute it. We call it commutation of penance, and I'll give them a certain number of prayers to say. A hard-line Catholic, and that could be anyone from twenty years of age to eighty, will be satisfied with that.

I like giving prayer as penance, because people can fulfill that penance more easily than a social penance.

Though Father Mulligan doesn't entirely disagree, he approaches penance from a more communal point of view:

> Penance is difficult to determine. It's important that the penitent repay society and find peace within himself. Penance must confirm the individual's humanity and the Father's love and forgiveness. In giving penance, the priest has to strengthen the will to change. If there's a serious problem, quite often I'll send a penitent to seek professional help as part of his penance.
>
> On the other hand, sometimes I'll give a penance designed to right a social wrong. For example, someone injures another's reputation by making a public statement, writing an article or simply gossiping. I always make the penitent rectify the situation by doing something positive for the wronged individual or totally withdrawing the hurtful remark.

Father DeLuca, fifty-six, a Dallas, Texas, parish priest, varies his penances according to the penitent and his needs:

> With an older person who confesses in a "by rote" way, I'll give one Hail Mary and one Our Father, because that's what they want to hear. They've been trained to think of sin according to species and number, and I don't want to traumatize them by asking them to do some charitable work.
>
> If someone confesses to having stolen something, I'll ask him to give money to a charity. If a man commits adultery, I'll ask him to do something to reestablish his relationship with his wife, such as taking her to dinner once a week. If someone misses Mass, I'll ask him to make an effort to attend a weekday Mass. Prayer is also an important part of the process, but I never ask them to recite more than one. I figure God has good hearing; he doesn't need repetition.
>
> When a person returns to Confession after a long pe-

riod of time, I never give him penance. I figure coming back is penance enough.

Father Benetto reminds us why the stringent penances of the Middle Ages were effective:

Penance can provide the discipline necessary to grow out of a sinning habit. That was the original idea of penance. It was supposed to be a healing process. You have a bad habit that requires ten or fifteen years to break. It's like going into therapy. People don't change overnight. It takes time and effort.

Deathbed Confession

God's finger touched him, and he slept.

—Alfred Lord Tennyson, *In Memoriam*

Deathbed confessions bring to mind two disparate images. The first conjures up someone who beats the devil in life's race and crosses the finish line into Heaven with a soul scrubbed fresh at the last moment. The second suggests a person taking a stately step from life to afterlife with the assistance of a priest. The latter is the image preferred by the Church, but it has never frowned on the morally fleet of foot.

Father Murphy, a hospital chaplain in Philadelphia for eleven years, explains how Confession is administered today to the ill and dying:

The Sacrament of the Anointing of the Sick used to be called Extreme Unction or Last Rites in pre-Vatican II days. When someone in the hospital is facing a serious operation and wants to receive the Sacrament of the Sick, I never request that they confess first. I simply explain that the Sacrament of the Sick is not meant for someone who

195

is dying, but that it represents the Christian community praying for the sick. Absolution from sin is incorporated in the Sacrament. A person facing a serious illness has enough on his mind without reviewing the sins of his past. On the other hand, if he says, "Father I want to confess," then I'll listen to the confession, absolve the penitent and then administer the Sacrament of the Sick. These days, we get few requests for Confession prior to the Sacrament of the Sick except from older Catholics. They've been going to Confession on a regular basis and believe that one Confession is good for only three or four Communions.

I've experenced a lot of death, to be sure, but I've experienced very few bona fide deathbed confessions. It rarely happens that a person who is dying says, "Father, I've been away from Confession for fifty years and now I'd like to get everything ready for God."

Father Murphy, like most priests familiar with administering the Sacrament of the Annointing of the Sick, points out that deathbed confessions are almost a thing of the past:

Prior to Vatican II, it was pretty much required by Church ritual that Confession precede Extreme Unction. But as a young priest, when I saw someone who was unconscious, I knew I wasn't going to ask him to confess. When we are administering the Sacraments, we should try to keep to the spirit of Christ rather than the letter of the law. I don't require any confession of sins from anyone who wants the Sacrament of the Sick. I believe most hospital chaplains and even parish priests would concur. However, before Vatican II, Confession would have been required.

He continues, speaking as an activist for the aged:

Older people, my mother's age, around eighty, see death, and they're frightened, nervous, unsure of everything. They have practical problems. They can't cook for themselves or pay their bills. A guy used to be an accountant, and now he can't go to the bank. Spiritually they're in bad shape too. We have to treat them carefully.

Whenever I hear a young priest complain about an older person, I tell him, that's my mother or someday your father that you're talking about. The advice I give a young priest is to put himself in the other guy's place. The person that comes into the confessional wants to be lifted up, not pushed down. The older person needs our help in the confessional and on the deathbed.

Father Benetto has the same sympathy for the elderly.

Last week, I was hearing the confession of a woman who was dying, and she said, "In order to live this life properly, you have to live it twice. I've made so many mistakes." The person of seventy has lived his life, gone through all the stages and faced the pain of growing. The person of seventy has the time to sit back and reflect on what's truly important. They realize that being at peace with themselves is essential. Their confessions are important.

Death does not burden most priests who see it as the peaceful passage from one life to another. To assist at that passage is a rewarding pastoral responsibility. Father Mulligan describes the experience:

One of the most beautiful experiences for a priest is to hear a deathbed confession. You can give a person of any age who's passing away something that nobody else can. All the scientists, all the doctors, all the teachers and bankers and friends can't do a darn thing at that point. But you can give peace of mind, and that should never be underestimated.

The confessions of the seriously ill resemble the new form of the Sacrament, and may well affect the future of Confession. Father Conrad, forty-nine, of Kansas City, explains:

Ninety-five percent of the confessions I hear as a hospital chaplain are face-to-face out of necessity. Face-to-face confessions are here to stay. Most people feel freer speaking of their sins this way rather than in a box, and I definitely prefer it. In the old days, there was never enough time—with people lining up on both sides of the confessional. We were looked upon as judges dispensing justice, one hopes with mercy. Now, people look at Confession as a way of receiving help and counseling, not simply listing sins, receiving absolution and reciting penance.

Seal of Confession

I know less about what I hear in confession than I know about those things of which I am entirely ignorant.

—St. Augustine, fifth century

The Seal of Confession dates from the Irish in the Dark Ages. During that time, the priests who heard confessions of the newly converted pagans wore keys around their necks to signify they were keeping the confessions locked and secret.

Today the Seal is still the categorical prohibition against revealing a confession. Because this injunction allows no exceptions, the Seal of Confession smacks of high drama and presents some tantalizing moral riddles. In films and in fiction, the question is repeatedly asked, "What does the priest do when somebody confesses he has just murdered someone?"

Father DeLuca tells of a priest who managed to preserve the confidentiality of the confessional and the laws of the state:

A few years ago a man who had killed five members of his family went to Confession. For the man's penance, the priest told him to turn himself in to the police. If the man was really sincere in wanting forgiveness, then the penance was appropriate. The man turned himself in.

Father DeNiro insists that the confidentiality of the confessional is essential to the peace of mind of the community:

> Suppose you came in and confessed that you'd murdered your mother. Once that confession is finished, I can't even mention to you that I heard it. You've got to mention it to me first. The Seal gives a priest credibility within the community. He can be brought into court of law and still not be forced to reveal a confession. Priests who work in prisons say that criminals always want to see the Catholic priest even if they're Presbyterian or Anglican. A priest is excommunicated if he directly or indirectly breaks the Seal.

Father DeLuca assuages the fears many penitents have of not being able to trust their priest:

> In the Sacrament of Penance, there's never any need to feel the slightest possibility of betrayal because the penitent is dealing with God through a stranger, even if the person knows the priest. It saddens me when my parishioners tell me that sometimes it's easier for them to confess to complete strangers, people they meet on an airplane, than to a priest in Confession.

Father Vincent, forty-eight, an Oblate from San Diego, relates the discipline in the seminary to the Seal of Confession:

> In my day you had what they called a "grand silence." From 9:30 P.M. to 5:30 A.M. there was no talk. It was excellent training for being alone with yourself and God. So when someone asks me how I can hear all those confessions and not divulge anything, I recall seven long years of having to be still for eight hours every night, and answer, "discipline."

Bless Me, Father, For I Have Sinned

Though confessional secrecy is a deadly serious business, Father DeNiro recounts an anecdote on the lighter side:

> There was a young priest who, whenever he was confronted by a woman who confessed to adultery, would ask her to bake a cake for her husband. Two women were having a chat, and one said to the other, "Father gave me an interesting penance. He asked me to bake a cake." And the other woman said, "That was my penance too." And suddenly it dawned on them that they were both being unfaithful to their husbands.

Father Quinlan, forty-three, a Washington-based professor, tells another story to lighten the priestly burden of the Seal:

> A young priest, recently ordained, was sitting at the dinner table with the older pastors, and one of them asked, "How was your first day at Confession?" "Well, it wasn't too bad," he answered, "except for the first person. She was awful, broke all Ten Commandments." And then he went on to detail all her complaints. A few minutes later, the loose housekeeper came in, all smiles, and announced, "Did you all know that I was the young Father's first penitent today?"

A curious aspect of the Seal of Confession was what we call the spillover effect. Awed by the stern demand for their priests to keep all confessions secret, most men and women interviewed revealed that as kids they'd never shared their confessional experiences with anyone else. Most kids didn't develop a street savvy for Confession as they did for almost all other aspects of growing up Catholic, from sex to survival. Few of them changed as adults.

Chapter 12

Penitents on Priests

In this chapter penitents are given the chance to judge their confessors. Both men and women recall the priests who confronted them in the confessionals, remembering the gentle compassion of some and the bitter condemnation of others. They recount their tales with a passionate urgency to right the wrongs and to set the record straight.

"Good" Confessors

When we asked the people we interviewed to describe their confessors, they instinctively divided them into two categories, the "good" and the "bad."

201

"What makes a 'good' confessor?" We found that the answer to that question depends largely upon the expectations of the penitent. Some seek only forgiveness for their sins; others want spiritual counseling to help change their behavior. Some want reparational penance, preferring to expiate their sins actively. The majority, however, feel more comfortable with traditional prayers.

For many, a close, continuing relationship with their confessors is integral to their religious life. Others want total anonymity. A few feel more comfortable with older confessors while some, as we've seen, search for a priest who might be more liberal. All, however, hope for a priest with compassion, a sense of humor and the wisdom of Solomon.

The majority of people who shared their "good" confessor stories are practicing Catholics who did not abandon the Church or the Sacrament during the turbulent sixties and seventies, but a few "good" confessor stories did come from those *born* in the sixties. These young people know only the Church of the Second Vatican Council.

Karen, a confident eighteen-year-old high school student from San Diego, describes the priest that she confesses to, face-to-face, in the reconciliation room every month.

> I have an ideal confessor. He's sympathetic, warm, talkative, understanding, flexible and knows his stuff. I like when I'm confessing and he makes a statement and then he backs it up with something from the Bible. Or when something happens in my life and he says, "That same thing happened to Sister Theresa and this is how she handled it." I like that. I like a priest having knowledge at his fingertips, so that when I go into Confession, I have something to contemplate as well as my penance. I have Sister Theresa as my role model and I can say to myself, "Wouldn't it be wonderful to deal with my problems in the same way?" I like that in my priest.

Penitents on Priests

Crystal does not fit the image of a good Catholic. The twenty-one-year-old singer in a New York heavy-metal band has chains around her waist, ankles and wrists—and a small silver cross tucked inside her leather vest.

People are always surprised to learn that I can be a singer in a heavy-metal band and still be a practicing Catholic. In the sixties they had all those groovy guitars in church, so why can't I love my religion in my own way today, too? I'm not a saint, but I really do try my best not to hurt anyone.

When I'm confused about something, I go to a wonderful priest I've known for years. I see him privately in the reconciliation room once a month or so, whenever I'm feeling bad, and he helps me sort myself out. Just last month, I learned that he also works in a small parish where most of the people are little old ladies in their seventies, and he hears confessions in the old-fashioned way, in a confessional box on Saturdays and before Mass in the mornings. I was real curious because my mother was always telling me about how she used to tremble before Confession and how she could never tell the priest about sexual things.

I wanted to know how it all felt, so one Saturday afternoon, I went to this little parish for Confession. There I was in that confessional, feeling so protected and close to God. I didn't even think about what sins I wanted to confess. I just started to confess things I now know were sins, but never really thought of as sins, like gossiping about other groups because of jealousy, doing a little drugs, a little sleeping around.

When I finished, the priest said, "Now say a rosary to yourself every time you catch yourself doing one of those things." I asked if he meant like every time, and he said, "Yes, my child, every time." When he called me "my child," I felt so warm inside, I almost started to cry.

Although a rosary can be a pain in the ass, I still go to

old-fashioned Confession sometimes. I think it's great. I can't understand why my mother never liked it.

Barbara, a forty-six-year-old Miami primary school educator, recalls how good sacramental preparation influenced her as a child and continues to color her life.

A good confessor is one who knows how to listen and ask questions, who understands what you're talking about. A compassionate priest knows he's a sinner himself so he doesn't sit judgmentally even though he does make a judgment. He realizes we are all sinners, but are loved and forgiven by God, that we are valuable people in God's eyes.

I truly believe that even before you get to the priest as an adult, your initial instruction in the Sacrament of Penance has a big influence on your attitude toward Confession. It's so important that you get good instruction initially, training that doesn't frighten you and make you fearful of God. I had good instruction, and I learned it well.

My father died when I was ten. He was seriously burned and lingered for two weeks before he died. I remember going down the stairs and hearing someone say, "How are we going to tell her?" I knew then he was dead. I asked if he'd had Extreme Unction and the priest said he had. Then I asked if he'd had the Holy Viaticum, and when I learned he had, I said, "Why are you so sad? He's in Heaven." My first-grade teacher and the priests had really given me a beautiful appreciation of the Sacraments that has carried me through all my life.

Stephen, fifty-five, a Los Angeles publishing executive, spent eight years in the monastery before going out into the world. He fondly recalls the therapeutic counseling he received in Confession.

For me, Confession was not the black box, but a conversation with a fellow monk. Several monks were outstanding, shining examples of good confessors in their method, their understanding, their ability to bring you along, so to speak. They knew me much better than someone in the darkness of a confessional would. They were really counseling sessions. We were all aiming for the same objective. We were all trying to perfect our lives, which is what the purpose of the monastic life is.

What happens, of course, in a monastic society, is that big things are taken care of and things that normally worry most people on the outside are not worries there. Since human beings have the capacity to worry, no matter about what, some of the smallest irritations would become the biggest. And the things that were huge on the outside, like murder or adultery, weren't even conceivable.

The major sins in the monastery were uncharitable acts. There's a great tendency toward scrupulosity in such a world. The good confessors put all this in context. They counsel, explain and set priorities. I found that extremely helpful when I left and joined the people outside.

Josie always knew what she wanted in a confessor and would accept no less. She admired her father very much and sought a priest who would possess his kindness and common sense. The forty-seven-year-old single magazine editor from San Francisco describes her fifteen-year relationship with her confessor:

I was a devout Catholic, at one time considered joining a convent and had little exposure to the secular culture. When I took a job at a magazine in the late sixties, I had to figure out how to relate to this secular male/female world.

My boss, a nonbelieving Protestant, was married. We began an intense relationship, my first, which became very important to both of us. I gave the relationship a lot of time and emotional energy, although I wasn't head over heels in love. I always knew that I would never marry him. He sometimes asked me, knowing in advance what my answer would be. My conscience was screaming bloody murder whenever we were together. He had a perfectly normal secular sex life which included a wife, three children and two mistresses before me. And here I was, a virgin who had chosen the single life because of religious convictions about sex. We had years of tenderness, during which time I came to understand why Catholicism puts such great value on the spiritual aspect of love and self-giving, but I stayed a virgin, at least technically. I would have to be married or no full sex. Half the time I was frigid. I also felt guilty about his wife, who would have appreciated a quarter of the attention he was lavishing on me. This relationship became a huge mark on my conscience for me. At this time, I started to look for a confessor. It had to be face-to-face and it had to be someone special.

I wrote a letter to a priest I respected who had been my professor at college and asked him if he would be my confessor. David is in his sixties, very bright and compassionate. When I started confessing to him, in 1969, I realized he had been on all kinds of emotional journeys. Just as the old culture of the Church had broken apart, he had suffered a nervous breakdown. He'd experienced a whole resynthesizing process, and in Confession we talked about his needs as well as mine.

For me, the central issue was the relationship with my boss and the questions it raised. My confessions became mutual explorations of good and evil in human living and loving. David was careful never to tell me what to do or to simply apply Church rules. He helped me move past the simplistic rules and to the level of living the question. We explored so many other things—like work and the idolatry of work.

Penitents on Priests

At first, I went to Confession once a month, then it became every Saturday morning for two and a half hours, face-to-face. My relationship with my boss ended when he was transferred to San Diego, but one of the many things it gave me, along with a whole new perception of what it meant to be a woman with a man, was a confessor, a real, spiritual brother. That's why I'm hooked on personal confession, because I've had the experience of a faithful, compassionate, responsible minister who loves me. I know that everyone won't be lucky enough to have this kind of relationship. Many of my friends don't go to Confession any more. I'm an advocate of Confession in the same way that somebody blessed with an excellent therapist is an advocate of psychiatry.

It was important for me that David give me absolution every time. He is a priest and speaks for the tradition. I kneel when I receive it. There are things in the Catholic culture that are more humanizing and expressive than in the secular conventions. I prize them and am glad they're still alive for me. He's respectful of me, but I don't think we're equals in the relationship. I give him authority, but am conscious that I am co-constituting that authority.

I obey him. Usually I have to ask him for a penance. He's a little shy with that part of the tradition, but when he gives me a penance, I do that before I do anything else.

Sometimes, as a penance, he'll tell me to go to a movie or do something relaxing because I work too hard. Sometimes, he'll tell me to take time off and pray because prayer is so important. In fact, prayer is often the first thing discussed in Confession. He's a bit more liberal than I am, although we're both middle-of-the-road, contemporary Catholics.

Occasionally, there has been a dramatic moment. A few years ago, I got emotionally close to a woman whom I met at a feminist conference. I discovered the world of women with great force and emotional energy at that time. Elaine had been married for eight years, had two children and was about to leave her husband. Our relationship became sexually charged. When I confessed this to David, he came close to panicking. He was shaken. He said that I shouldn't have a personal relationship with this woman. That was the most direct thing he ever said in fifteen years. We both prayed about it, stopped the conversation there and then and prayed. Was I abdicating my responsibility if I did as he told me to do? Would I be regressing to a more dependent way of life? We did a lot of probing and praying. At the end of the Confession, I said I would try.

Being a compulsively candid person, I told Elaine about my confessor and my decision. In short, I told her the truth. Not only was she angry, she was genuinely scandalized. She saw it as some priest telling me what I could or could not do with my emotional life. She was a Protestant and given the way she had seen Catholicism all her life, from a distance and as an inferior religion, I could understand her reaction. I was sorry I'd told her the truth.

Elaine and I wrestled with our relationship for two weeks. I phoned David and told him I wasn't going to break off with her.

When Elaine and I began to see each other again, I stopped going to Confession. Three months later, she moved to the Midwest. I wish I had kept in touch with her after she moved away, but I didn't. I'm not proud of the way I finally concluded the relationship. I still feel there was some unfaithfulness on my part because I told David. But David is my confessor and I share everything with him.

Ralph, a thirty-nine-year-old television repairman in Baltimore, describes himself as a shy guy, which is why finding the right confessor was essential for him.

I searched out this priest because he was a real talker during Confession, not just a listener. I never wanted someone who would just give me my penance. I needed someone who would go a little further to explain why I feel like I do, almost like a psychiatrist, although I've never been to one. I have such a hard time relating to myself, putting myself across, that it's important for me to find someone who'll really talk to me first, kind of open me up.

About three years ago, Lindsay, a thirty-two-year-old single airline stewardess from Boston, began an active search for her ideal confessor.

I decided to go to Confession on a regular basis when I realized there was no continuity in my life. I was always traveling, never feeling I had any roots. Both my parents had died within the past five years, and I was an only child.

So I asked my friends about their confessors and visited a couple of parishes. I wanted a serious relationship with my confessor, one that would allow me to grow spiritually. I wanted a father-figure kind of priest. Not somebody too close to my own age or somebody who was too good-looking or contemporary. Somebody who wouldn't lecture me or patronize me either, but who would take me seriously. After shopping around for three months, I found my confessor. I see him every month, face-to-face in the reconciliation room, and he's terrific.

Virginia was part of the burgeoning American Catholic intellectual elite of the fifties and sixties. A well-respected journalist, the forty-seven-year-old native New Yorker describes why she began to priest-shop at the age of eighteen:

Most young people have their biggest conflicts with the overt laws of the Church when they become sexually active. The problem came much later for me, and not very strongly. I was someone for whom ideas came first. It took me a long time before I became more a heart than a head. My sexual life was slow in developing. My social life was pretty pale in comparison with many of my contemporaries.

Bless Me, Father, For I Have Sinned

Gradually, God and Jesus began to be less part of the furniture and more persons I could relate to and get excited about. During high school, I didn't go to Confession because I considered it to be a marginal experience, although I did pray regularly and wrote religious poetry. I began to consciously choose confessors when I was eighteen, because I would no longer go to Confession just to get absolution from any anonymous priest. It had to be a mutual relationship. I needed to have respect for the priest as a person. That's true for a lot of people now, but I came to that realization earlier than most because of my strong Catholic intellectual background. In college I began to choose priests who would serve as spiritual guides because they inspired me.

The following three women have much in common. All in their mid-thirties, they abandoned the Sacrament when they started to have premarital sex. Each has just had her first experience with a good confessor and, as a result, vows to return to Confession.

Diedre, thirty-four, a Cincinnati theater manager, describes her confessor:

I never felt good enough. I felt if you could look into my soul, you'd see little black bits on the edge, even right after I'd been to Confession. Sometimes I tried to talk about sex, which gave me great pleasure, but the priests always told me I was committing a mortal sin and gave me a routine penance. I stopped confessing altogether. They wanted to make me a nun, a celibate until I got married.

I went back to Church when my father died because I had to go to Communion at his Requiem Mass. The priest recognized me and asked me to see him in the rectory. I wasn't nervous. I felt at home. I gave him my confession. I told him why I was there, which was to make my mother happy because my father had just died. I said there were lots of things wrong in the Church's eyes that weren't wrong in mine, but unless I confessed them I thought I was being a hypocrite about coming to Church. He nicely disagreed. He twisted it all around to make me feel good. He told me going to Confession for my mother was a perfectly good reason, and he was glad I wasn't being hypocritical and hoped that I would do it again. He was very sympathetic. I've been to Confession three times since then and hope to continue.

Robin, thirty-four, is a Winston-Salem, North Carolina, interior designer. She and her husband had a similar experience.

I was so grateful to the priest who married us and heard our confessions because it was the first face-to-face encounter I'd ever had with a confessor. It had been so long since I'd been to Confession, I even forgot to say "Bless me, Father." But the confession was so natural; he made me feel at ease right away.

He said, "Okay, Robin, what's happened to you in the last ten years of your life." I was astounded that he hadn't come down on me really hard. We laughed, talked like we were friends.

When it was over, my husband and I took Communion for the first time in years. Then we started to attend Church and go back to that priest to confess. It never would have occurred to us to go back to Confession if it hadn't been for him.

Sometimes I feel guilty about letting the Church slip away from me for such a long time, because here was this wonderful opportunity and I blew it, in a sense. That priest reminded me of it. I will go back.

Pamela, thirty-six, a divorced New York stockbroker, tells of a confessor who gave her the stiff penance she was seeking:

When I walked through the Church, I wasn't even sure how to get to the confessional, so I asked a man who was standing in the back. I told him I hadn't been to Confession in a long time and wasn't sure how to go about it. He was sympathetic and said, "Well, let's start by seeing if the light's on." He brought me over to the confessional and I went in. I was very nervous. Then the slot opened, and the priest immediately launched into a reading from the Bible. I was used to saying, "Bless me, Father, for I have sinned, it's been a long time since my last Confession." And I thought, isn't that nice, because the priest was giving me an invitation, like "Let's talk."

And then I told him about my past thirteen years, and my sins. He was quiet for about five seconds. Those five seconds were important to me because what it meant was that he'd really listened. There were some pretty big sins in there. Then he asked me how many times, and what did this mean to me? And all of a sudden, I felt that, finally, an official of the Church was really talking to me. He wasn't judgmental. He took me seriously. And he gave me more of a penance than is normally meted out, although before I went to him I'd decided what I could do to satisfy my own sense of penance. I'd had the feeling that whatever priest I went to wouldn't give me a penance as strong as I deserved because the things that I'd done were sinful against humanity as well as myself. I'm glad I went.

Cora, thirty-one, a physician from St. Louis, describes a penance she received from an unforgettable confessor.

I had a serious problem but going to Confession never occurred to me as a solution. I had done something in the past which had never been resolved. It was very personal, troubling, and I frequently discussed it with close friends. One of them said I should confess. I laughed, and said that wasn't what I needed. He insisted, as friends can, and we reached a funny sort of compromise. He was going to Confession the following day and he suggested I go to the church with him, no more than that.

We were both kneeling when a woman came out of one of the reconciliation rooms. That was it. I didn't pause. I knew if I hesitated I would never do it. So I got up and ran across the church. Just as I arrived, the priest peeked out of the room and said, "Hi, I'm Father So-and-So, what's your name?" My name? I'm going to confess and on top of that he wants to know my name! This wasn't at all what I'd bargained for.

He showed me in and indicated I had a choice of either kneeling at the screen or sitting facing him. Now that we had exchanged names, it seemed silly to pretend to be anonymous, so I sat down. I went straight to it. I told him about the terribly personal thing that was troubling me. Right away, he said he had experienced something like that a few years ago, and he understood the pain I was suffering. He asked me to tell him more about it, how it happened.

Before he gave me penance, he asked if I had time to go to Mass. I said I did, and he then said that for my penance he wanted me to attend that afternoon's Mass. At the Offertory, he wanted me to review my experience of a few years back, to look at it from all sides, and then mentally roll it away. I was then to symbolically take it up to the altar and leave it there. That was my penance. It was extraordinary!

When I left the reconciliation room, he left with me to celebrate the Mass. The ironic part of the story is that we spent so long in the reconciliation room that the friend I came with never got to confess that day.

Occasionally an extraordinary priest assigns an extraordinary penance for an extraordinary sin. Thierry, a fifty-five-year-old foreign correspondent for a leading French magazine, who currently lives in New York, speaks in a tone of reverence:

I will tell you a true story about Confession. I was told it by the priest who was involved.

There was a Russian man during the Revolution. He had a small son and they had nothing to eat. He couldn't bear to hear the child crying because he was starving, so he killed him in the snow. Then he went to Confession, told the Orthodox priest, "I have killed my child," and explained the circumstances. The man was very crazy with grief. And the priest said, "If I had been in the same situation, I would have done the same. So I'll give you absolution and good-bye."

But the man could find no peace. So, twenty years later, he met another priest in a German war camp, this was the priest I knew who told me this tale, and the man confessed his sin to him. And this priest said, "I suggest, when you go home to your country, you take in five or six orphans, and raise them as your own." He did so, and found peace.

Sometimes "good" confessors can save a marriage, a child and much more. Lorraine, a fifty-two-year-old Cincinnati housewife, is still grateful to such a priest.

We were at the University of Michigan. My husband was getting his doctorate, working all the time, literally all the time. The housing was cramped and inadequate, and we had two small children. I could feel my marriage falling apart. There was no love, no sex, only anger. One day, my husband, who isn't a Catholic, said out of the blue, "If you believe in your Church so much, then by God, go to it and get some help."

I went to a Dominican to confess. Although I started out "Bless me, Father . . ." it soon stopped being a confession. I told him everything. He asked if I thought I could get my husband to come to see him. I said it was he who'd sent me in the first place. That night, we went to the rectory and had coffee and chatted about other things. Then he suddenly asked my husband, "When was the last time you took your wife out for dinner?" Brian admitted he couldn't remember. "Do me a favor," the priest said, "once a week go out by yourselves."

For the next twenty years we followed his advice, and

we've never had a serious problem in our marriage. If I knew a priest like that now, one I could go to for insight, it would make a big difference. I don't miss confessing. I miss the counseling.

Many priests schooled in the post-Vatican II mentality have turned into excellent marriage counselors. Daniel, a thirty-nine-year-old photographic-supplies salesman from Akron, Ohio, thanks a confessor for his happy marriage.

I'd been living with Sharon for about five years, and we were fairly content. Though we weren't married, we both knew it was for all time. We'd started out insisting on our individual freedom, but over the years, we'd come to think of ourselves as a couple for the foreseeable future.

At the same time we both started thinking it would be nice to get married. Then I began to drag my feet. I couldn't figure out my reluctance at first, but finally I understood. We were practicing birth control. I say we, because we'd both decided that Sharon would take the Pill. I respected the Church's position on birth control—respected it rather than agreed with it—but I did believe if you want to belong to a club, you've got to abide by its rules. I purposely stayed away from Confession because I couldn't promise myself, the priest or God that we were going to stop using the Pill. Sharon had no problem with the Pill; she simply felt it wasn't a sin, not a confessable offense. I wish it was that easy for me.

I couldn't drag my feet any longer. We started making marriage plans, but I wasn't happy. I wanted my marriage to start right and beginning it in sin was definitely the wrong way to set out. I wanted to go to Confession before the wedding, and I had a little speech all prepared about how I felt about the Church, the Pill and marriage. The priest stopped me half way through and explained that things were a little more liberal now. If I wanted to put off starting a family for a while it was all right. He asked, however, that we leave ourselves open to children for at least the period of a month, to symbolically respect the Church's teaching. He also gave me a book that surprised me because it was by a priest and said that anything a husband and wife do to each other to stimulate or add pleasure is perfectly all right. This was a new Church! I had been taught sex was only acceptable in the missionary position and that was it.

After that confession, I felt the way I used to feel as a kid after I'd confessed swiping a candy bar and suddenly realized I wasn't going to Hell for it because I'd been absolved. Oh, the exhilaration! I felt fabulous! I can't tell you how important that guy was to my marriage. I am so grateful.

Sometimes these new counseling priests are responsible for saving a penitent's sanity. Rebecca, a thirty-nine-year-old New Haven doctoral student, tells of her uncontrollable grief and the consolation she found in the confessional:

When my husband was shot down in Vietnam, I couldn't stop crying. I went to Mass every day, but for some reason I didn't think about Confession. Then after about two weeks, I called and asked if I could make a confession in the chaplain's office. When I went, the priest spoke with hope and enthusiasm, but I couldn't cope with it. I wept. I sobbed. He reached out and held my hands. He put his arms around my shoulders and just held me. It was like a spiritual nurturing. Nothing was said while he held me. Later, he gave me a book by Aquinas. After that, every day on his advice I randomly dipped into Aquinas for my message for that day. It was truly as if God were talking to me. That man and that confession were so important. I love that priest for being there when I desperately needed him.

Nancy, a thirty-nine-year-old Los Angeles television producer, also found the spiritual strength she needed with the help of a priest.

About six months ago, I was involved in a relationship with a woman who was twelve years my junior. After the first few months, it became evident that she had developed a deep dependency upon me. The relationship had become, for her, one of reparenting, and for me, one of excessive hand-holding. It was very tense. She began accusing me of not treating her properly, insisted that nothing she did was ever good enough for me. It soon degenerated into one of those relationships where two people are always looking over each other's shoulders and analyzing every word and action. It all became very tedious. But the point was that I really liked her and knew she cared for me. We had shared some very special moments.

For the past eight years, I've been seeing a confessor on a regular basis, face-to-face, once a month. I told him about the relationship and how it was draining all my energies just trying to keep it alive. I asked him what I should do. I didn't want to break it off, but I couldn't keep on living like that, either. Right there, in the middle of my confession, he laid his hands on my head and prayed intensely, as though he were in the middle of an exorcism. At that moment, I clearly felt that my confessor had brought God to my side so that my relationship with this woman could grow from the point at which it had become stultified. Within the next few days, I noticed a marked difference between us. The pattern of dependency and suspicion had ended, and we continued being together for many years after that. I credit it all to my confessor.

Frequently the priest must give concrete as well as spiritual help, and sometimes he must step out of the confessional to do it. Allison, a thirty-five-year-old Chicago housewife, tells of such an instance.

My son knew a girl who was being sexually abused by both her parents who were alcoholics. She told my son that she had gone to Confession to seek the help of her priest, but he said he couldn't actively intervene because of the Seal

217

of Confession. He asked her to come to see him away from the church and to tell him again. It seemed silly to me at the time, but then I understood. When she told him outside of the confessional, he took steps and had her put in a foster home.

I know another case where the woman was an alcoholic and also had drug problems. She'd been drinking heavily for years but never admitted she had a problem. It was in Confession to this same priest that she talked for the first time of being an alcoholic. He saved her life. She's fine now. I'm proud of her, but we should also be proud of the priest.

Margie, a forty-four-year-old Long Island, New York, housewife, has benefited somewhat from the practical counseling the priest gave her husband in the confessional.

I wish I could say that the priest made my husband be nice to me and the kids, but I can't. All I can say is that since he's started to go to Confession again regularly, he's stopped hitting us. After our youngest daughter was born, Bob would come home from the factory around four in the afternoon, have some beers, watch the news, eat supper, have some more beers, watch TV until eleven and then go to sleep. As long as me and the kids didn't speak to him, everything would be fine but if we said just one word, he'd fly into a rage and blame me because we've got four kids and he's got a dumb factory job.

Over the past year, his drinking became worse and he started to slap me around in front of the kids. Then he started to whack the kids with his leather belt. One time, he hit our oldest son so badly I had to take him to the hospital for stitches on his chin. It was at that time I told my husband either he goes to a priest or I'm going to the police.

I don't know what the priest is saying to Bob. He still drinks a lot and yells at me and the kids when he drinks too much. Last week, he got real mad because one of our daughters stayed out until three in the morning. I thought he was going to beat her up when she got home, but he just put his fist through the wall instead. I guess you could say the priest is helping. I mean, I'd rather have Bob hurt himself than one of the kids.

Deborah, thirty-seven, a Wilmington, Delaware, graphic artist, belongs to the Catholic Charismatic Renewal movement. She describes what she looks for in a confessor:

My ideals are the priests in the Charismatic movement who realize their potential power in the confessional. There is power to heal relationships, memories. I do believe in demon spirits and I'm not talking about Satan or being exorcized like in the movies. I'm talking about the legion of spirits that oppress people. I've seen it happen to people who have been driven bonkers by something for years. And I've seen deliverance by priests and by lay people.

The ideal confessor is someone who recognizes that power and knows how to use it. He must have the spiritual discernment to sense when somebody has an emotional or mental problem, or even a demon streak. If you have that ability and use it in the name of Jesus Christ who has given that gift, it's a beautiful thing. It's a beautiful thing to watch a person being instantly freed. I've seen it.

Next to sex, politics is probably the most explosive topic in the Church. Sometimes both penitent and priest are caught in the crossfire. The following stories took place in different countries and times but in each of them the Church and politics got dangerously mixed up.

Joseph, forty-seven, a Buffalo high school English teacher, describes an America very different from today:

My father and I always had a good relationship, not exactly "Father Knows Best," but one of mutual respect and occasionally of fun. However, when I was fourteen, I turned against him and accused him of being a traitor to the United States and to the Church.

I was a freshman at St. Paul's and really proud to be there. I worked on the school paper, joined the debating society, played basketball, thought the priests were terrific, went to Confession once a week and was having a great time. It was during the fifties, the time of Joe McCarthy, and everybody at St. Paul's, me included, thought the senator was one of the greatest men in America.

One day at school, I was given some inflammatory anti-Communist, pro-McCarthy propaganda and told to take it home to my parents.

When my father read it, he hit the roof. He called it a piece of undemocratic filth. I had never seen him like that before, a whirling madman, sputtering with rage all over the house. When he calmed down, he blamed me for bringing such garbage into our home. Then I made the greatest mistake of my youth. I said it wasn't garbage—it was true—and everybody except pinkos knew it. I called my father, right to his face and in front of my mother, a traitor to the Church and to the United States of America.

He walked out of the living room quietly, closing the door behind him, and I didn't see him again that night. The next day was Saturday and after basketball practice at St. Paul's I went to Father Kelly to confess that I hated my father. I explained my father's reaction to the propaganda I'd brought home and confessed I'd called him a pinko traitor. Father Kelly said for my penance I should say a rosary and ask God to forgive my father and show him the way back to the Church and away from the scourge of atheistic communism.

Over the next few days, home became a no-man's land. My father stayed in the kitchen and I stayed in my room. Neither of us would give in. Then came the confrontation.

Penitents on Priests

It was around nine o'clock on a chilly December evening. My father came up to my room and yelled that he was going to take me out of St. Paul's. I yelled back that if he did it would be a mortal sin—and I'd report him to the police for being a communist. I still had my back to him because I'd been praying and he wrenched me around to face him straight in the eyes. His face was purple with rage. He couldn't believe his own son would threaten to report him. "Report me?" he shrieked. He didn't even give me a chance to put on my coat. He dragged me, hand in hand, down the four blocks to the rectory and banged on the door like a policeman. He shouted to Mrs. Malloy that he wanted Father Herman to hear my confession right there and then. I was really bewildered, because I thought it was my father who should be confessing. He was the one espousing international Godless communism.

My father threw me at Father Herman's feet. "Those bastards at St. Paul's have turned my own son against me, Jim. Talk to him." Then my father stormed out, leaving me with Father Herman, who acted as if these scenes happened every night. He sat me down in a comfortable chair, and I told him what had happened. All the while, he just kept nodding. He explained how murky it can get sometimes when you mix religion and politics. The Church has been doing it for two thousand years and I shouldn't expect things to change so quickly. Then he gave me as penance one Our Father and one Hail Mary. I didn't even realize I had been confessing.

When I came out of his office, my father was standing in the hall, looking expectant, probably like he looked when I was born. I started crying and hugged him and we walked home arm in arm. I left St. Paul's at the end of the term.

Carla, a fifty-six-year-old Catholic educator living in Richmond, Virginia, has done considerable research into the activities of the

Vatican during World War II. She describes an incident she heard on a radio documentary about the survivors of the Holocaust:

> A Jewish woman in her fifties, living in New York, was recounting her experiences growing up in Warsaw during the war. She began by saying that when she was eleven years old a Jesuit who was hearing her confession saved her life. The story goes as follows. Her father, a professor at the university, had been taken to Auschwitz and never heard from again. Her mother, an indomitable spirit, decided that she wasn't going to wait for death to knock on her door. She and her daughter joined the Polish resistance movement and subsequently got false identifications. For two years this mother and child lived as Polish Catholics with assumed identities until the Germans discovered their branch of the underground. They took her mother to jail, tried and executed her as a Polish citizen, and buried her in a Catholic cemetery.
>
> Now this eleven-year-old Jewish girl, all alone in the world, living with a false identification, went to Confession. She told the priest she was Jewish and pleaded with him to give her absolution so that she could continue receiving Communion along with the Catholic community in which she was living. In the midst of this madness of war, this Jewish orphan was concerned about making a sacrilegious Communion.
>
> The priest told her that he'd give her absolution and that her Communion would not be sacrilegious if she promised him only one thing. In her whole life, she must never make this same confession again to another priest. He explained that the Germans went into the confessionals and, posing as priests, warned the Polish people that they were committing a mortal sin, condemning their souls to Hell, if they concealed the whereabouts of any Jews, helped any Jews, or worst of all, hid any Jews.

Over and over, men and women contended that a good confessor was solace for their soul and Confession was an oasis of sanctity. These were the people who nurtured their relationships with their priests both in and out of the confessional, allowing them to become part of their lives.

Some men and women we interviewed, however, recalled times when they had become more attached to the good confessor than to the Sacrament. When the priest was transferred to another church, or if he died or when they moved to another parish, they were reluctant to search for another confessor. As a result, they went to Confession less, if at all.

Some who had fallen away from the Church stated that a good confessor would provide the impetus to return to the Sacrament and their faith. They described those priests as the Church's goodwill ambassadors.

"Bad" Confessors

The majority of the men and women who told stories of "bad" confessors are long-lapsed Catholics. Some left the Church as disgruntled teenagers. Others broke away in confusion and anger in the sixties and seventies when it was fashionable to do so. None of them was willing to give the Sacrament or another confessor a second chance.

These people were furious with confessors who had failed to live up to their expectations. They accused these priests of everything from using foul language to withholding absolution, dispensing inappropriate penance and being oblivious to their pain. Many people complained about the priest's indifference, comparing him to a computer, a tape recorder, a blank wall; some weren't even sure there was a live human being sitting on the other side of the box. The rage with which these people spoke reveals how deeply they feel the Church hurt them.

For Vincent, a thirty-six-year-old Chicago insurance salesman, a priest's indifference was devastating.

223

Until I was about twenty-five I went pretty regularly to Confession, but I could never tell the priest what bothered me most. I hated my father. Every week I planned in my mind how I was going to confess, and every time I became so ashamed I couldn't get the words out. For months, the need to tell the priest just kept building up until I thought I was going to burst. I could feel the beads of sweat on my forehead as I started to confess that I hated my father. Then finally I blurted it out. It was the hardest thing I'd ever done in my life.

The priest wasn't even paying attention. It was like I hadn't spoken. He gave me my regular penance. I was destroyed. It had taken so much out of me to confess that I hated my father, and the priest didn't even listen. That was the last time I went to Confession. Now I only go to Church at Christmas.

Ronald, a forty-year-old New York advertising copywriter, describes himself as a Zen Buddhist with Catholic guilts:

In the confessional, you could have killed your mother and father and all of your sisters and brothers and then gone out and robbed three banks, and all the priest would say was, "Three Hail Marys and three Our Fathers."

I mean, this guy was not there! That used to bug the hell out of me. That and the fact that I could never get any answers from anybody. I used to ask the priests questions and they'd refer me to the Bible. I'd get stuff like, "Pray to the Lord and all your sins will be forgiven. Trust and all will be well." Empty words if you don't understand the meaning behind them. Nobody could break the code for me until I started studying Buddhism, then I began to understand the symbolism behind religion.

Akira, born in Japan, now lives in Los Angeles. The thirty-six-year-old computer programmer recounts a confession that took place more than twenty years ago, and marked a turning point in his life:

I grew up in a Catholic orphanage in Japan, and throughout my early life all I ever wanted to be was a priest. My
dream was killed by a priest in Confession.

Though illegitimacy is a great stigma in Japan, the
French nuns that cared for us never told me where I came
from and that didn't bother me at all. It was only later,
when I attended a minor seminary at the age of sixteen,
that my being a bastard became important to my lifelong
dream.

We used to confess every day, and the confessions were
more like spiritual conversations. I recall telling my Italian
confessor what I considered to be the grave sin of pride.
I said I equated myself with Jesus. I had convoluted reasoning but it went something like this. I was proud that I
didn't know who my father was because I was like little
Jesus whose father wasn't his real father, either.

The Italian immediately sat up straight in the confessional. I could hear him moving around. I thought he was
angry about my presumption. He asked me what I meant
about not knowing who my father was. I innocently explained that I was illegitimate, a bastard. I heard him sigh,
as though he were very sad. I could hardly hear him when
he whispered, "In this order, we have a rule that illegitimate boys cannot become priests." I didn't understand at
first. Then I felt like I wanted to break out of the confessional and destroy it, destroy the whole Church because
they were destroying my life.

I left the seminary that day in humiliation, in despera-
tion, feeling like nothing. I never went back to Confession.

The following stories are about two penitents who were reluctantly given absolution. Both women still go to Confession at least
once a year, and consider themselves practicing Catholics—despite
the uncharitable acts of their confessors.

Gina, a twenty-eight-year-old designer who lives in Rome, was
married in New York last year.

When I went to confess in New York, prior to my marriage, I just walked into a church around the corner and somehow I got a Polish confessor. I could tell by his accent. He was so shocked that I had not confessed in six years that he almost didn't want to hear my confession or even give me absolution. I had to beg him. I said, "Look, I want to get married and I want to go through the Sacrament." He gave me a hard time, but he finally gave me absolution.

Afterward I started feeling very upset. I was trying to come back to the Church in a formal way, and this man was doing his best to keep me away. I hoped he wasn't typical of confessors in America. He almost made me walk out forever.

Grace, a sixty-five-year-old Worcester, Massachusetts, grandmother, is still furious at a priest's intransigence.

When I was in my twenties, I had an experience with a priest that really rocked me, but luckily I didn't let it drive me away from the Church. I won't mention any names because that particular monsignor is long dead. I remember trudging through the snow in the dead of winter to go to Confession, and he wouldn't give me absolution. You know why? Because I hadn't been to Confession for a year. I was so angry when I got home. My sister calmed me down and sent me to another priest who gave me absolution right away. This other priest told me that the monsignor probably had a lot on his mind. Maybe he did, but I'm still wondering, after all these years, what would have happened if I'd been killed in an accident between those two confessions. Because of that man, I could be in Hell.

Many people complained not only about what the priest said, but also about the way in which he said it. Whether inadvertently or purposely, many confessors cause their penitents great embarrassment.

Penitents on Priests

Marvin, a forty-six-year-old Forth Worth, Texas, accountant, recalls his teenage confessions:

> The thing I hated about Confession was that my priest would attack me right there in the confessional, and the son of a bitch would scream so loud all the other people in line could hear him.
> Everybody tells you that what you say to a priest is totally private. You can torture him and he won't talk—except when you tell him you're screwing around with one of the girls in the parish. Then he gets so mad the whole church can hear. "Why can't you keep your hands off good clean Catholic girls," he said. I always wanted to ask him if Jesus wanted me to sleep around with only Jews and Protestants, but I never had the nerve.

Denise, a thirty-five-year-old Los Angeles tennis pro, relates her mother's experiences:

> My mother used to tell me stories about her childhood. All the parishes were ethnic; German, Irish, Polish. She was in a German one and those priests were so authoritarian. She told me that once she went into the confessional and told a priest she'd been to the carnival and consulted a fortune teller. In his broken accent, he shouted at her at the top of his voice, "You silly thing, you silly thing, why did you do that?" Everyone in line heard him yell, and she was so embarrassed to face them as she came out because they were all wondering what kind of silly thing she did.

David, a thirty-four-year-old New York taxi driver, is cavalier about his own language but not about his priest.

> The language used by a priest in Confession when I was in Navy boot camp really pissed me off. I hadn't done anything serious so I made up some things. I mean, you don't go to Confession and say, "Father, I'm clean." So I made up a half-truth, a little exaggeration about something that had to do with a young lady.

I started my confession and said, "Father, this girl and I . . ." and he said, "Yes, I know," and took it from there. He just went on and on, in graphic sexual detail, about what he assumed we did. He wanted to know everything from start to finish and kept prodding me with details from his own imagination. Was I taken aback! I went along with it, but boy, was I shocked to hear that kind of language coming from a priest. Maybe it was because he was a Navy chaplain.

Many claimed that their penances had no relation to their sins and guilts but were merely meaningless assignments meted out in assembly line fashion.

George, a sixty-seven-year-old retired police lieutenant living in Atlanta, remembers his penances ruefully:

The penances were a joke. Ten Hail Marys for committing a sin that I thought was monumental. I remember Father Callaghan very clearly. He always gave me the same penance. Whether I had impure thoughts all week or threw my sister down the stairs, it was always the same. Why didn't he tell me to do something worthwhile, like visiting old people in the hospital or spending time with handicapped kids? Lots of times I wanted to talk to him about my penance, but he never let me get a word in. He'd just give me penance and kick me out of the confessional. I used to get so angry and frustrated.

A priest who breaks the inviolate Seal of Confession is beyond the pale. Church law dictates excommunication for the offense, but there have been circumstances under which the law has not been carried out. Angela, a fifty-six-year-old dressmaker born in Seville and currently living in Philadelphia, recalls the dangers of confessing to the wrong priest during the fearful days of the Spanish Civil War:

Those were dreadful times in every part of Spain, and the Church played a part. You'd see a good man being marched off to be shot and you'd ask what he had done. Somebody would comment that his wife went to Mass. The rumor was that his wife had denounced him as a Red to the priest in Confession. It was common for men to get caught through denunciations in the confessional. I remember clearly the priest asking us in Confession if our fathers or their friends were on the right or the left. Going to Mass suddenly made you suspicious.

Alfredo, a thirty-eight-year-old photographer born in Madrid and now living in Washington, D.C., feels his confessor broke the spirit rather than the letter of the Seal.

I am a homosexual. I started to play sexually very early, maybe seven or eight. Those boyfriends of our maids were so handsome, I followed them all over the place. Then I'd have to confess. But I enjoyed my sins so much I'd do them again, so I'd confess again and commit them again. The priest, sometimes he asked me how I did it? Did he touch you? Did you touch him? Then he asked me how many times. He wanted all the details. Then he told me not to do it again. I don't think he was shocked. He was probably used to it.

My last confession was to a priest who was very influential and was once a military man. I told him about my homosexuality and he asked where I went to meet people. I told him we went to the main bull ring at night because it was dark. And guess what?—one week later, a crew came and put lights in the place. I connected it with my confession. The priest didn't have to reveal my confession, all he had to say was, "I want lights put there." So he didn't actually break the rule, but he certainly bent it.

Jason, the thirty-three-year-old owner of a Washington, D.C., carwash, was so devastated by a careless priest that he didn't return to the Sacrament until he was about to be married.

When I was thirteen, a priest who had been a longtime friend of the family destroyed my entire confidence in him and in the Church. I confessed something to him that was troubling me a lot, something I'd done that I really felt horrible about.

A few days later, a bunch of us were playing baseball and he drove by in the car. He stopped, got out and said, in front of all the guys, "Keeping your nose out of trouble, are ya' Jason?" Then he went on to elaborate with an example or two. Fortunately, none of the guys understood what he was saying, but I was so embarrassed I ran home crying all the way. The priest left the Church soon afterward. I think he was fired. His own sins must have caught up with him somewhere along the line.

Many people criticized confessors for their inability or refusal to give counseling and spiritual direction. Norman, a thirty-seven-year-old Los Angeles film location manager, spent his teenage years in parochial boarding schools. He, like many others, recalls the priests who were insensitive to his sexual anxieties:

At school there was never any understanding from my confessor about the important sexual things. Impure thoughts, impure actions, they were just driving me crazy. I had a Polish priest who kept making fun of my sexual confessions. He'd go "tsk, tsk, tsk," every time I said something that I thought was important. As I look back now, I was confused as hell and he was really doing a number on me. What a vindictive thing to do to a kid in school.

Janet, a thirty-six-year-old Boston college professor, had problems far more desperate than impure thoughts.

I remember going to a priest in my early twenties when I wanted to commit suicide. He just wasn't equipped to deal with deeper philosophical and psychological problems. He was equipped only to give axioms and penance.

It was very disappointing, because in my romantic way I pictured the priest as the one person who could help me out of my quandary. But all he said was that it would be a mortal sin to take my own life. Now isn't that the stupidest thing to say? As if that would deter someone desperate enough to commit suicide! All he could think about was sin. He didn't even begin to realize I'd come to him for help, not forgiveness. It took about eight months of severe depression, and eventually I came out of it—no thanks to the priest. Maybe a psychiatrist would have helped.

Some of the men and women interviewed said that when they'd become disenchanted with their confessors, they'd turned to psychiatrists. If the priest wasn't going to relieve their guilt, perhaps the psychiatrist could explain it.

Sharon, a twenty-five-year-old reformed drug addict from Washington, D.C., is currently enrolled in an adult retraining program and hopes to be come a hairdresser. She talks about her priest and her psychiatrist:

How can three minutes in a box talking to a priest who doesn't know who I am do me any good? It's not helping me to change my behavior. I've been seeing a shrink for the past year. I finally have a better understanding of myself and I'm beginning to change my life. Priests never helped me do that. All they kept telling me was that I was committing all these so-called sins. Well, I knew I was doing that because I was telling him first! All I ever got was penance. Three Hail Marys and three Our Fathers. You're forgiven, back on the street and don't do it again. The other thing I hated about my priest was that everything was my fault because I didn't love God enough. Well, the reason I took drugs in the first place was because the priest and the Church made me feel like such a piece of worthless scum. That's what the shrink said anyway.

Juan, thirty-three, a recent immigrant from Ecquador currently working on his doctorate in computer science in Houston, compares his former confessor and his current psychiatrist:

> My priest never had the training that my psychiatrist has. His point of view was one-sided. What else could it be since he lived such a sheltered life. He might have been an expert on the spiritual, but certainly not on things in real life.
>
> My psychiatrist opens me up. I go to him out of an awareness that I want to change, to grow. My priest never allowed me to do that. He always treated me like a child, even after I was married, even after our first baby was born.

On the other hand, many Catholics, both lapsed and practicing, argued that a psychiatrist was not and would never be a substitute for sacramental confession.

Tom, a fifty-five-year-old Chicago art director, explains his preference:

> Confession conjures up a whole mystical, religious cosmic thing. You get absolution and grace. It's high drama in the box. Psychiatry is, well, you pay some guy fifty bucks and he sits there and listens to you and gives you some suggestions.

Joan, a forty-seven-year-old Philadelphia housewife, recalled the words of her uncle:

> He was a priest and he used to tell me how important it was for people to get things off their chests. He said Confession was just that. The best thing the Church ever got into. He said psychiatry was an expensive way of getting something off your chest, and Confession let you do it for free.

A few penitents realized that they were as responsible as their priests for the failure or success of their sacramental encounters.

Penitents on Priests

Some penitents, trained in a childlike consciousness of Confession, approached the Sacrament as indifferently as the priests they criticized. Others harbored unreasonable expectations, demanding from their confessors a sophistication of counseling that only a professional can provide.

Many men and women who renounced the Sacrament were unaware of what they could say to the priest in the confessional. "I didn't even know you could talk to the guy, other than just rattling off your sins," explained a fifty-year-old Detroit lawyer who left the Church in the fifties. "I never thought of shopping for a confessor," said another lapsed Catholic in his fifties. "I just took whoever was around and figured he'd be okay."

The people who were satisfied with their experience of the Sacrament had made the effort to find a confessor who they felt was responsive to their spiritual—and sometimes personal—needs. But for many the successful administration of the Sacrament required the involvement of both priest and penitent. As a sixty-eight-year-old retired New York doctor aptly sums up, "You never get out, unless you put out. If you want God's grace, then you're going to have to do something about it. It's as much your responsibility as the priest's."

Chapter 13
Women and Confession

"There cannot be the slightest doubt that hearing the confessions of women is the most dangerous and fatal rock which the minister of God has to encounter in the stormy sea of this world. Pray to God to preserve him in that state of indifference and insensibility."

These words, taken from *The New Parish Priests' Practical Manual*, published in 1883, crystallize the Church's 2,000 year history of regarding women as occasions of sin. The Church traces its condemnation directly to Eve.

Tertullian, in the third century, claimed, "Woman should dress as Eve, mourning and repentant, that by every garb of penitence, she might the more fully expiate that which she derives from Eve —the ignominy of the first sin, and the odium of human perdition. And do you not know that you are each an Eve? The sentence of

235

God on this sex of yours lives in this age: the guilt must of necessity live too."

Twelve hundred years later, St. Charles Borromeo devised the confessional to maintain the decorum of the Sacrament by separating the priest from his female penitent. Four hundred years later, Pope John XXIII wrote in his diary at the age of fourteen, "With women of any kind, be they even relatives, or saintly, I shall be especially careful, fleeing from their friendship, their companionship or their conversation, especially if they are young. Nor will I ever look them in the face, remembering what is taught by the Holy Spirit, 'Let not thy eyes linger on a maid unwed whose very beauty may take thee unawares' " (Ecclesiastes 9:15).

In the following pages, women, the majority over thirty-five, all products of the pre-Vatican II Church, describe their confessions and confessors. Their stories vary. There is no consensus. There is, however, a recurring question. If a woman is, *a priori*, regarded as an occasion of sin by her priest, can she receive the same treatment as a male penitent, especially when confessing sins of a sexual nature?

Many of the women interviewed stated that, as teenagers, confessing their sexual sins to a priest caused them a great deal of embarrassment. Some had little trust in their confessor, fearing he would divulge their secrets to their parents. More important, many believed that a celibate male could never understand their sexual anxieties. Some wished that their priest had been a woman.

Gloria, a forty-seven-year-old secretary from Detroit, believed her impure desires would shock her pristine male confessor.

> I've often thought that if the person sitting in the confessional were a woman, I might have been more honest, especially when my problems were of a sexual nature. As a teenager, sex really kept me from going to Confession. I could never say those things to a man because I felt too embarrassed and guilty at the same time. I had all these urges to experiment with men, but I just didn't know what to do about it.

Women and Confession

The late fifties in a close-knit Catholic community wasn't the time or place for a nice Catholic girl to sow her wild oats. When I was twenty-one, just after I graduated from college, I ran away to Europe for the summer and slept with so many men I lost count. When I returned I was consumed with guilt, but how could I confess my sexual escapades to a priest who knew my parents and had known me since I was born? I never said a word about any of it. Fortunately, I had a very close girl friend who was going through the same kind of sexual experimentation that I was. We became confessors to each other, every Sunday afternoon. We never gave each other absolution, but we sure gave each other a lot of love and support.

Whenever she went to confess, Alexandra, a thirty-seven-year-old Los Angeles mother of three, couldn't get the words out. Soon, the inability to voice her sexual anxiety to the male priest kept her away from the confessional entirely.

In my teens I met a boy who was a Catholic, and a relationship developed. It was really pretty pure because at that time I thought petting—anything below the neck but above the waist—was pretty racy stuff. Lots of times I really wanted to go further, even all the way, as we used to say, but I could never confess these things to a priest. I mean, how can you tell a priest you've got these evil desires which turn out to be very normal after all? If the priest were a woman, I know I would have confessed.

Carmen, a sixty-two-year-old cosmetician, currently living in New York, grew up in Spain during the thirties. She recalled that her parish priest represented terror both in and out of the confessional:

My confessions during my youth were terrible because I knew the priest spoke to my father, and if I didn't go on Saturdays, he went to him immediately. All through my youth the priest was a dictator in my village. In church we

237

had to have sleeves to the wrist even in midsummer, and the girls couldn't wear makeup. He used to close down the dances. If a few friends got together to play records, he put an end to it. In the movies, fiancés could not sit together.

My youth during that postwar period was terrible because of him. If a girl confessed she kissed a boy, *Madre Mia!* You couldn't even imagine it. That was the first thing he asked, whether you went with boys. He made the town an unnatural place, an unhappy place. That was why I left Spain. I was only twenty.

Lina is a forty-seven-year-old housewife, born in Italy, at present living in Atlanta. She speaks softly when describing the sexual advice given her by the priest in her native Milan:

A priest in Confession told me many years ago, before I was about to be married, that I must submit to everything my husband demanded of me sexually. He also said that my husband had absolute rights over my body and that if I didn't do everything my husband demanded, he might begin to wander elsewhere for his sexual gratifications and that I would be to blame. We've been married for twenty-six years, have five children and I've done everything my husband ever wanted, everything the priest ever wanted, and I still never felt that I satisfied either one of them.

In the confessional women frequently have to choose between lovers and absolution. Doris, an unmarried forty-six-year-old public school teacher in Washington, D.C., blames a priest for her loneliness today.

I was engaged when I was twenty-six. At that time, twenty years ago, I went to Confession and the priest said that the kisses between engaged people are not a sin, so long as they don't last long. He also warned me that kisses on the mouth were unhygienic and capable of evoking animalistic instincts. As for caressing, the priest said it wasn't a sin

either, as long as we didn't get excited. He told me that
if I had sexual relations with my fiancé, I would lose the
grace of God.

I told all this to Bernard, my fiancé, who prided himself
on being a lapsed Catholic. He said if I ever went back to
the priest or any priest for that matter, he would never
marry me.

In all my life, I never had so many sleepless nights. I
realized that I had to choose between my fiancé and my
church. I never married Bernard, and when I consider
how lonely I sometimes get, I wish that priest would have
been a little more understanding.

Erica, a forty-two-year-old woman from New Haven, listened to
her instincts rather than the words of her confessor, and hasn't
regretted it for a moment.

When I was forty years old, I was intimate with a man for
the first time in my life, and shortly after, I swore I would
never set foot in a church or a confessional again. To tell
the truth, I've mellowed a bit since then. I've been to Mass
several times, but I won't go to Confession or take Communion.

I'm a librarian, not exactly the old-maid kind with the
bun and glasses, but there are some similarities. I'm an
only child, very shy and have spent most of my life being
quiet. My father died when I was twenty-two, and I lived
with my mother until I was thirty-seven. When she had a
stroke five years ago, I put her in a nursing home. She's
totally paralyzed now and has difficulty recognizing me.

I never felt comfortable with men, probably because I
had always been taught by the nuns that sex was something that women endured in the name of Our Lord for
procreation. I was such a good little Catholic girl, so fearful of committing any sins, that I never dared to discover
for myself what sex was all about.

Two years ago, I met a man. I feel a bit embarrassed to

239

tell you about it because it reads like a romance novel you buy at the supermarket. Howard is an accountant, transferred here from California. Every week, Wednesdays at noon, he'd come in to the library to browse, and we'd talk. One day he asked me to have lunch with him and then he asked me to meet him after work for a bite to eat and a movie. Before I knew it, I was meeting him regularly and really enjoying it.

For the first time in my life, I wanted to be with a man. I realized the loneliness I'd been suffering all my life. It wasn't that I thought of Howard as my last chance—I thought of him as the right chance.

So, like a nice Catholic girl, I went to the priest I'd known all my life and told him all about Howard—fifty-four, a non-Catholic, separated from his wife who still lived in California with his twin daughters, one married, the other engaged. I told him Howard was responsible, caring and had a corny sense of humor I loved. We wanted to live together. Perhaps we'd get married when he got his divorce, perhaps not.

When I told the priest how lonely we both were, he reminded me of the suffering of Christ and the everlasting fires of Hell. I told him that before I met Howard, I was living in Hell and left the confessional immediately. It's been two years, and thank God, Howard and I are still together and very much in love.

Many women criticized the Church's whore /Madonna attitude. Since a woman is either someone's mother or a tramp, it behooves her to keep herself barefoot and pregnant, or at least pregnant. St. Augustine claimed that woman's purpose was to bring forth children and tend to the men as they got older.

Rosita, a forty-one-year-old actress who has been living in Los Angeles for the past ten years, tells about the priests in her native Barcelona:

Women and Confession

In school, they always told me that to be a virgin was better than anything else, but there was my mother. I love my mother and she has eight children. She is a beautiful person. But the priest tells me in Confession that virginity is better. What is he talking about? His mother wasn't a virgin. What a problem they had with the Virgin Mother!

Carmella, a thirty-seven-year-old New York advertising executive of Italian descent, suffered from this same hypocrisy.

If the Church thought that Confession worked like a cold shower, it was wrong. I could never make that man in the box understand that, although I was a good Catholic girl, I had sexual needs that made me feel like a cat on a hot tin roof. According to the Church, I wasn't supposed to get those needs until I was married, and probably not then either. If a single Italian girl isn't the Blessed Virgin she must be a whore. There's no middle ground.

I was never promiscuous, but for about a year I hit the singles bar scene. There were some nights I thought I'd never get through alone, without a body beside me, and on those nights I found someone.

Afterward I'd confess because I knew, down deep, it was wrong, and didn't want to do it. Some priests talked to me as if I were a common prostitute. Others wanted to hear the tackiest details of my sexual activities. A few were nice, but when they spoke of sexual desires, they made it clear that only men were allowed to have them, and there was something wrong with me. That's when I decided the Church should allow women to become priests. It would be wonderful to confess my sexual sins to someone who understood and cared.

The probing priest who wants to know the intimate details of a woman's sexual life is a source of embarrassment and irritation to many female penitents. Such priests became part of Catholic folklore as they leeringly inquired, "Tell me how many times, my daughter . . ."

Some women rebelled at being forced to describe and enumerate those special moments shared with husbands or lovers. They argued that probing is an invasion of privacy and an assault on their dignity. Others were timid and, in reverence to their priests, dutifully answered all questions.

Lorraine, a devout forty-seven-year-old mother of five living in Orlando, Florida, recalls a confession that took place twenty years ago:

> All you have to do is go to a bad priest once, and he can turn you off Confession for life—and scare the hell out of you as well. Fortunately, I have a very strong faith.
>
> When I was twenty-seven, I went to an old priest to confess. I told him all my sins and then, instead of giving me a penance, he started questioning me about sex. I could have told him I'd murdered my mother, but all he wanted to know about was if I had sex, and how and how often. I resisted but he said, "I have to know. How many times a week? With the same guy? A different guy every night? Do you perform any unnatural acts? Describe them." That was the first time in my life I almost told a priest off. I kept thinking of the penitent who hasn't been to Confession for years and winds up with this priest. Afterwards, I came out feeling terribly dirty. In fact, it was the first time in my life that I didn't feel totally cleansed after Confession. I felt as if I should go home and shower for five hours.

Cheryl, a thirty-nine-year-old divorced Chicago saleswoman, describes herself as a lapsed Catholic and blames the state of her faith upon a priest in the confessional fifteen years ago.

> When I was twenty-four, I married a Protestant and a Justice of the Peace performed the ceremony because the Catholic priest at the university wouldn't. He said he

wouldn't carry the burden of my soul on his shoulders. Six months later, I got married again, in the Church by my brother who was a priest, but for the six months before I was technically living in mortal sin.

A few months after my marriage by the Justice of the Peace, I was going to be a bridesmaid at my girl friend's wedding, and she wanted all the wedding party to go to Mass and Communion together. Well, in those days, I didn't dare go to Communion in a state of sin because I knew I'd be sucked into the depths of Hell. So I went to a large downtown Church called St. John's. There were always crowds of people there, and I felt better about that. I wasn't looking forward to confessing I'd been living in sin for two months. The line was long and suddenly a priest came down the aisle, pointed to me with his finger and told me to get into the new line he was forming. I could have said no and told the person in back of me to go first, but I was frightened because the priest pointed his finger at me. It was like the finger of God.

Right off the bat, I said I had been married by a Justice of the Peace and was technically living in sin. He asked for how long and wanted to know how many times I'd for-nicated with this man. All he kept asking me was how many times I had been with this man sexually. He was reducing my young love, my romance and my marriage to the number of times we'd slept together.

He said I had to stay in the confessional until I gave him a number. The tears were rolling down my face, and the sobbing was getting louder and louder. I was becoming hysterical because I couldn't come up with a number. I was trying to figure when my husband had gone away on busi-ness and when he'd come home, the priest kept mention-ing numbers and the whole time I was crying uncontrolla-bly. Finally we came up with a number. I can't remember the number now, but I remember the confession. It will stay with me forever. I went to Communion with the other bridesmaids, but after that it was all downhill for me and the Church.

Amy, a thirty-two-year-old San Francisco stockbroker and another lapsed Catholic, also blames a priest in the confessional for her loss of faith.

> The worst experience I had with Confession was right before my first marriage. I decided to go across town to another parish where I didn't know anybody and the priest wouldn't know me, because I thought it would be easier to confess a mortal sin to a stranger. After I'd told him a few sins, he asked me if there was anything else. That was when I admitted I'd been sleeping with my fiancé. He shrieked, "You wait until now to tell me! Don't you know that if I hadn't asked you, you would have gone before that altar with a black soul, and the whole Sacrament would have been canceled." He went on and on at the top of his voice. Then he gave me twenty-five Our Fathers and twenty-five Hail Marys, but said they weren't nearly enough for the terrible thing I'd almost done. He didn't prepare me for the Sacrament of Marriage, but he did ruin the wedding for me.

Some women believe that the younger the priest, the more liberal his attitude. Andrea, a recently divorced forty-two-year-Chicago advertising executive, was one of these. She, and many others, were proven wrong.

> After I got my annulment from the Church five years ago I went on a retreat where I confessed face-to-face with the priest. It was my first time out of the box, as well as my first time with a priest who appeared young enough to be my son. He said to me, "You do understand don't you, young lady, that you now have to conduct yourself like an unmarried woman again." And I asked how the Church could come so far as to annul marriages and have confessions face-to-face, and then be so narrow-mined about something so important. I was thirty-seven

years old, I had been married for twenty years, I had four children, and this priest who looked as though he wasn't even old enough to shave was telling me that I had to go back to being celibate. That was the last time I ever went to Confession.

Many women felt there was a conspiracy among confessors to keep them single and pure, or married and pregnant, with no option in between.

Evelyn, a thirty-five-year-old secretary from Austin, Texas, who was married at seventeen, remembers:

> I think that to hurt someone deliberately is a mortal sin, but I didn't think it was a mortal sin to go to bed with a guy I'd been dating for two years. And I had been going out with Jack for almost two years before we started to sleep together. We wanted to be sure about each other before we got married.
>
> When I confessed my sexual relationship to my priest, he became angry. He said I was threatening my immortal soul with everlasting punishment and the only way to save myself was to get married right away. So we did, and had three kids in five years. I think I did the right thing, but sometimes when the kids get on my nerves, I keep thinking that the only reason I got married was to save my soul from Hell, or so the priest said. Is that enough reason to get married these days? Maybe I was born twenty years too early?

Lydia, a thirty-six-year-old single nursery school teacher from Providence, Rhode Island, is angry with the Church and with her mother.

> My mother and the priest are still furious because I slept with a man before I was married. I was twenty-eight at the time. I'm thirty-six now. What happens if I'm sixty-five and still not married? Nobody thinks of that. Nobody thinks of me! They only think of God and the Church and the neighbors.

245

The advice some confessors gave to their female penitents was occasionally harmful to their marriage.

Loretta, a fifty-seven-year-old woman from Nashville, showed us the pictures of her five children while lamenting the words of her parish priest many years ago:

> Before I was about to be married, my priest told me in Confession that it was a sin if I took the initiative in love-making with my husband. I never did, and I often wonder if that was one of the reasons Jack left me ten years ago. Jack and I never talked about sex because the priest said that even bringing up the subject for discussion was a sin. Did I do wrong? The priest says no, but now Jack is living with a woman half his age, and I'm alone.

Joan, a forty-five-year-old Boston waitress, feels more anger than regret about priests' inability to understand female sexuality. She declared:

> Because of Confession and all those priests and all that guilt, I didn't have a goddamn orgasm until I was thirty-nine!

The following two women have committed adultery. The reactions from their priests had a great influence on their future confessions as well as their relationships with the Church and their lovers.

Ann, a forty-three-year-old lab technician from Baltimore, explains:

> I went to an Irish priest when I was going through a bad patch in my relationship with my boyfriend. I was getting bitter about the affair. I thought my soul was blackened, and I was taking it out on other people. I tried to explain to the priest that I was angry with my boyfriend, with the world and with God. He asked me why I didn't marry the man, and I explained he'd been married before and had a grownup son. He didn't want to go through all that again. The priest said that if he'd been married, he still

246

was married, and that I was committing adultery. I almost keeled over. That was the last time I went to Confession because suddenly the priest made me an adulteress.

Cathy, a thirty-five-year-old Tucson, Arizona, saleswoman, praises her priest for taking her seriously and treating her like an adult:

A year ago I was having a bad time with my conscience because I was having an affair with a married man. A friend recommended I confess to a certain priest, and it was the best thing I ever did. As soon as I confessed, he said, "I'm human too," and made me feel so at ease. He had been an alcoholic and could see past the strict Catholic laws. He explained that I had to deal with my conscience as well as the Church. "The reason you're so uncomfortable with yourself is because what you're doing is not right for you." And he was right because I'd always believed that you can destroy a whole family by committing adultery. That's why my affair was the hardest thing for me to confess.

The priest never told me to stop seeing the man, he just asked me if I thought it was right. I admitted that if I thought it was right, I wouldn't be in the confessional. He said, "I can't tell you what to do, but if you keep it up you'll just feel worse. You've got to decide for yourself. But if that marriage breaks up, can you really live with yourself knowing that you were responsible for it?" The affair was over the moment I walked out of that confessional.

On Birth Control and Abortion

Birth control is one of the thorniest problems facing the Church today. For the conservative confessor, the answer is simply no. For others, the issue is more complex.

To circumvent the wrath of the traditional priest, as well as to relieve their own guilt, many women on the Pill resort to ingenious rationalizations. Lise, a thirty-three-year-old Houston, Texas, secretary, rationalizes the Pill as follows:

> Every month, before I begin a new cycle of pills, I confess that it's absolutely necessary that I regulate my menstrual cycles. By telling the priest that, we never have to deal with the sin of birth control.

Adelle, a forty-five-year-old Atlanta housewife, was prepared to go on the Pill regardless of what her confessor said. His approval, however, meant a great deal to her.

> When my fourth child had been born, I didn't want any more children. My priest told me categorically that I couldn't take birth control pills. So I went to another priest, from Holland, real "old school." I was about thirty and scared to go in and ask him if I could use birth control pills. This priest also disapproved of the Pill and told me I should use the rhythm method. I told him that was how I'd conceived the last two. He finally gave me permission to use the Pill by rationalizing that the rhythm did not work for me and I had had all the children I could physically, emotionally and financially handle.
>
> I think he knew I was going to take them anyway. But he did tell me not to tell anybody he said I could take them. He was so concerned about that he made me promise.

When Brenda began to speak of the grandmother she never knew, she became enraged. The forty-year-old computer programmer from Denver recounts a story similar to those told by many others:

> My father didn't go to Confession. I only learned why when I was in my twenties. My father's mother died when he was ten. She died in childbirth. And she died in childbirth because the doctor had told her she should not have

another baby but the priest in Confession had told her he would not give her absolution if she did anything artificial not to have one.

My husband and I decided that we would use birth control devices from the day we got married. And we never felt a pang of guilt.

Jennifer, a thirty-five-year-old Kansas City mother of two, has been on and off the Pill for over eight years. Whether it was semantics or sympathy, she came away from her confessional experience with her dignity and faith intact.

The most sympathetic priest I ever met was a Jesuit. He was sensitive because he accommodated me rather than having me accommodate the Church. He was a university chaplain.

I had been reticent to go to Confession because I didn't want to be harassed about birth control. I had made friends with this priest previously, and I suspected I could go to him and confess as a person, not just an anonymous body in the box. I told him I wasn't confessing birth control, but I wanted a clarification of the issue because I didn't think it was a sin. He said I had an "erroneous conscience" and explained that that means a Catholic is doing something which is conceivably a sin, but not in her own heart. It was as simple as that.

While some women rationalized their use of birth control, others went shopping for a priest who would support their views. Eleanor, a forty-five-year-old Boston public-relations consultant, chose the latter path. She had to if she wanted to save her marriage.

After I gave birth to my third child in six years, I went to see our family priest to talk about the Pill. And right there, in the same confessional I've been going to all my life, he said that it would be a mortal sin every time I put a Pill in my mouth. So I didn't take it. It was especially awful because I couldn't discuss it with my husband because he'd refused to have anything to do with the Church a long time ago.

The only choice I had was to avoid making love. One night when he was on the verge of practically raping me, I told him the truth about the priest and the Pill. He said that if I wanted to save our marriage, I'd better find a pro-Pill priest. That was eighteen years ago. Liberal priests were rare.

I didn't know how to find an obliging priest except by going to Confession. The following Saturday, I went to the nearest parish and confessed to the first available priest. He forbade the Pill and refused to discuss the subject any further. I went to four priests that afternoon—people must have thought I was crazy—and not one showed any understanding. One priest said that taking the Pill was like pouring sulphuric acid down Our Savior's throat.

During the next few months, I spoke with fifteen different priests in five parishes before I found one who assured me that God would understand and forgive me. This priest only insisted that I never make public what I was doing.

While some priests are becoming more liberal regarding birth control, the Church's position regarding abortion stands firm. Abortion is murder. The following two women approached their priests from opposite directions. One had already had an abortion, while the other was contemplating one.

Randy, a thirty-year-old high school drop-out from Washington, D.C., had spent most of her early life in foster homes. She explained that she had had an abortion at age eighteen which she confessed to a priest. The following year, she took her younger sister to the same priest to confess the same sin.

I did find a good priest once who helped me when I felt terrible after my abortion. He wasn't mean or anything. Just very nice. He said it was a bad thing, but that everything could be forgiven. That made me feel better, but at the same time he let me know that it was wrong. You want to know when you're wrong. Grownups need that too, not just kids.

Joyce, a forty-five-year-old Denver housewife, speaks glowingly about a priest who helped her to make her own decision:

> When I found out I was pregnant with my fourth, I considered abortion, but it was a bit late. My husband and even my mother thought it was the right thing to do. I wasn't sure so I went to Confession. The priest told me he had a lot of experience with women and abortion. He said if I were able to have the child and could cope with it, the Church's position was that it would be wrong to go through with the abortion.
>
> He was very understanding, and he wasn't dogmatic; he didn't say I shouldn't do it. He said that was the Church's official position, but I had to examine my own thoughts because I had to live with my own decisions. He gave me some histories of women who'd had a hard time after abortions because they'd made the wrong decision. I think he was giving me a way to discover my feelings. I came away satisfied. He'd tried to sway me from having an abortion, but he never mentioned the word sin. I didn't have an abortion. In fact, I gave birth to twin girls—wonderful, healthy children.

Yesterday and Today

An early twentieth-century guide for confessors entitled "Theory and Practice of the Confessional," offers an example of the type of training a priest would have received more than seventy years ago:

> The confessor must not be overready to believe the complaints of wives about their husbands. But if he finds the complaints are justified, he will tell the woman how to act and gravely comfort her. If she complains of the severity

and bad temper of her husband, he must advise her to remain patient and obedient to him, to perform every service which he desires, to show her love for him by the greatest willingness and kindness, to be silent when her husband is angry or intoxicated, not to drive him to greater violence even when she suffers injustice, and admonish him affectionately when he has become calm and sober and good-natured, but not until then.

Another guide for confessors gave the following advice regarding the confessions of women:

. . . Moreover, it is the greatest importance to keep these devout penitents very simple-minded and humble because there is no accounting for the freaks of female levity. They easily yield to temptations of vanity, suffer themselves to become the victims of delusion and stray from the right path.

Today most priests do not subscribed to the teachings cited above, though some older priests have undoubtedly been influenced by these prejudices and assumptions. Nonetheless, the influence of the Second Vatican Council, the changing role of women in society and the emergence of well-educated, liberal sisters have all contributed to the way most priests relate to women in and out of the confessional.

As John XXIII wrote in *Pacem in Terris,* in 1963, "Since women are becoming ever more conscious of their human dignity, they will not tolerate being treated as mere material instruments, but demand rights befitting a human person both in domestic and in public life."

The painful encounters recalled in these pages still occasionally take place whenever a woman encounters a dogmatic, chauvinistic confessor. But as society and the Church continue to change their attitude toward women, one can hope these tales will fade into history.

Chapter 14

First Confession Today

For almost seventy-five years children have made their First Confession before their First Communion, at the average age of seven. Traditionalists claim early initiation into the Sacrament helps develop disciplined and devout Catholic adults. Today Church liberals maintain that the Eucharist, the Sacrament of love, and not Confession, is the healthiest way to introduce children to the Church. As a result, many Catholic youngsters are now making their First Confession at the average age of nine, two or three years after their First Communion. Although this reversal of the sacramental order pleases many parents and priests, the Vatican refuses to formalize the change.

Monsignor George Kelly writes in *The Battle for the American Church:*

Bless Me, Father, For I Have Sinned

Rarely has a conflict in the American Church been so trifling, yet diverse, as the one over making children go to Confession before they make their first Holy Communion. Family spats over eight-year-olds seems inanity for a Church in turmoil on more serious counts, yet if anger is a measure of seriousness, then this battle between Rome and professional catechists in the United States is not a small skirmish.

Father Hart, a thirty-year-old Wilmington, Delaware, priest, feels that many kids come to First Confession in a state of confusion because their parents have mixed up discipline with sin.

Lots of kids, even at six or seven years of age, are in conflict with their parents. I remember a little girl in First Confession who told me that she sucked her thumb and that it was a serious sin because her mother told her so. "That's not a sin," I explained as gently as I could. "It might be bad for your teeth, but it's definitely not a sin."

Father O'Brien, a forty-five-year-old Los Angeles priest, also favors First Confession at a later age.

What's happening is that we're forcing kids to go take the Sacrament when they're not ready for it. A brief examination of conscience and the teacher traipses them down to confess, one after the other, like little parrots.

Father McMillan, who has been hearing children's confessions in his Toronto parish for the past forty-five years is in favor of the change.

What sins can a seven-year-old commit? I've got a problem with First Confessions when they're from children that young. Most priests do. The kids are still too immature and you've got to explain over and over what a sin is.

Father Henreid, thirty-one, a parish priest in Detroit, Michigan, introduces First Confessions in his own way:

First Confession Today

When teaching children about Reconciliation today, I start with the goodness of the love of God, how much He cherishes us and how much He wants us to be happy. I explain sin is not just an action, the things we do and say, but sometimes the things we think about doing or saying. A sin for kids would be not living up to their potential. Sin is relational too because it affects our relationships with friends and parents. I set up mock confessions, and we do a lot of role-playing.

Kids here have First Communion about two years before First Confession, although that varies from parish to parish. I don't know any parishes in this area where First Confession precedes First Communion. It all depends on the pastor, though guidelines are given by the diocese. I defend this order wholeheartedly because the child is establishing a relationship with God, making Jesus rather than guilt his friend.

The bishop said in a letter that, "Children should be familiar with the Sacraments when they are making their First Communion." So we'll make them familiar. If parents demand that their kid makes First Confession before First Communion, I'll sit down with the kid and have a little chat. If he tells me something that matters, we'll call it of a sinful nature, I'll give him absolution. But if there's nothing there, I'll just send the kid away with a blessing. This way everybody's happy.

First Confession with kids today is entirely face-to-face. Though they're intrigued by the box, its dark, exotic mystery, I don't use it. I can't reach out and get close to the kids, and it doesn't lead to real communication. I never ask them the number of times they did something. It discourages them. Their parents may want them to confess that way, but I don't. And I never talk to them about Heaven, Hell or Purgatory in reconciliation. I focus in on the immediacy of their lives rather than the fear of judgment or the pearly gates. I won't have the kids entrusted to me worrying about burning in Hell. I want them to love God, not fear him.

Father Amerty, thirty-three, discusses how First Confession is handled in his Washington, D.C., parish:

> At the Cathedral, the kids have a choice of the box or face-to-face, but most priests prefer face-to-face because you can hold the kids' hands, and really talk to them. There are also priests at the back to hear the parents' confessions, so it becomes an experience that the whole family can share. Most priests are trying to introduce the habit of going to Confession often and, therefore, we want to make it as light and airy as possible.

Estelle, a fifty-six-year-old New York lawyer, takes a similar approach:

> I made my First Confession when I was about seven. I now feel the whole idea of children of that age going to confess in the box is ridiculous and traumatic. I'd never send a child of mine for First Confession unless it's in a reconciliation room or General Absolution and well after First Communion.

Vera, an outspoken thirty-eight-year-old mother from Bennington, Vermont, is determined to protect her daughter from what she herself experienced many years ago.

> I won't let them have her young. I intend to delay her First Confession for as long as possible. First Confession at seven is ridiculous. I wouldn't call it First Confession anyway. I'd call it first guilt.
>
> Getting a child ready for Confession before First Communion—what you are really doing is teaching kids to feel guilty about things that are natural. Now we know from psychology that in order to grow up and grow away from parents, kids go through a normal period of resentment

toward their parents. I know from my own sons that when they rebel, it's because they have to rebel. It's the only way they'll grow up. But if you have bad thoughts about your parents and you tell them to the priest in Confession, all this becomes a serious sin in the eyes of the Church. Some things all kids say, like taking the Lord's name in vain or swearing, are only linguistic habits. How can you possibly make eight-year-old children feel guilty about that? The Church found a way.

Many Catholics still prefer the old way in all things, including early First Confessions. Maria, sixty-five, born in Italy, a resident of Miami for forty years, speaks for many of those who liked things the way they were:

> I believe it is very important that children make their First Confession when they are seven years old. From the time my kids were born, I told them that I couldn't be with them every minute to make sure that they didn't sin, but that God was always with them. He sees everything, absolutely everything. I wanted them to learn about sin and God from a very early age. I believe that if they are afraid of me and afraid of God, they won't commit sins. When they develop, from childhood, this fear of doing something wrong, then they will never do anything wrong throughout their lives.

Nine-year-old Claudia lives in a suburb of Philadelphia and made her First Communion at seven. Five days before being interviewed, she made her First Confession.

> I had my First Confession last week and I was so excited. I really looked forward to it. We had a party afterwards with cake and ginger ale. After it was over, I felt like I wanted another Confession. At the beginning, the priest took my hands, asked me if I knew that Jesus loved me, and I said, "Yes, I know that." Then I told him I usually

fight with my brother and hit him when he hits me back. I also argue with my mom sometimes, and I want to stop doing that.

I confessed at the front of the church. Everyone was there, at the back of the church. I've never been in a box. Isn't it only for people who have very, very bad sins? For my penance, Father Michael told me to say a Hail Mary and do something nice for my mom. I already did. I helped her around the house and I made her bed. After our First Confession, we all wrote letters to Father Michael thanking him for everything he did for us. When I came home, my mother had baked a cake especially for me. Later, we all went to celebrate at the Pizza Palace. Some adults say that they feel clean after Confession, but I don't know what they mean. I don't feel like a sinner or a bad person, because everybody sins, except for Jesus.

The following are some excerpts from the dozens of letters Father Michael received from his young, first-time penitents.

Thank you for spending your time with me so that I could learn more about God, Jesus and our world. I was so nervous until the whole ceremony was over.

I was very nervous about going to Confession until I knew I was only going to confess my sins.

I liked the party, the cakes and the drinks. I had a very wonderful time. You showed me that God always forgives.

Thank you for the Reconciliation. My mother made a surprise party with tacos and rhubarb crisps.

It was so much fun making our Sacrament of Reconciliation. I told my parents, and they were surprised.

The Church has drawn no conclusions about the benefits of delayed First Confession, nor have many Catholics. According to

First Confession Today

Alphonse, fifty-two, an engineer from Brooklyn, New York, it's a toss-up as far as his family goes.

> We've got eight kids. The first four were brought up the old way; the last four the new way, with the "Come to the Father" series and Confession after Communion. Don't see any difference in the kids.

Chapter 15

Reconciliation

In this chapter, both priests and penitents speak out about the Catholic Church of today. Some complain that the new post-Vatican II freedoms threaten the Church's very foundation and future; others maintain the new freedoms *are* its future.

Current changes in the Church, generally, and Confession, specifically, are driving many of the faithful to distraction. Practicing Catholics can't keep up with the liturgical and philosophical changes that began in the mid-sixties and are still going on. While many progressives applaud the new Church, others, moderates as well as conservatives, have their reservations.

A priest in his mid-fifties complains, "Today's churches are so modern I don't know whether to bring a Bible or a basketball." A mother in her thirties laments, "My kids don't even know what a

261

rosary is!" A former deacon moans, "Even the Holy Days are up for grabs."

The following people discuss the confusion which challenges their very faith in Roman Catholicism.

Lee, forty-four, a liquor store manager from Baltimore, typifies the dismay felt by many:

> It saddens me, all these radical changes in the Church. When Latin went out and they said Mass in English, it wasn't the same. Some of the medieval touches I liked, even the confessional box. They were special, mysterious, exciting. I'll tell you something, I can feel more religion watching an old Victor Mature movie than going to church today.

Francis, thirty-nine, a Denver accountant who hasn't "been inside a church in ten years," speaks as if he were recalling a dear, lost friend:

> In some ways I was happy to see the spirit emerging from all those dusty old rules and regulations, but I'm not sure it hasn't lost all the magic. My biggest regret is the disappearance of Latin. There's nothing mystical about my own language. Latin suggested the rigor and discipline we need, plus the universality of the Church. You used to be able to go to any church in the world and understand what was going on. I miss that.

Christina, forty-one, a Catholic journalist based in Baltimore, talks about being caught between the old Church and the new:

> In 1963 and 1964 the culture in which we had all been born and raised cracked up. It had died, and we were in the birth pangs of a new one. The older people remained committed to the tradition they knew and felt comfortable in. The younger ones left. These were bright people, liberal, and they left the Church the way they were leaving marriages. They'd gone out into the world, seen things

and been changed by them. But the Church hadn't changed yet, so they left it, the way they might leave a husband or wife they'd married right out of high school and outgrown.

Being Catholic since 1965 is a completely different proposition from being a Catholic when I was born. It's hard to exaggerate how different it is culturally and emotionally.

It started at birth. I was born in a hospital staffed by nuns. Nuns made all the decisions, did most of the nursing, ran the floors. There were hundreds of them. I went to a school staffed by nuns with very few lay teachers. The principal was a nun, and her boss was a nun. The layers and layers of women religious who controlled my life filled the sky as far as I could see. The year I graduated from high school, 1955, was the first year in the whole 150-year history of the school that nobody entered the convent.

Now that culture which held people so firmly and clearly is all gone. Its passing changed the way people understood the world and conceived of themselves. We're more individualistic. Today the individualism of the Protestant Reformation has penentrated the Church as well as secular culture.

Since the sixties people assume they've been brainwashed by the Church and have to break free of it to find their true selves. They turn from the religious to the secular. The secular culture doesn't send nuns to convents. It also doesn't do such a hot job of sustaining people in marriages or in other lifelong commitments. Catholics are more like everybody else now than when I was growing up.

Luke, forty-five, a Cleveland sports executive, is a practicing Catholic. He's aware of all the changes but in agreement with only some of them.

Catholics over the centuries were big on cause and effect. When you do this novena, you get this indulgence. You don't hear about things like that in the modern Church. You don't have to do as much, but you don't get as much. I think we need to get rewards from the Church, but the modern Church doesn't offer any. There are no more carrots. They hardly mention Heaven or even Hell. In Reconciliation, you don't feel you've cleared your conscience the way you used to in the old box.

Of course, there's less to confess. A lot of things that used to be sins aren't anymore. They're even demoting saints. A person has got to wonder whether he was wrong in the past or right now, or the reverse. Was the Church right all along? They've changed so many things, you can't be absolutely certain about anything.

Jennifer, a thirty-four-year-old dental hygienist from Houston, is one of those who would prefer to attend mass with the traditional dignity.

I went to a service at Easter and they had a five-piece band complete with saxophone, and they were screening the words to the hymns above the altar, like follow-the-bouncing-ball. I hated it. There wasn't ten minutes of silence in the whole ceremony. And then they got to this General Absolution thing, with all these people. To me, it's not confession, it's show biz. The whole thing is far too liberal.

Kevin, fifty-six, a U.S. Army officer based in Georgia, prefers a down-home priest as well as a downhome church.

We had a priest here a couple of years ago, really flaky, Volkswagens down the aisle at Easter, mops on his head, all fun and games. He was very antinuclear, antiwar. He drove most of the military out of the parish. He was really off the wall and very political. For me he typified the new movement. This was the first time I'd run into it head on. And if that's the new Church, you can have it. It's all going too far, too fast. There was nothing positive. No, it's worse than that. There was nothing sacred.

Terry, thirty, a New Haven university public-relations officer, had difficulty accepting the Church's new "evangelical, Protestant trimmings."

> I started going to church at college but I stopped when I realized they were into groovy Catholicism. It got on my nerves, all this love and peace bullshit, and then the General Absolution, with all those goody-two-shoes people, all together, forgiving each other's sins.

Pauline, forty-one, a Des Moines teacher, loves the changes in the Church, and wishes they were more widespread.

> I loved the Catholic Church in the sixties when I went to college. They were just introducing General Absolution and for me it was heaven. I hated confessing in the box and feeling guilty and ashamed. We had wonderful services, wonderful preachers who dealt with real issues that really touched the world. The Catholicism at college wasn't rigid. I've spent the last fifteen years of my life trying to find it again. I know it's still on the campuses of the Catholic colleges or at the Newman centers today, but I haven't found that open, liberal, exciting warmth in ordinary parish churches. Today, in local parishes, you get too much rigidity. It's that rigidity that keeps me from coming back to the Church, although I still feel that I'm a Catholic in essence.

Father Morrison, thirty-seven, a diocesan administrator from Chicago, speaks with the care of an arbitrator as he tries to balance the old and the new:

> The upheaval of the sixties hit the Catholic Church harder than any other religion because the Church is the most restrictive. It demanded things of you, didn't ask, just demanded. If you were Catholic, you ate fish on Friday,

didn't sleep around and went to church on Sundays. If you didn't obey, the Church said you were in sin, and it was a social stigma. Now we're saying, don't come to church because you're afraid of criticism from your parents or neighbors. Come because you want to. Come because of the positive things it has to offer.

The Church says that it's not a mortal sin if you eat meat on Friday. But the Church also says that this is very important, that it is a greater act of love for the family to decide on their own that they are not going to eat meat on Fridays. The emphasis now is on doing something because you love God, not because it's the law of the Church.

Father Arnott, thirty-eight, a San Francisco parish priest, explains what it was like to straddle the two disparate eras:

I was ordained with Vatican II. When I went into the seminary, we were learning everything in Latin. When I left, all that had changed. But in some ways I suppose it was an advantage because I lived through the change and it gave me a tremendous insight.

It was a frustrating time to be studying because things kept changing. And there was a huge exodus of priests. Lots of my classmates left. I'd say about twenty-five to thirty percent. Normally ninety-five percent survive to ordination. In the early seventies we lost a lot of good men. Outsiders maintained they left because of the celibacy issue, but that's not true. Their leaving reflected the times. We went through a five- to six-year period of drifting. People like stability, and at that time there just wasn't any.

Today the seminarians and the young priests are a new breed because the changes have taken place, and things have settled down. The pendulum has almost swung back.

Father Ford, forty-five, a mathematics teacher from New Orleans, is typical of many priests who successfully blend the best of both worlds.

Reconciliation

In the old days, the Church was all black-and-white. That made it rough on a lot of young priests in Confession. I always saw the gray, so I'm glad now the Church does too.

  I've served the Church almost half my life, under the old regime and the new, and I like the modern Church. But I guess I'm a traditionalist too. Yet I wouldn't want to go back to a lot of the old ways. What I do is pick and choose along the way.

Father Francis, fifty-three, a teacher at a New York seminary, is another veteran of the transition.

When the older priests watched the values they'd based their lives on swept away, they saw red. And you can't blame them. At sixty-five or seventy it isn't easy to change.

  Somebody my age can still cope. When Vatican II came in, half of those in my priesthood were unable to cope. I always felt sorry for those who were ten years older than me. They were just too far set in their ways and couldn't adjust.

Anthony, forty-four, a financial journalist from Miami, is weary of the changes, but sticks with the Church. Like so many of the faithful, he is willing to put up with almost anything for his faith, but he prays the changes will soon stop.

I grew up being taught only a priest's hands could touch the Host. Today any son of a bitch who wants to walk down the aisle and reach for it can have it. Now they're talking about women priests. You'd think only the young fellas would support that. Not on your life. My pastor's seventy-five years old, probably of the old order. He taught in the seminary. You'd think he'd hate the idea, but he can't wait to see women ordained. He thinks they would make terrific priests. In many ways, some of the qualities that make a good woman are much more suited to the priesthood.

  Worse is that they can't seem to make up their minds

about anything anymore. It's a shame to see the Church going through these throes and agonies and finally coming around to say what we did before is wrong. Now they're saying we want you to do the exact opposite of what you did before. I only hope all these changes are the end of it. I can't take much more. Funny, before you'd have to confess to feeling that way, and it would be a sin. Now it's a virtue.

For many, the confusion becomes disorientation. Irene, thirty-eight, a Santa Fe mother of three, has lost her way in the Church.

Things have changed so much. A lot of things I was raised on in the Church aren't true anymore. I was told God has a little book and He writes down all your sins, and that's not true. I was told that when someone dies, God wills it, and that's not true. And now that the Mass is in English, I hear words like eat of the body and the blood. That sounds barbaric to me.

Louise, thirty-seven, a Cleveland cocktail waitress, poses a very Catholic question:

Fifteen years ago if you ate meat on Friday and didn't confess, it was a sin. You went to Hell. Now you can eat meat on any day you want and nothing happens. So the people who didn't go to Confession in those days, theoretically they're all in Hell. And the guys nowadays who do exactly the same thing, they get off scot-free. Is that fair? What can you do about somebody who ate meat on Friday twenty years ago? Pull him out of Hell?

The New Rite

The Church in North America has failed to effectively spread the word about the new forms of Confession. In an uneven publicity campaign, some practicing Catholics were oversold on the New Rite, while others barely heard about it. Neither did the Church reach the great majority of the lapsed or the "Christmas and Easter Catholics," the men and women who could have benefited most.

Allison, thirty-seven, a Toronto housewife, knew nothing of the changes in Confession.

> I've been going to church for the past two years, five or six times a year and I never heard a word about how people might catch up on what's been happening in the Church. I've read all the newsletters, but nothing, not a word. I wonder how many millions of Catholics are out there who don't know that the Church has changed? Take General Absolution, for example. I remember friends vaguely talking about going to a Confession service in a group, but I never heard anything from the Church itself about it. Why are they keeping it a secret?

Sister Renata, forty-four, a coordinator of diocesan social workers in Detroit, discusses the American Church's effort to promote the New Rite:

> I think it's going to take a long time before the New Rite will be fully accepted. As the changes in Vatican II came about, there wasn't enough education. I don't remember receiving any instruction on the New Rite. Whatever I learned, I got from my own reading. When I was a child they changed the Act of Contrition, and I still call it the "new" Act of Contrition. People change slowly, maybe even more slowly than the Church. It's going to take time, a long time.

To make matters worse, many Catholics aren't accustomed to asking questions of their Church. Father Roberts, forty-five, a par-

269

ish priest from Portland, Maine, deplores this lack of intellectual curiosity:

> I think most Catholics have a juvenile understanding of their faith, as well as the Sacrament, even those who went to Catholic high schools and colleges. Their additional knowledge has come through newspapers that distort many things. Within parishes we've attempted to have adult education classes to teach them about the new rites, but few people show up. Sometimes we'll sneak in an adult education class in parent meetings. If a child is making a First Confession we insist that the parents come to a meeting where we give them a brief history of the Sacrament and the New Rite. We've spent a lot of time and resources on educating children, but I think we've done a real disservice to our adults because we've left them back in grade school. Until I got to the seminary, that's where my understanding of the Church was.

Father Josephs, forty-two, a Jesuit based in Philadelphia, traces the Catholic's lack of religious curiosity to pre-Vatican II Church policy. Catholics weren't supposed to concern themselves with doctrinal details—that was the province of the priest, who told the laity only what they had to know. In the old days Catholics were not encouraged to learn more about their religion, and until they are and given the means to do so, there will be very little change.

> You can't expect the laity to become intellectually stimulated overnight. Except for a few alert Catholics, the elitist intellectuals, nobody knows about the New Rite. Lots of parishes have interesting and vital adult education classes, but in a parish of 1,800 families you might get 40 to 50 who show up for such programs. For 400 years all you had to do was memorize. You're not going to undo 400 years in 20.

Take Your Pick: Box, Room or General Absolution

So many changes in the Church during the past two decades bear the word "new." There's the new Rite of Reconciliation, the new theology, the new consciousness. There's even a new awareness of sin, community, self and God. For the progressives, the word implies a more flexible Church that allows room for debate and growth.

Many of the people we interviewed dismissed the old-time confessional box as anxiety-ridden, medieval and totally out of sync with the times. They embraced the reconciliation room as the humane wave of the future.

An equally large number, who knew of and understood the New Rite still preferred the anonymity of the box and the intimacy of the one-to-one encounter with their priest. They felt they would be intimidated or constrained in a face-to-face-situation and unable to reveal intimate details. Although the New Rite was officially promulgated in the mid-seventies, more than one half of all American Catholics still confess their sins to the priest in the confessional box.

Many people resist General Absolution as well. This newest form of practicing the Sacrament is potentially the greatest challenge to Confession since the abusive sale of indulgences triggered the Reformation over 400 years ago. Some find General Absolution invigorating; others infuriating. It has been praised as a ritual with great meaning for the socially conscious, ecumenical eighties. For those countless Catholics who regard the confessional and the reconciliation room as outmoded or frightening, General Absolution can be an attractive alternative. However, many traditionalists fear that General Absolution may spell the end of private confession. The practice also confuses many of the devout who question its spiritual efficacy. If there is no penance, can it really work? Will the sinner still be forgiven?

Father Arnott, forty-nine, a Vancouver priest, has known the old and adjusted to the new.

271

Vatican II tried to take people from the fear of God to the love of God. When I was growing up, the Church used the Baltimore Catechism, and it was, "Why do I love God? I love God because . . . boom, boom, boom." Now the Cathechism the kids study is called the "Come to Father," and the whole concept is of a loving father who is asking for love from you in return.

Young people today, who never knew the harsher earlier system, see the loving Father and trust Him. They're coming to understand the reality of the new Church.

If you tried to teach pre-Vatican II moral theology today, people would laugh at you. Back then, if our professors tried to teach anything else, they would have been condemned as heretics. They taught what they had to teach, and we learned what we had to learn.

Father Porter, a fifty-six-year-old Chicago parish priest, describes the enthusiasm that many of the older laity feel toward the New Rite:

They're all coming to General Absolution. These people in their seventies, who have lived their lives, are no longer concerned about the mortgages and the food bill. Now they have time to spend with God, to discard nonessential things and get down to business. They've seen the suffering, they've seen change in every part of their lives. They've come looking for God, and they've found Him in the New Rite.

On the other hand, he goes on to describe a personal friend, a seventy-five-year-old Canadian nun, who has turned toward the New Rite with a vengeance:

Elizabeth visited her relatives in New York two years ago and went up to take Holy Communion in their parish church. She put out her hands, like this, to take the Host because that's the practice in Canada. The priest said, "We only give Communion on the tongue here." Eliza-

272

beth didn't say a word, but kept her hands out. He repeated "Our rule is Communion on the tongue," but she stood her ground. He finally put the Host in her hands. She's a tough lady and isn't going to be pushed around.

Father Stewart, thirty-nine, a New York parish priest, is optimistic about the New Rite and bases his judgment on the quality rather than the number of his penitents.

Reconciliation is the Sacrament of the eighties. In my ten years as a priest, the caliber of confessions has improved immensely. People don't come in with shopping lists of sins anymore. There are fewer and fewer rote weekly confessions, and more and more soul-searching monthly confessions which is a very good sign. It means people are taking the Sacrament more seriously. Twenty-five percent of confessions used to be routine weekly affairs. Now it's fewer than five percent.

People are bringing their family problems into the confessional. Mothers with teenage problems; single people with lifestyle questions; homosexuals; older people concerned about their relationships with their peers. People aren't confessing to avoid Hell and gain Heaven, but rather to be reconciled with the Church, the community and God.

Today's theologians have difficulty saying that God condemns us to Hell. No more emphasis on one act and you're condemned. People used to leave Confession and say, "Phew, saved from Hell this time," but hardly anymore. It used to be a mortal sin, really, if you missed Mass on Sunday. Right to Hell, not even to Purgatory. People were taught that was it, their soul wasn't open to God's grace. Now, if a person goes to Mass fifty-one weeks of the year and misses one week, it's pretty hard to say that he's in mortal sin. The individual act is less important than the motivation.

Most priests are flexible regarding the reconciliation room or the confessional. The penitent's comfort is the deciding factor. Father Stephens, thirty-four, a Chicago innercity priest, explains the importance of giving people the option:

> The important thing today is that we give penitents their dignity by treating them like adults. I work well in the confessional and don't mind spending time there. Of the three options, I prefer face-to-face confession because it's more relaxed and I don't feel the pressure of time. Most people raised on the box still prefer it, but many like the reconciliation room because they have the option of face-to-face or the screen.

Father Innes, fifty-six, a former professor of theology, is currently a parish priest in Dallas. He believes there is room for more than one way of confessing in the Church.

> There are people who come to Confession and want the reconciliation room because they need a personal exchange for twenty minutes or a half hour. Others prefer the confessional box because they want anonymity and to confess in what they think is a more sacred way. That choice has a lot to do with the way the person was brought up as well as his individual chemistry. Some people are, by nature, shy and find it impossible to tell me, face-to-face, they slept with someone or how much they're ripping off from their employer. They feel more comfortable kneeling in a dark confessional, pouring their heart out and asking me for forgiveness. There's a shyness, that part of their humanity that must be respected. Either way, these people find the peace and the comfort they need.

Father Jordan, fifty-four, who has adopted the New Rite wholeheartedly, describes a General Absolution service in his Louisville, Kentucky, parish:

Reconciliation

I believe that General Confession and General Absolution are going to help people recognize the need of the Sacrament in their lives. I was pastor in a small city, 30,000 people, and there were 5 parishes. During Holy Week we had General Absolution, and they were hanging off the rafters. It was a beautiful experience . . . and the joy! People are still talking about it. Older people, seventy or eighty, coming up saying it was the best experience in Church they've ever had. My own brother had stopped going to private Confession, but he went to General Absolution because he found it so meaningful.

The following two priests describe how the New Rite has been accepted abroad. Father O'Neill tells of the Irish experience; Father Marcel, the French.

Prior to being assigned to his American parish, Father O'Neill, 55, served for 5 years in his native Ireland. He tells how the Irish, responsible for the first major changes in the practice of the Sacrament more than 1,400 years ago, have responded to Reconciliation today:

I remember when the confessional was heavily patronized. There would be three particularly busy occasions, Christmas, Easter and All Soul's Day. In Ireland the introduction of the New Rite of Penance broke the pattern of continuity. People who were happy with the old way look upon the New Rite as irrelevant. The New Rite addressed a failure in Confession which had surfaced in Europe, but worked to the detriment of the practice that was flourishing in Ireland.

Father Marcel, eighty, is a Benedictine who has lived in Paris most of his life. He explains that the introduction of the New Rite in France was not so very new:

Vatican II wasn't a revolution but more of a confirmation of what had been passed before in the other assemblies

275

and councils. There was always the possibility of having a communal examination of conscience, with several priests available to give Confession individually and then absolution together followed by an exhortation. It was an evolution, not a revolution.

Frequently, the examination of conscience was done by the laity who often knew things better than the priests. They could also better understand the faults and sins that were being discussed.

Confession used to be horrible. The conversation part of Confession has changed. The accent today is not on what is confessed but on the reconciliation. I was always a bit progressive though it frequently wasn't easy. When the change in attitude occurred, I said, "At last, we are in the verity." Although many Christians may not have been prepared for the changes, three quarters of the priests were ready before Vatican II. For them, Vatican II was a confirmation. I prefer the reconciliation room, of course. I never go in the box at all anymore. I refuse to go when people ask me. They want to hide behind a gate. Only ten percent of the confessionals originally in use remain in France today.

Occasionally, General Absolution meets practical as well as spiritual needs. Father Harley, thirty-four, a parish priest from Milwaukee, tells of such an instance:

One evening during Holy Week, forty people showed up for private confession, and I was the only priest on duty. So I said, "Look, I could hear all your confessions tonight, but I'd get a headache, and I don't want to have a headache, so let's all have General Absolution." We did, and they thought it was terrific.

Martin, sixty-four, a Buffalo lawyer and deacon of his church, speaks with the passion of a convert although he has been a Catho-

lic all his life. He and his wife have totally embraced the New
Theology.

> One of the biggest changes that has taken place over the
> past ten years is the Church's encouragement of indepen-
> dence of thought. Before Vatican II, it was simply, "Do it,
> or else!" Being a Catholic meant being passive. I could
> never go back to that.
>
> Since Vatican II a question leads to an answer which
> leads to another question. Sometimes it isn't easy. We have
> to learn to be comfortable living with the possibility that we
> may never have absolute answers. But living in uncertainty
> and constant change causes us to continually grow.
>
> Reconciliation means to be at peace, with yourself and
> with God, rather than to be violent and aggressive. I be-
> lieve it's the best thing that's ever happened in the
> Church.

Rocco, sixty-eight, a retired grocer from Flushing, New York,
emphasizes that the new theology is not the province only of the
young:

> The older people who you'd expect to be wrapped up in
> the letter of the law, aren't. They're in the spirit of the law.
> My mother has got to be as strait-laced as you can imagine.
> In our family, we've got a divorce, with another one com-
> ing up. We've had a shack-up, a single parent and two
> mixed marriages, and every time we've lived in dread of
> my mother. But she's the most understanding of all, and
> she'll be ninety-one years old next year. You should see
> her at General Absolution; she beams.

Brenda, a thirty-nine-year-old Boston social worker, loves the
warmth of the New Rite.

> In the past, Confession was like taking a bath. As a kid, you
> didn't want to take one, but somehow, after it was over,

you were glad you had. Today, Confession is like talking
with a friend, face-to-face, and seeking the kind of guidance that only a friend can give. Today the "friend" is the
priest and I think that's wonderful. My daughter has just
learned a new song in school and the kids call God their
"Buddy." It's such a welcome change from my day!

Lorne is a fifty-seven-year-old lawyer from Fairfax, Virginia. He
and his entire family have been attending General Absolution services for the past five years.

Thank God I was still young enough to get in on the New
Rite. I haven't been in the penalty box in almost twenty
years. Confession never became a meaningful or helpful
Sacrament until General Absolution. Before General Absolution, I went to Confession only because it was the
thing to do.

To keep it in the family, we spoke with Lorne's older brother,
Thomas, fifty-nine, also a lawyer, whose attitude to the New Rite
was just as enthusiastic.

As kids, we were fortunate enough to learn that you don't
go to Confession to tell your sins; you go to receive grace,
and that kept me going. New General Absolution has become even more meaningful to me. I spent four years in
the seminary. During that time I went once a week to my
spiritual director for Confession, and I'm still not sure
what it was all about.

Henry, thirty-four, a Trenton architect who's active in his church,
practices all forms of the New Rite.

I attend two General Absolution services every year in my
parish and probably three more at the Cathedral. On
weekdays, I confess in the box. I can't say I prefer one to
the other, because they complement each other. I'm on
the liturgy committee of my church, and we were remark-
ing on the sense of joy that people express after General

Absolution. They linger at the back of the church more than they do at any other time, including Easter Vigil or midnight Mass. At General Absolution, they seem friendly, more at peace with themselves and each other.

When you go to Confession privately, you bring all the guilt you've been feeling for the whole year into the box. At General Absolution you have the knowledge that everyone has the same problems and same guilt. You have a communal examination of conscience and realize there's no cause for despair. Then you carry that joy back with you to your private confession.

From the ages of six to fourteen, Joanna confessed only in the box. These days the seventeen-year-old Denver high school student attends only General Absolution:

Confessing in the open instead of the enclosed box makes you face another reality, the reality around you. The box always made me feel like a sinner, a bad person. General Absolution is an active joyous thing.

In General Absolution, everybody's quiet, only the priest is speaking, and when the "I absolve you" comes, everyone breathes a sigh of relief. I'll try harder, and I now know I can make a new start. It's terrific.

Many Would Opt for the Old Way

Many priests and penitents, however, aren't thrilled with General Absolution. These detractors, coming from all ages and backgrounds, fear that the practice might some day supplant private confession. They contend that General Absolution is capable of bringing about the demise of private confession and even the Sacrament.

Father Jennings, thirty-four, a New York City parish priest, explains:

It certainly doesn't substitute for individual confession. I don't think General Absolution works and I don't think it's good.

It's easy to walk into a church, kneel down and say "I'm sorry" to God. It's not too easy to kneel down in the confessional or sit down in the reconciliation room and say "I'm weak, I'm human and I've made a mess of my life and maybe somebody else's as well." It's difficult, but the person who does it is growing.

Individual confession allows for growth and introspection. We'd be gravely mistaken to underestimate the power of individual confession. I think General Absolution is good in the sense of peace that obviously follows. We may be saving ourselves a lot of work with General Absolution, but we're also cheating people.

Father Caruso, forty-eight, from Boston, agrees with Father Jennings.

As a priest, I would like to see private confession emphasized a little more. Since Vatican II, I think we've gone too far in insisting that whatever you do is between you and God. If kids grow up today with the attitude that they never need to go to Confession, or if it's only a matter of routinely going once a year, then they're not pursuing the ideal of being honest with themselves. There's no greater way of being honest with yourself than being honest with another human being.

Father Briar, fifty-four, a Buffalo parish priest, regrets the loss of intimacy in confession.

One-on-one confession has many advantages. Chief among them is that you can discuss your problem with somebody who is in a position of authority. And if you know the confessor, you're at an even greater advantage.

Then the priest can view your problem and understand it better because of his knowledge of you.

In General Absolution, the intimacy is gone. If you don't have a problem, it's fine, but if you do have a problem, you're left alone with a lot of people looking up at a statue trying to figure out what to do.

Father Allan, fifty-seven, an Atlanta parish priest, also fears that General Absolution cheats the penitent.

I'm not entirely sold on General Absolution, even though people have prepared for it in advance. I really think individual face-to-face confession is more important because someone reaches out and touches you. That's important in Catholic theology. When you are baptized, go to Communion or get married, you receive something. In Confession, it is important that there is a laying on of hands, an outward sign of the Sacrament. You can't get that in General Absolution, but you can get it in a reconciliation room.

Father Amery's Washington, D.C., parish is popular with the diplomatic community. He notes that people from India and various Third World countries, as well as the Mediterranean area, don't feel comfortable with General Absolution:

They'll always prefer the confessional box. It's a matter of tradition and habit. Some of them don't feel that they've got their money's worth when they leave General Absolution. We've got a long way to go in teaching people about it. General Absolution has caught on faster in America, and certainly in the larger cities.

Raj, twenty-nine, who has recently arrived in Ottawa from New Delhi, is wary of General Absolution for pragmatic reasons.

I believe that since priests can give General Absolution, they aren't always available. I think it is necessary to have a priest in church at regular times, especially before Mass.

At home in India there was always a priest in the confessional waiting from five forty-five in the morning onward. Now here in Ottawa, you can never be sure one's around. I miss that very much.

As a result of his interview for this book, Brian, a forty-four-year-old advertising copywriter from Chicago, attended General Absolution service, "just to check it out."

I went to General Absolution, just as you suggested, and you're right, I was astounded. I hadn't been in a Catholic church for twenty-seven years, and I couldn't begin to grasp all the changes. There were so many, and I didn't like them at all.

For me, the General Absolution service I attended proves that Luther, after all these years, not only won the battle but the war. Catholicism has become downright Protestant. There was absolutely no sense of a Sacrament, no emphasis on atonement and nothing about a purpose of amendment. Where the hell is penance in this thing? The hymns and scripture readings were so evangelical I could have been in a Presbyterian church.

I have nothing against Protestantism. I just don't want to be one. If I can't buy real Catholicism, I'm certainly not going to buy a watered-down version.

What does everybody being nice to everybody else in church have to do with sin and repentance? Yes, it was a nice social event, but you should go to church to communicate with God. Go to the supermarket if you want to socialize with your neighbor.

The only thing I can say about the changes is that this face-to-face confession makes more sense than a confessional. That box was directly out of the Dark Ages. I would like to have a one-on-one conversation with a priest, but that's about the only thing I could tolerate about the New Rite. I want to know why they sold the store in the first place!

Reconciliation

Bruno, forty-seven, an insurance agent from Miami, proudly described himself as a lapsed Catholic who hasn't been in a church in more than twenty-five years. Unlike Brian, he has no desire to return to the church to witness recent changes. When we told him about the New Rite, the reconciliation room and the option of face-to-face confession, he snickered.

> Do you mean to tell me that any one of those priests I used to know is going to be psychologically equipped to listen to confessions—and without anonymity? Those guys aren't psychiatrists. They'd never be able to look someone in the face and tell them anything straight. What training are they getting for such delicate stuff? Look, the guys that were bad under the old system are going to be worse with the new. I heard someplace there were some changes, but having a face-to-face confession with a priest is going too far. What about the people who still want to be anonymous? They never make small changes anymore. It's now got to be all or nothing. No wonder the number of Catholics is plummeting.

Silvester, thirty-four, a photographer's assistant in Los Angeles, voices a doubt echoed by many on the subject of penance:

> Don't I have to do penance anymore? In General Absolution—those innermost sins I might be afraid of revealing to a priest or even in my own conscience—am I really absolved of them? Does it really work as well as when I confess to a priest? I just have the feeling it's not the same. I wouldn't want to risk my soul on it. Maybe they're wrong, and I'll end up in Hell.

Father Jordan has an answer to Silvester's question about penance and General Absolution:

> Penance is built into the service to enable people to share in the acceptance of peace and the reconciliation experience.

Bless Me, Father, For I Have Sinned

Constance, fifty, a devout Catholic from Chicago, speaks passionately about her particular concern:

I've a lot of problems with General Absolution. My main concern is how the sacraments are understood. I work very hard to expand people's consciousness and explain that sacraments aren't magical dances of the gods. It's how you live your life and how you communally present those acts of love. With General Absolution, everyone comes in, they don't know what they're looking for and somebody says I absolve you. And I'm saying, "Big deal, who absolves you? And who absolves the absolver?"

Father Clinton, forty-seven, a parish priest from Annapolis, Maryland, puts the argument into perspective:

You're never going to find the perfect way to celebrate the Sacrament. General Absolution, for me and for many others, symbolizes the real meaning of the word "reconciliation" because it involves the social aspect of sin. You just don't get this in face-to-face confession.

Father Mackie, sixty-seven, a pastor in a Detroit suburb, has been hearing confessions for more than forty years. He voices the same fear as the Vatican about General Absolution:

I think the Church is going to have to pull back a bit on General Absolution. People are losing contact with sacramental Confession, as we know it. They are losing one-on-one contact with the priest as well as the medicinal aspect of the Sacrament. They're losing the chance to talk their problems over. One thousand people at a time is not the Confession that I know. And priests as well as penitents are taking advantage of it. I think the younger priests may get into such a habit with General Absolution that they'll never hear a confession. That's a frightening thing.

Some priests will say it's a matter of logistics, that they can't hear all the confessions of their parishioners, but before I arrived here, I was the pastor of a parish for 21 years with 2,220 families and I heard all their confessions. First, you import priests to help you. Second, you make Confession available at all times. During Holy Week we'd have priests hearing confessions for one hour at a time all through the night. Once I counted 24 people at 6 in the morning. If a priest judiciously used the manpower that's available and kept a close track, there'd be no problem.

Stephen, a Los Angeles publishing executive, refuses to accept the New Rite. His years in the monastery cemented his confessional habits, and he's not about to change for the sake of change.

I'm confessing today more or less the way I did when I left the monastery, thirty-three years ago. My attitude is the same. I'll never be convinced that Confession is a sharing or communal thing or that the priest and I are on an equal level. Absolution isn't something I can conjure up myself, and it isn't going to be more powerful because of my participation. I have none of those feelings, although I've heard them expressed. Then again, I don't believe that man created God. You have to believe that in order to accept the New Rite.

Sin Today

When I was a kid, everything was a sin. Now, the only sins are those we commit against our neighbors.

—Fifty-seven-year-old New York executive

If two decades ago it was a sin to eat meat on Friday, it now might be judged a sin to eat grapes from South Africa. Some people no longer confess to missing Mass, premarital sex or masturbation. They confess selfishness, jealousy and prejudice. Today, sin has as many definitions as beauty, and it, too, is in the eye of the beholder.

Bless Me, Father, For I Have Sinned

Sister Renata, a fifty-one-year-old New Orleans nun, discusses sin and confession today:

> Our whole sense of sin has changed. It started before Vatican II in the sixties, when all the theologians were writing about the fundamental option. It changed our sense of sin and relationship with Our Lord. People who have accepted the teachings of Vatican II, and have kept up with what has happened since then, concentrate more on their faith relationship with the Lord than on Confession. The Eucharist is central in their lives and they are aware that the Eucharist forgives sin. Unless there is a major event in their lives where they feel they need an outward gesture of forgiveness, a lot of people just don't go to Confession.

Father Martino, thirty-seven, a parish priest in Toronto, offers a historical overview of sin:

> I don't think sin has changed as much as people's attitudes about what they think is a sin. Today the communal aspect of sin, rather than individual guilt, is far more important. People are more apt to confess how they hurt their family than they were twenty years ago. There is a deeper consciousness of our effect on other people rather than on our individual relationship to God.
>
> In the past, people talked about sin as offending God. That's what my mother told me and she still believes it, but she can't explain how an all-powerful being can be offended. Perhaps the way to look at it is not offending God, but offending yourself. A sin makes you less human and that thwarts God's ultimate plan for you.
>
> Pre-Vatican II went back to the Irish Penitentials, a legalistic approach, that emphasized the specific definition of sin and the number of times committed. The emphasis now is on the attitude that you bring to Confession. If

someone comes in and lists all his sins, I'll say, "that's fine, but are you sorry? That's ultimately what counts."

Father Jennings, thirty-six, a parish priest from Detroit, considers the social dimensions of sin to be most important.

How have I hurt other people by my actions? Even drinking coffee produced in South American countries can be troublesome to some people today. I'd never go probing about personal matters—tell me about your sex life or who you're living with. If they don't bring it up in Confession, neither do I. But if they do, then obviously they've got a twinge of conscience and I respond to their need to talk.

John is a deacon in his suburban Chicago church. The sixty-seven-year-old architect claims that people today still consider themselves serious sinners, when most of them really aren't.

People are far too hard on themselves. But that's all coming from the Irish boys. They laid a pretty stiff trip on us. A fear of God rather than a love of God.

We have need of public prayer, as well as private prayer. When we come together in the New Rite of Reconciliation, we are coming together as a community to celebrate. The emphasis now is on a God of love, not a God of fear, not on the God that's coming down with an anvil to smash you over the knuckles. All you have to do is ask for forgiveness. The emphasis isn't even on the penance as it was.

Father Humphries, fifty-seven, an American theologian, offers his comments:

In the past, we overemphasized mortal sin and underemphasized venial sin. In the future, I would see it as the other way around. Mortal sin is the breaking of one's multiple relationships with God–neighbor–world. Frankly, there's a much less frequent occurrence of that than people thought there was in the past.

In the past, the moral life was seen primarily in terms of the Ten Commandments, and sin was, therefore, an act against the law. Interestingly enough, the best Catholic theology did not agree. For Aquinas, mortal sin was not an act against the law of God; mortal sin was the breaking of our relationship with God. He comes very close to the way some people look at sin today.

Aquinas said most people's mortal sins are forgiven before they come to the Sacrament. What you have in the Sacrament is a celebration of a reality of forgiveness and reconciliation that has already occurred. It is not something that takes place in a moment in a church.

There is no doubt the Church has warmly embraced a contemporary interpretation of sin, one in keeping with a philosophy which seeks to return Catholicism to the communal responsibility of its first centuries. What is in doubt, however, is how many Catholics understand the difference between the letter of the law and the spirit of the law? How many define God in terms of love rather than in terms of retribution? The numbers are steadily growing. It is a question of time.

Confession Tomorrow

Today, many Catholics are tampering with the new forms of practicing the Sacrament as revised by the Second Vatican Council. Nuns are hearing confessions in many cities throughout North America. Their regular counseling sessions, offered to both laity and clergy, are reminiscent of the *anmchara* or soul friend, in the Irish monasteries of the fifth and sixth centuries. Upon the completion of their spiritual direction, these sisters urge their penitents to attend General Absolution services.

The Church takes exception to the use of the word "confession" in these nonsacramental encounters and refers to them as "spiritual counseling." The people who speak out in these pages, however, insist that as far as they're concerned, it's "confession."

Sister Renata recalls the climate twenty years ago, in the midst of the Second Vatican Council. She recounts a conversation that took place with her bishop:

> During the Second Vatican Council the bishop in my diocese returned from one of the sessions and came to say Mass. At breakfast afterward he sat back and said, "Sister, what do you think? Did we do a good job at the Council?" I said, "Bishop, there's one thing you didn't address that I think you should have addressed and you're going to have to address it sometime." He asked what and I told him the role of women in the Church. He said, "Oh, Sister, come on, don't tell me you're one of those nuns who wants to be a priest?" I said, "No, *I* don't particularly want to be a priest, but there are women who should be priests." He maintained we could never ordain women because no one would go to confess to them. Then I sat back and said, "Well, Bishop, many of your priests go to Confession with me. I just can't give them absolution." That was in the sixties, when a lot of the priests were having difficulties with their vocations and the exodus was beginning. A lot of priests came to me to talk.
>
> There are lots of nuns who are hearing confessions. The thing is they're not empowered to give absolution, and they feel that they don't have to be. They can say to a priest or a sister that he or she is forgiven. I see a great deal of this going on, and to me, it's very refreshing because more and more people realize that they are the Church. Women who are in the feminist movement and who are pushing for the ordination of women are saying, "You're not going to get rid of me, I'm staying inside." Otherwise, who's going to push it? They are convinced that they are the Church. Eventually they'll succeed. I'm sure they will.

Bless Me, Father, For I Have Sinned

Sister Gabriella puts the concept of women confessors into a pastoral context:

> I belong to a community that doesn't have any schools or hospitals, which is what most nuns are involved in. We are a catechetical community and our main responsibility is to proclaim the word of God and to teach religion. We often visit a parish, negotiate with the pastor and go door-to-door to do census. When you do that you meet people who are no longer Catholic and don't go to Confession, but they do confess to you. And the irony of it is that if we could give them absolution, they'd automatically be back in the Church. To get them to go to a priest is almost impossible. Now, if you're in a good parish, a priest will follow up on your visit and give them absolution. I think in many instances women find it much easier to confess to women.

Sister Rebecca comments on some of the priests she has known in the confessional:

> Women can definitely be priests because they live on a more personal level and are more compassionate. In the confessional, the male priests definitely harassed us. Their heads were turned away or tilted upward. They never spoke to us or offered any help with problems. I don't believe a female priest would behave that way.

Father Evans, thirty-four, a parish priest from Cleveland, favors the ordination of women.

> I have no doubts we will have female priests in the future. How far in the future remains to be seen. I know some sisters who demanded it yesterday, others who pray for it today, some who will be happy whenever it comes. Many aren't legislating for it for themselves, but because they believe it will be better for the Church. I agree with them. I know many exceptional sisters I would go to for advice, for spiritual direction.

Reconciliation

Some men had positive reactions to the possibility of female priests and female confessors. Andrew, forty-four, owner of a Denver hardware store, recalls the women who gave him religious training in his youth:

> Women confessors would be a good thing. A woman tends to be kinder and more compassionate than a man. She is more loving than a man and perhaps she would be more understanding of the frailties of a man as such. Certainly as spiritual advisor she would be very good. In my youth, our spiritual advisors were our teachers, and they were nuns. It was the nuns who prepared us for Confession, and they did so with the feeling of human kindness.

Others had reservations. Richard, forty-eight, a Miami musician, recalled the ruler that was frequently smacked upon his palm:

> Women confessors? Probably revolutionize Confession. Like speaking to a mother figure, probably less frightening, get a better turnout. But then, I've known some Mother Superiors who were nasty, real, real, nasty.

While some people are confessing to sisters and subsequently attending General Absolution services, others are confessing to spiritually gifted lay women. Gregory, thirty-eight, a U.S. Navy officer, has been confessing to a lay woman for the past four years.

> My spiritual director is very important to me for many reasons. She's a good listener who gives me feedback from a true Christian perspective when we discuss what's going on in my life. This is important to me. She also has the gift of healing and counseling, but she encourages me to lead as well as to follow. She is my spiritual companion all the way. Wherever I am, knowing I can communicate with and confess to her is crucial to my well-being. Oddly, I have hardly spoken to her in person over the last year. She's on the West Coast, and I've been on the East or in Europe. The first time I confessed to her on the telephone was

awkward, but just for the first moments. Then it was as natural as when we are together. I attend General Absolution services to complete the Sacrament. I doubt if I would ever go back to a priest in the confessional.

In discussing the future of the Sacrament, Father Morrison takes us through the past and present and into the future:

We're now going into a third stage of the Sacrament. The first thousand years saw public confession, once in a lifetime with great emphasis on penance. The second stage was influenced by the Irish penitentials, with the emphasis on what you did wrong. I think the next one thousand years of the Sacrament will focus on man's hopeful nature.

While there are undoubtedly Catholics who will continue to hold to the pre-Vatican II form of Confession, the practice of the Sacrament has indeed changed remarkably over the past two thousand years, beginning with public, once-in-a-lifetime confession and slowly evolving into private, frequent confession. Despite the unending debate over how sins are to be confessed, the Church's new attitude toward the Sacrament has taken it a near-full circle to its simple beginnings, embodying the sense of communal sin and forgiveness as taught by Christ.

What struck us most in recording the many confessional stories in this book was the overwhelming power of the Sacrament in people's lives. We also found ourselves comparing Confession to a carpenter's tool—if used carelessly or with insufficient understanding, Confession can result in pain, even have negative consequences, as evidenced by many of the pre-Vatican II confessional experiences we heard. But when used purposefully, with knowledge and insight, Confession can result in a sense of hopefulness and peace in the lives of penitents. Those who celebrated the Sacrament with understanding were the most deeply rewarded, experiencing, as they said, a spiritual renewal and a meaningful sense of community within the Church.

Glossary

The Sacrament of Penance, the Sacrament, Penance, Confession, the Rite of Reconciliation, Reconciliation, the New Rite are all used interchangeably to signify the Roman Catholic Sacrament of confessing one's sins to a priest to obtain absolution.

In the Sacrament, people guilty of mortal or venial sin committed after Baptism are reconciled with God and the Church. According to pre-Vatican II tradition, unless a person is in the state of grace at the moment of death, he or she cannot attain Heaven, and is in danger of eternal damnation in Hell.

Absenteeism: The practice of landlords or bishops to live away from their estates or dioceses.

Absolution: God's forgiveness and remission of a person's sins as conveyed by a priest in the Sacrament of Penance.

Glossary

Apostasy: The abandonment or renunciation of one's religious faith or moral allegiance.

Baptism: see Sacrament

Bishopric: The province of a bishop, a diocese.

Canonical: Having reference to an edict or canon law, or belonging to the canon of Scripture.

Charismatic Renewal: Also called the Pentecostal Movement, concerned with the renewal of the Christian spirit and typified by such phenomena as prophesy, discernment of spirits, healing and speaking in tongues.

Contrition, Act of: "Oh, my God, I am heartily sorry for having offended Thee, and I detest all my sins because of Thy just punishments, but most of all because they offend Thee, my God, Who art all good and deserving of all my love. I firmly resolve, with the help of grace, to sin no more and avoid the near occasions of sin."

Encyclical: An ecclesiastical epistle; a circular intended for extensive circulation. Now, chiefly the letters issued by the Pope.

Eucharist: see Sacrament

Excommunication: The action of excluding an offending Christian from the communion of the Church.

Grace: The presence of God.

Heaven: In traditional pre-Vatican II terminology, the dwelling place of the Deity, a celestial abode of bliss. In Catholic theology, Heaven is synonymous with the "Beatific Vision," or eternal life, that full union with God which is the goal of all human existence.

Hell: Traditionally, a place for the damned; a place in the netherworld where the damned must suffer everlasting punishment. Today, Hell is more likely to be defined as an absence of God and a state of ultimate failure to achieve full union with God after death.

Heretic: Baptized persons who call themselves Christians, yet deny or doubt some article of faith. This doubt must be externally manifested.

Glossary

Limbo: A place or state of being, which is neither Heaven nor a state of eternal punishment, designated for the just who died before Christ's coming as well as for unbaptized infants. Today, Limbo is not a required article of faith for Catholics.

Liturgy: The service of the Holy Eucharist, i.e. the Mass, as well as the entire official public worship of the Church conducted in accordance with a prescribed form.

Magisterium: The teaching authority of the Church, particularly as represented by the hierarchy of bishops and pope.

Mortifications: The subjection of one's appetites and passions by the practice of austere living and the self-infliction of bodily pain or discomfort.

Occasion of Sin: Circumstances, persons, places, situations, things, etc. which easily lead to sin.

Offertory: The portion of the Mass following the Liturgy of the Word, i.e. Scripture and other readings, when the bread and wine are brought to and placed upon the altar and are consecrated and offered to God.

Patristic: Relating to the early Church fathers and their writings.

Pluralism: The practice of holding more than one benefice by one person, i.e. a bishop holding more than one bishopric. Today, pluralism can refer to the beneficial coexistence of many traditions, ideologies and histories within one denomination or church community.

Prelate: An ecclesiastical dignitary of exalted rank and authority, as a bishop or archbishop. Formerly, an abbot of a monastery.

Presbyter: An elder in the Christian Church. In the early Church, one of a number of officers who had the oversight and management of the affairs of the local church and congregation. Some also had the function of teaching.

Purgatory: Traditionally, a place for the accommodation of the dead until the Last Judgment. A place where the souls of the dead, not guilty of unrepented mortal sin, expiate their venial sins. Today,

Purgatory is seen as a state of purification and maturation in preparation for full reunion with God after death.

Sacraments: Traditionally, "outward signs instituted by Christ to give grace." Today, Sacraments may be described as any outward ritual or sign performed by members of the community which expresses the community's faith in Christ's presence among them and communicates the saving truth and reality of God. Often the community itself, as the physical and mystical body of Jesus, is seen as the basic Sacrament from which the others flow.

Seven specific rituals, the "seven Sacraments," have been designated as signs of specific truths which the Catholic community proclaims as central to its faith. These are the Sacraments of initiation: Baptism, Eucharist, Confirmation; the Sacraments of healing: Reconciliation, Anointing of the Sick; and the Sacraments of vocation and commitment: Matrimony and Orders.

Baptism: Signifies dying to sin and rising to the new life in Christ; the Sacrament of entry into the Christian community of faith, marked by the ritual use of water. In the early Church, all three Sacraments of initiation were administered in the same ceremony.

Eucharist: A joyous spiritual communion with God. A Sacrament literally meaning "thanksgiving," in which the body and blood of Jesus Christ, under the appearances of bread and wine, are contained, offered and received by the community at worship. Often used interchangeably with "the Mass" or "the Lord's Supper."

Confirmation: A Sacrament by which a Catholic ratifies and "confirms" the promises made at Baptism and focuses upon the missionary call given at Baptism to serve and to preach the "good news" of Jesus to all. In the Middle Ages, the notion developed that Confirmation robed a person with special strength to be a "soldier of Christ," carrying out the demands of a more mature Christian life.

Reconciliation: A Sacrament of healing, administered by a priest, in which Catholics come to be forgiven for their sins by God and are reconciled with God and the community. It is the Sacrament that enables Catholics to carry out the words of Jesus, "Repent. Change your lives. The Kingdom of God is at hand." The Sacrament symbolizes the humanity of each member of the Christian community, calls for constant conversion from sin and recognizes God's abundant mercy, love and forgiveness.

Anointing of the Sick: A Sacrament of Healing which was called Extreme Unction prior to Vatican II. Through prayer and anointing with oil, the Sacrament brings health of mind and body in the name of Christ the Healer. It symbolizes the Catholic belief in Christ as Savior of the whole person, body and soul, and the constant need of the community to be healed. Traditionally, the Sacrament has been associated with old age and imminent death.

Matrimony: A Sacrament of vocation and commitment whereby two Christians symbolize Christ's union with his Church by committing their lives to each other in fidelity and exclusivity.

Orders: The Sacrament of vocation and commitment through which structure and order is given to the ritual life of the Church. In the Sacrament, priests, bishops and other ministers are called out from among the community to proclaim the Gospel, celebrate the Sacraments, provide pastoral care, and perform other functions.

Simony: The act of buying or selling ecclesiastical benefices, such as Holy Orders or bishoprics; traffic in sacred things.

Sin: A selfish act which breaks or damages a person's relationship to God, to the community members or to self. A willful turning away from the convenantal love relationship with God; a failure to love.

Mortal Sin: Traditionally, a grave offense performed with full consent after sufficient reflection upon the act. In pre-Vatican II tradition, one mortal sin was thought to deprive the sinner of all grace and condemn him or her to everlasting punishment in Hell. Today, reflective of a new knowledge of the complexity of a person's mind, body and soul, mortal sin may be described as a deep-rooted break or turning away from one's love relationship with

God. This severance may be reflected in a pattern of damaging acts, but is not generally considered to occur in one irreparable action.

Venial Sin: Traditionally, a less serious act which does not threaten the sinner with everlasting punishment in Hell. Today, venial sin may be viewed as any erosion or violation of a person's love relationship with God. This violation takes place at the level of the act, and is not reflective of one's total Christian orientation. Venial sins do not cause a complete break in the love relationship with God and community.

Original Sin: Traditionally, Adam and Eve's biblical rebellion, their initial act of self-will in violation of God's will. Today, Original Sin may be described as the human condition, the probability of sin to occur, the tendency of people not to achieve that which God intended for them.

Temptation: The creation of a desire incompatible with the proper loving relationship with god.

Viaticum: The Eucharist given to a person in danger of death. The last communion before death.

Bibliography

Abbott, Walter M., S.J., ed., *The Documents of Vatican II.* New York: Guild Press, 1966.

Ayerst, David and Fisher, A.S.T., *Records of Christianity, Volume II.* Oxford: B. Blackwell, 1971.

Bach, Marcus, *Strange Sects & Curious Cults.* New York: Dodd, Mead & Co., 1961.

Barraclough, Geoffrey, *The Medieval Papacy.* London: Thames & Hudson, 1968.

Bokenkotter, Thomas, *A Concise History of the Catholic Church.* Garden City, N.Y.: Doubleday & Company, 1977.

The Catholic Theological Society of America, *Human Sexuality, New Directions in American Catholic Thought.* New York: Paulist Press, 1977.

Cavendish, Richard, *Visions of Heaven and Hell.* New York: Harmony Books, 1977.

Chiniquy, Rev. Charles, *The Priest, The Woman and The Confessional.* New York: Fleming H. Revell Company, 1880.

Bibliography

Cogley, John, *Catholic America*. New York: Dial Press, 1973.

The Collected Speeches of John Paul II in Ireland and the United States. London: Collins, 1980.

Dacio, Juan, *Dictionnaire des Papes*. Paris: Editions France Empire, 1963.

Danielou, Jean and Marrou, Henri, *The Christian Centuries, The First 600 Years*. London: Darton, Longman & Todd, 1964.

Davies, J.G., *Early Christian Church*. New York: Holt, Rinehart and Winston, 1965.

Deansly, Margaret, *A History of the Medieval Church, 590–1500*. London: Metheun & Co., 1925.

Delaney, John J., *Dictionary of Saints*. Garden City, N.Y.: Doubleday & Co., 1980.

Doyle, Charles Hugo, *What to Say to the Penitent: Instructive Counsels for Use by Confessors*. New York: The Nugent Press, 1953.

Dunney, Rev. Jos. A., *Church History in the Light of the Saints*. New York: MacMillan & Co., 1944.

Ellis, John Tracey, *American Catholicism*. Chicago: University of Chicago Press, 1956.

Encyclopedia Judaica. New York: Macmillan & Co., 1971–72.

Fazzalaro, Rev. Francis J., *The Place for Hearing Confessions*. Washington, D.C.: The Catholic University of America Press, 1950.

Flannery, Austin, *Vatican Council II, The Conciliar and Post Conciliar Documents*. New York: Castello, 1975.

Flood, J.M., *Ireland, Its Saints and Scholars*. Dublin: The Talbot Press Ltd., 1930.

Foucault, Michel, *The History of Sexuality*. New York: Random House, 1980.

Forner, Rev. B.N., *The Story of the Church*. Detroit: The Basilian Press, 1935.

Foy, Felician A., O.F.M, editor, *Catholic Almanac, 1980*. Huntington, Indiana: Our Sunday Visitor Inc., 1980.

Frassinetti, Joseph, *The New Parish Priests' Practical Manual*. London: Burns and Oates, 1883.

Friedenthal, Richard, *Luther, His Life & Times*. New York: Harcourt, Brace, Jovanovich, 1967.

Glock, Charles Y., ed., *Prejudice USA*. New York: Frederick A. Praeger, 1969.

Gontard, Friedrich, *The Popes*. London: Barrie & Rochliff, 1964.

Gough, Michael, *The Early Christians*. New York: Frederick A. Praeger, 1961.

Grimm, Harold, *The Reformation Era, 1500–1650*. New York: Macmillan & Co., 1954.

Grun, Bernard, *The Timetables of History*. New York: Simon & Schuster, 1975.

Bibliography

Guzie, Tad and McIlhon, John, *The Forgiveness of Sin.* Chicago: The Thomas More Press, 1979.

Guzie, Tad, *What a Modern Catholic Believes about Confession.* Chicago: The Thomas More Press, 1974.

Hardon, John A., S.J., *The Catholic Catechism.* Garden City, N.Y.: Doubleday & Company, 1975.

Hastings, James, ed., *Encyclopedia of Religion and Ethics.* Edinburgh: T. & T. Clark, 1910.

Hebblethwaite, Peter, *The Runaway Church.* London: Collins, 1975.

Hennesey, James, S.J., *American Catholics.* New York/Oxford: Oxford University Press, 1981.

Hertling, Ludwig, S.M., *History of the Catholic Church.* Maryland: The Newman Press, 1957.

Hughson, Shirley C., *Athletes of God.* London: Society For Promoting Christian Knowledge, 1930.

Hurtscheid, Rev. Bertrand, O.F.M, *The Seal of Confession.* London: B. Herder, 1927.

Kelly, George Msgr., *The Battle for the American Church.* Garden City, N.Y.: Doubleday & Company, 1979.

Kelly, Gerald, S.J., *The Good Confessor.* New York: The Sentinel Press, 1951.

Kennedy, Eugene, *A Sense of Life, a Sense of Sin.* Garden City, N.Y.: Doubleday & Company, 1975.

Lea, Henry Charles, *The History of Auricular Confession and Indulgences.* Philadelphia: Lea Brothers & Co., 1896.

Leech, Kenneth, *Soul Friend, The Practice of Christian Spirituality.* San Francisco: Harper & Row, Publishers, 1977.

Lunn, Brian, *Martin Luther: The Man & His God.* London: Nicholson & Watson, 1934.

McAvoy, Thomas T., C.S.C., edited by, *Roman Catholicism & the American Way of Life.* South Bend, Indiana: Notre Dame Press, 1960.

McGrath, Sister Albertus Magnus, *What a Modern Catholic Believes about Women.* Chicago: The Thomas More Press, 1972.

McLaughlin, Loretta, *The Pill, John Rock and the Church: The Biography of a Revolution.* Boston: Little, Brown, 1982.

McNeill, John T., and Gamer, Helena M., *Medieval Handbooks of Penance.* New York: Octagon Books, 1965.

Martin, Malachy, *The Decline and Fall of the Roman Church.* New York: Bantam, 1983.

Martos, Joseph, *Doors to the Sacred.* New York: Image Books, 1982.

Bibliography

Maynard, Theodore, *The Catholic Church & the American Idea.* New York: Appleton Century Crofts, 1953.

The New Catholic Encyclopedia. New York: McGraw-Hill Book Company, 1967.

Obst, Lynda Rosen, *The Sixties, The Decade Remembered Now by People Who Lived It Then.* New York: Random House/Rolling Stone Press, 1977.

Olmstead, Clifton O., *History of Religion in the U.S.* Englewood Cliffs, N.J.: Prentice-Hall, 1960.

Orsenigo, Cesare, *St. Charles Borromeo.* Freiburg, Germany: B. Herder, 1947.

Riga, Rev. Peter, *Sin and Penance.* Milwaukee: The Bruce Publishing Co., 1962.

Roeggle, Rt. Rev. Aloysius, D.D., *The Confessional.* New York: Benziger Brothers, 1882.

Rogge, Oetje John, *Why Men Confess.* New York: De Capo Press, 1975.

Ryan, Rev. John, *Irish Monasticism, Origins and Early Development.* Dublin: The Talbot Press, 1931.

Sann, Paul, *The Angry Decade: A Pictorial History.* New York: Crown Publishers, Inc., 1979.

Schieler, Prof. Caspar E., *Theory and Practice of the Confessional: A Guide in the Administration of the Sacrament of Penance.* New York: Benziger Brothers, 1905.

Searle, G.W., *The Counter Reformation.* London: University of London Press Ltd., 1974.

Sheed, Francis Joseph, *Saint Jerome, The Early Years.* London: Sheed & Ward, 1933.

Simon, Edith, *Luther Alive.* Garden City, N.Y.: Doubleday & Company, 1968.

Spitz, Lewis W., *The Protestant Reformation.* Englewood, N.J.: Prentice-Hall, 1966.

Tentler, Thomas N., *Sin & Confession on the Eve of the Reformation.* Princeton, N.J.: Princeton University Press, 1977.

Thompson, Edward Healey, *The Life of St. Charles Borromeo.* London: Burns and Lambert, 1858.

Twain, Mark, *Letters from the Earth.* New York: Harper & Row, 1962.

Valentini, Norberto, and di Meglio, Clara, *Sex and the Confessional,* trans. Milton S. Davis. New York: Stein and Day, 1974.

Vann, F. Joseph, edited by, *Lives of Saints.* New York: John J. Crawley Co., 1954.

Von Galli, Mario, *The Council and the Future.* New York: McGraw-Hill Book Company, 1966.

Bibliography

Weiss, Johannes, *Earliest Christianity, A History of the Period A.D. 30–150, Volume I.* New York: Harper Torchbooks, 1959.

Wills, Garry, *Bare Ruined Choirs: Doubt, Prophecy and Radical Religion.* Garden City, N.Y.: Doubleday & Company, 1971.

Ziegler, Philip, *The Black Death.* London: Collins, 1969.